*Counseling Gay Men
and Lesbians*

Brodly
2002

Counseling Gay Men and Lesbians

A PRACTICE PRIMER

BOB BARRET
The University of North Carolina at Charlotte

COLLEEN LOGAN
The University of Houston–Victoria

BROOKS/COLE

THOMSON LEARNING

Australia • Canada • Mexico • Singapore • Spain • United Kingdom • United States

BROOKS/COLE

THOMSON LEARNING

Sponsoring Editor: *Julie Martinez*
Marketing Team: *Caroline Concilla,*
  Tami Strang
Associate Editor: *Shelley Gesicki*
Editorial Assistant: *Catherine Broz*
Production Coordinator: *Kelsey McGee*
Permissions Editor: *Sue Ewing*

Cover Design and Illustration: *Roger Knox*
Print Buyer: *Vena M. Dyer*
Production and Typesetting:
  G & S Typesetters, Inc.
Cover Printing, Printing, and Binding:
  Webcom, Limited

For more information about this or any other Brooks/Cole product, contact:
BROOKS/COLE
511 Forest Lodge Road
Pacific Grove, CA 93950 USA
www.brookscole.com
1-800-423-0563 (Thomson Learning Academic Resource Center)

For permission to use material from this work, contact us by
www.thomsonrights.com
fax: 1-800-730-2215
phone: 1-800-730-2214

Printed in Canada

10 9 8 7 6 5 4 3 2 1

Library of Congress Cataloging-in-Publication Data
Barret, Bob, [date]
    Counseling gay men and lesbians : a practice primer / Bob Barret,
  Colleen R. Logan.
        p.   cm.
    Includes bibliographical references and index.
    ISBN 0-534-55084-3
    1. Gays—Counseling of. I. Logan, Colleen R., [date] II. Title.

RC558 .B374   2001
616.89′14′08664—dc21   2001035495

To the memory of the many men
and women who have died or otherwise
suffered as a result of their sexual
orientation and in honor of the many
courageous gay men and lesbians
who go out each day into a world
that is not always safe or welcoming
to them.

Contents

Chapter 5

Counseling Gay and Lesbian Couples   87

Chapter 6

Counseling Bisexual and Transgendered Clients   106

Chapter 9

Gay and Lesbian Parenting   163

Chapter 10

Gay and Lesbian Health Issues   180

Preface

This book is a product of a shared vision. Given the bare mention or absence of gay men and lesbians in our graduate counseling programs, we have both faced the situation that most counselors soon discover: The client, a gay man or lesbian, begins to talk about aspects of her/his life that may be at best vaguely familiar, and we are forced to choose between applying heterosexual counseling models or creative improvisation. Looking for resources to serve as a guide left both of us astonished. There simply are no books that provide solid clinical direction for mental-health professionals who want to know what to *do* to help their gay and lesbian clients.

This book is unique because of its focus on predicting potential challenges and developing clinical skills. In every chapter you will become acutely aware of the impact of homoprejudice and the toll it takes on sexual minority clients. It is our hope that you will read this book and not only be a better counselor but also a better human being committed to making this world a safer and better place to live—a world where everyone is afforded the opportunity to live out and fully participate in the global community.

One of the challenges in such an undertaking is that each topic is extremely complex. Distilling background information to provide the context for clinical interventions means that much material must be omitted. We have been confounded by difficulties caused by the paucity of research studies, the absence of comprehensive theory, the challenges of language, and the confines of space. In addition, we recognize that we certainly did not give multicultural issues the attention they require and deserve. This occurred not because we want to ignore or devalue the issues, as they are critical to our work with sexual minorities, but due to the enormity and complexity of the core issues, we found ourselves limited by space. We strongly encourage others to pick up the torch and write a book that is solely dedicated to issues associated with managing multiple identities. Nevertheless, we believe that this book will serve as a valuable guide and a source for new insight.

Each chapter begins with a hypothetical case that will help you understand the counselor's dilemma, provides important background context, and ends with specific suggestions for clinical practice. Clinical examples provide real-life demonstrations of many of the issues that clients and counselors face. Rather than ending each chapter with a resource list that would be dated in short order, we end the book with a resource section that will direct you to Internet sites containing more information.

Chapters 1 and 2 provide background information so you will understand better the context in which counseling gay men and lesbians occurs. Although recent great strides have improved the general public's knowledge of gay men and lesbians, oppression and discrimination continue to challenge those who have a minority sexual identity. These chapters examine theories behind homosexual development, the impact of homosexuality on individual development, a discussion of the misrepresentation of those who claim that reparative or conversion therapies offer a way to change from minority to majority sexual orientation, and a clear presentation about the benefits of living totally out.

Chapters 3, 4, and 5 focus on the counseling issues presented by gay men, lesbians, and gay and lesbian couples. Chapters 6 and 7 examine the particular issues faced by gay and lesbian youth and by the often overlooked bisexual and transgendered client. Finally, Chapters 8, 9, and 10 examine specific issues (spirituality, parenting, and health) that transcend each population covered in earlier chapters.

Among the challenges in writing about gay and lesbian issues is that rapid change in the gay and lesbian community may cause sources as recent as five years ago to reflect knowledge that has become out of date. The decade of the 1990s has seen radical change in the acceptance and understanding of gays and lesbians. Because oppression has lifted significantly in many large cities, research drawn from samples of gay men and lesbians who have been deeply closeted may report findings that no longer are accurate.

Another challenge is that of language. Because both of us identify as counselors, we use that term throughout the book. However, because we recognize that psychologists, social workers, pastors, and other helping professionals will use this book, we also use the term *mental-health practitioner*. We hope the reader will see these terms as interchangeable.

This book is drawn, by and large, from our clinical work and therefore presents counseling skills that are not often found in the literature. The history of gay and lesbian people in the mental-health system is not a source of pride. We hope that as a result of this book, direct service delivery for gay and lesbian clients will improve and that these valuable human beings will not be so challenged to find counselors who truly understand them.

Acknowledgments

From **Bob Barret:** I acknowledge the pivotal role played by my colleagues at the University of North Carolina at Charlotte. Provost Denise Trauth and Dean Mary Lynne Calhoun gave encouragement in the form of a semester's leave to allow time for the completion of this and two other book projects. My fellow faculty members in the Counseling Program asked about this work and were steadfast in expressing their support. Rob Mate, my professional buddy at Purdue University, read and made comments on several chapters. My friend, Paul Cockrell, has listened to me drone on hour after hour about ideas for this book. I am grateful to each of them for their belief in me and for their presence in my life. I owe the greatest thanks to the many gay and lesbian clients who have sought my assistance over the years. Sitting with them as they addressed the complex issues of forming stable and rich lives has taught me more than I suspect they gained from me and has been a steady source of inspiration. Finally, I thank Colleen Logan for her enthusiasm, comments on my writing, and for the ways she challenges all around her to live out more fully.

From **Colleen Logan:** I am forever indebted to my life partner and soul mate, Deborah Bloom. Her steady presence and unwavering love helped me find my voice and passion for writing. She is my greatest inspiration and sweetest distraction, often carrying the load of our lives while I pursued this dream. I am also grateful for the support of my colleague Dr. Mary Natividad. So many times she gave me the gift of time and space to do this work. I am also grateful to my parents, Ernest and Muriel Logan, and my birth parents, Marilyn Glithero and Patrick Coghlin. Along this journey and throughout my life, I am steadily reminded of the many gifts my parents gave me, gifts that allow me to live and love with pride. And it is during this process of writing my first book that I was given yet another amazing gift, the joy of meeting my birth parents. None of this would be possible without the many clients I have learned from along the way; I am continually humbled by their courage and willingness to share their lives with me. And finally, I am thankful for and to Bob Barret. His presence and influence in my life has helped make the ordinary extraordinary. His amazing vision, attention to detail, and gentle guidance helped make my first book a challenging and exciting experience.

We also thank our reviewers for their thoughtful comments: C. Emmanuel Ahia of Rider University; Fernando Cordero of Alan Hancock University; Patricia E. Hudson of St. John's University; Wanda Lee of San Francisco State University; Judith Lewis of Governors State University; Beth Rienzi of California State University, Bakersfield; Mary K. Stroube of California State University, Sacramento; Gil Torre of AGLBIC; and Susan Wycoff of California State University, Sacramento.

Bob Barret
Colleen Logan

SEXUAL ORIENTATION: SOCIAL AND CULTURAL CONTEXT

The Case of Mary ▼

For the last seven years, Mary has been a counselor in an employee assistance program (EAP) operated by a bank. During this time she has become a Licensed Professional Counselor (LPC) and has distinguished herself as one who can deal with a broad range of client concerns. Particularly effective in marriage counseling, she is recognized by her peers as a fine and competent counselor. In the past seven months she has become aware of a growing number of clients who present with concerns about their sexual orientation. At first taken aback when the clients would mention that they might be gay or lesbian, she has learned ways to listen to them and thinks she has been helpful. Recently she was reviewing a journal she has kept for years and realized that these clients had crept into her personal reflections.

Jan. 29 Today I saw a young gay man named John at the office. He was so conflicted about how he was going to let his parents know he is gay. He talked on and on about how they might reject him, and at times his distress was hard for me to understand. His parents live 1500 miles away, and they hardly ever come to see him. I can't understand why he is feeling so much pressure to tell them, but I tried to be supportive and encouraged him to let them know soon. I wish I had had more training about working with gay and lesbian clients when I was in graduate school. I have never known any gay people, and I really do not understand them at all, but when one comes into the office I have to be as helpful as I can. If I were lesbian I don't think I would bring that up with an EAP counselor where I work. I would see someone privately to discuss something like this.

Feb. 16 John came back in today. He was a wreck. He had gone to see his parents last weekend to tell them that he is gay, and it was a disaster! His mom just fell apart, crying and telling him that he needed to pray to God to take this curse from him. His dad got angry and told him there was no place for him in the family if he was going to parade around letting everyone know that he is a fairy. They convinced him to talk to their preacher who told John he was going to hell if he did not get this out of his system right away! They want him to go to some kind of religious counselor who will change him back to straight. John has agreed to go even though he does not believe it is possible to change. He said he had prayed about this for years, and nothing had happened. The church counselor told him he would have to pledge not to see any of his old friends again, and John does not want to do that. They are good friends to him and he likes them because of who they are, not because they are gay. Since he is now working with the Christian counselor I don't expect to see him again so we said our goodbyes. After he left I found myself shaking my head wondering why he had to go tell his parents. He could have never told them and his life would have been so much easier. That's one thing I don't think I will ever understand—Why can't gay people just keep it to themselves? They can move away from their families and have their lives without getting everyone so upset.

Apr. 4 I found myself thinking about John again today. My new lesbian client, Janie, was telling me about her family's reaction to her coming out. She had made careful plans to tell them, and I had warned her that they might reject her. But, unlike John's parents, Janie's whole family was so loving to her. Her father hugged her and told her that he would always love her, and both her parents seemed eager to meet her friends. Her brother is coming for a visit this weekend just to hang out with her. I am happy for her, but I was stunned when she started talking about telling her boss. She wants to bring the woman she has been dating to the office picnic in June, and she wants to make sure her boss is ok with it. Honestly, I can't see why she would do this. She's even talking about marching in the gay parade. Janie is a bright and attractive woman who has a solid future with this company. Why would she risk losing all of that? I can't believe her boss will be supportive about her bringing a girlfriend to the picnic. Wouldn't that just make everyone uncomfortable? I'm glad her family was supportive. But, for the life of me, I can't see why gay people have to shove it in your face all the time. Straight people don't do that. And why must they have these parades where people are practically having sex with each other in public! I can't imagine Janie at that kind of event. Her career is about to go down the tubes!

June 23 Mr. S, one of the department heads, came in to see me today. At first he was very nervous and kept beating around the bush. Finally he told me that his son is gay and that he is not sure what to do about it. I told him I had seen several gay and lesbian clients and that I would be glad to listen. Just about everything he said was exactly what

I have been thinking! He wants his son to move to another city where he can live the gay lifestyle without anyone having to know. And he told his son that he would always be welcome in the family home but not to expect to bring any boyfriends around. Mr. S does not want his younger children exposed to gay people. I thought everything he said was reasonable, and was surprised when he told me that he needed to talk about them with me. His son had cried at the new rules and left saying he would not be back until the family could accept him as he is. And Mr. S is thinking that maybe he is wrong. I recently learned about an organization called Parents and Friends of Lesbians and Gays—PFLAG, I think they call it—and I suggested that he go there and see what other parents were doing. This gay thing gets so complicated.

Aug. 30 John came back in to see me today. He has given up on the church counselor. It turns out that he had seen the man twice a week and even spent his vacation time at a retreat just for ex-gays. In all, I think he has paid more than $1500 for this treatment. And nothing has changed! He is still attracted to men, and he is lonelier than before. He does not have so much in common with the friends in the church group and he misses his old friends. He asked if I could refer him to an openly gay or lesbian counselor, someone who might understand and be able to help him out. When he said that, I was startled. I thought I had been very supportive of him, and, anyway, I didn't know there were gay and lesbian counselors in our community. I asked a colleague and she gave me several names. Two of those people were friends of mine when I was in graduate school! They were great students and had so much compassion. I was shocked that they were both gay. Still, I gave John their names, and I hope he can find some peace. He is a neat guy, but he sure is confused.

Oct. 26 Mr. S came back to see me today. I thought he was going to tell me that his son had decided to accept the rules, but instead he told me that he wanted to talk about something that happened to him. He has been going to PFLAG regularly since I referred him, and the group has really been helpful. He told me he now accepted his son fully, and that he and his friends were welcome at all family gatherings. He said that those who oppose gay men and lesbians are the ones with the problem. He wants his son to move to a new community where gays are more accepted than they are here. Last week, a group of guys beat up his son, and he is still in the hospital. I was stunned when he told me that they had called him awful names and beat him up before he could get in his car. Mr. S wants to see what might be done here at the bank to help gay employees feel more safe. When he said that I thought about Janie and wondered if she might want to work with him on this. I asked Mr. S if I could give his name to another employee who might be willing to assist him and he agreed. Before he left, he thanked me for encouraging him to go to PFLAG. It has changed him and made his family life so much better.

Oct. 27 Janie came in today after I called to tell her I wanted to see her. She looked awful! She told me that things had gone very well after she came out to her boss and that she and her girlfriend had attended the office picnic without any trouble. She had continued to work hard and had some wonderful successes. But at her annual review last week she had been marked down in several categories. She said her boss said she was "pushy" and "aggressive" and that he was threatening to remove her from a project she has managed well for the past 18 months! And to cap all of that off, he told her she would not get a raise this year. I had such mixed feelings about that. I knew she should never have come out at work, and part of me was saying she got what she could have predicted. On the other hand, Janie is a young woman with many talents, one who has had a great future at the bank. I can't understand why she is being treated this way. When I told her about Mr. S, she got so excited. She thinks her negative evaluation reflects the bank's negative attitude toward gay and lesbian employees, and she told me she would get in touch with Mr. S right away. After she left, I wondered if maybe I might want to help them myself. Obviously there is a lot more I need to understand about gay people. Looking back I can see that I failed John. I wish I could make it up to him now, but it's too late for that!

UNDERSTANDING THE GAY AND LESBIAN EXPERIENCE

Empathizing with Mary is easy. She is like many counselors who have had no training in working with sexual minorities who now are confronted with real clients facing real issues, and find themselves lost in their internal reactions to the clients' situations. For years gay men and lesbians have reported negative and prejudicial interactions with mental-health professionals. Determining the number of gay men and lesbians in the general population is difficult: estimates range from 4–17% (Gonsiorek & Weinrich, 1991). Few graduate training programs provide information about the unique experiences facing sexual minorities, so what most mental-health professionals know about them is based on a combination of personal experience and what has been gleaned from media reports. Utilizing sources like these can result in a belief that gay men and lesbians live in monolithic cultures filled with stereotypes. In fact, the cultures in which all sexual minorities live are as diverse within as the general culture is without.

The absence of pedagogical training about a culture that has largely been invisible means that by and large the quality of mental-health services for gay men and lesbians is below standard. It is estimated that 25–65% of gay men and lesbians seek counseling (a rate two to four times that of the general population), and studies reflect a high level of dissatisfaction (Bell & Weinberg, 1978; Jay & Young, 1980; Rudolph, 1988). Gay and lesbian clients report that counselors are not informed about the situations they face and frequently make negative or rejecting, if not judgmental, comments. This homonegativity exists in spite of the fact that the American Psychiatric Association removed homosexuality from the *Diagnostic and Statistical Manual (DSM)* in 1973.

To understand gay and lesbian clients, counselors need to become familiar with the environments in which they live. Heterosexism is the belief that it is normal (and best) to be heterosexual. This oppressive belief creates a part of the pressure that keeps gay men and lesbians invisible. As John, Janie, and Mr. S learned in the case at the beginning of this chapter, being openly gay or lesbian can place one at risk of social and political discrimination and potential harassment. To understand this better, take a look at the way two human developmental theories have been constructed around heterosexist values.

Human Development and Homosexuality

Whatever the origin of homosexuality may be, understanding its influence on development will enable counselors like Mary to provide a safer and more effective therapeutic environment for sexual minority clients. Theories of human development attempt to shed light on universal developmental stages. These developmental tasks can be determined by age and time (stages) or may represent themes that extend across the life cycle. Adlerian psychology identifies five life tasks (Dreikurs, 1953; Mosak & Dreikurs, 1967):

- Society
- Work
- Sex
- Self
- Spirituality

These five life tasks are not static. Rather, they function throughout our lives. The task of *society* is to establish a relationship with the larger communities in which we live. *Work* demands that we make a decision about the role of work in our lives and how we define ourselves as workers. *Sex* suggests that all of us must come to terms with our sexual selves and become comfortable with the ways we express our sexuality with others. The task of *self* requires that we develop an understanding and appreciation for our uniqueness and find security in the ways we live out our selves in the world. Finally, *spirituality* calls us to take a look at the spiritual realm and make some decision about its role in our lives.

Levinson (1978) defines two tasks that adults face across the life span. Forming a *dream* of adult life begins early as children imagine themselves as adults. This dream is shaped and reshaped across the years as individuals develop a more realistic picture of the demands and rewards of being an adult. According to Levinson the dream will become more central at particular points in life. Creating a *life structure* is another task of development. We structure our lives with people, school and work, activities and interests, and various other ways that help us define who we are. Like the dream, the life structure is a dynamic phenomenon that needs attention at specific points during adolescence and adulthood.

In most communities, social institutions are charged with the responsibility of helping people resolve each of the tasks defined by Adler and Levinson. Schools and religious organizations assist young people to relate to larger social environments, stressing cooperation and competition and offering models of social interaction such as clubs and sports teams. During adolescence, the tasks of work, life structure, and shaping the dream are most intense. Schools and families support youth as they begin to define their goals for adult life. Sexual contacts are generally monitored during adolescence. Freedom is gradually expanded, and parents closely watch the ways their children behave sexually. From chaperoned events at school or religious organizations, young people are encouraged to mix, to form couples, and to create primary relationships. Improving self-esteem is another goal that social institutions have for adolescents. And finally, most religious organizations have created rituals where adolescents move to a more adult status that affirms their spiritual understandings.

Most adults can remember the turbulence they felt as these life tasks became more of their individual responsibility, and most can also remember the normalcy of these expectations and the sense of excitement they felt as they anticipated their futures. Few will have given much thought to the ways these developmental experiences are infused with heterosexism, or the belief that all people are heterosexual. In resolving these tasks, the adult world structures the challenge and the solution in terms of the goal of living a heterosexual life. Gay and lesbian persons report knowing of their same-sex attraction early in life. Because of their fear and the real threat of oppression and discrimination, few let others know what is going on within. These children head into adolescence with a deeply held secret that leaves them feeling out of step with their nongay peers. For example, the emphasis on dating and conversations about life goals that take place in schools and religious organizations assumes that all are heterosexual. Sexual minority youth mature without the kind of support they need to resolve the life tasks. Their development has been interrupted, leaving a number of tasks that must be resolved as a part of the coming out process. In Chapter 3 you will learn more about these challenges. While gay and lesbian persons participate in social conditioning along with their nongay peers, they rarely have a chance to learn about the ways their sexual orientation will impact their lives.

Much of the depression and anxiety reported by gay youth is tied to their lack of support as they attempt to resolve Adler's life tasks at the same time they are encountering questions about their sexual orientation. Until very recently, when gay and lesbian youth groups began to appear in urban areas, sexual minority adolescents were left alone to resolve these very complex tasks. If the developmental tasks proposed by Adler and Levinson are valid, it is apparent that when one comes out as gay or lesbian, the tasks identified by both theorists have to be reexamined. It is not difficult to understand how one's self-image must be altered or why reassessing a relationship with an oppressive religious organization would be necessary. Finding new ways to express the sexual self and figuring out how minority sexual orientation changes one's ability to relate to society can combine with the other challenges to create a sense of being overwhelmed. As these five tasks are reshaped, the dream of adult life and the life structure likewise change. What happens is virtually a complete reinvention of self. The fact that this recreation occurs in an oppressive atmosphere leads many gay and lesbian people to become involved in political organizations that seek equal rights for all citizens.

Cultural Understandings About Homosexuality

As with all other issues, various cultures describe and understand homosexuality in different ways. While most of the research on homosexuality has been conducted using white, middleclass respondents, in recent years a growing body of literature attests to the ways other cultures understand this population. Brown (1997) describes the Native American belief that gay men and lesbians are **two-spirited people** who possess magical powers that are not available to heterosexual (one-spirited) persons. In the African American culture and in certain Hispanic cultures, men who have sex with men may never self-identify as homosexual, but instead see their behavior as unrelated to their sexual orientation. Chicana lesbians may be seen as threatening the established order of male dominance, and African American gay men and lesbians have been shown to be more vulnerable than their white counterparts to negative psychological outcomes (Greene, 1994). Given the patriarchal nature of Asian American families and the traditional expectations placed on the eldest son, it is not surprising that many Asian homosexuals stay deeply closeted because of fears of family rejection. As with all counseling relationships, it is critical that the counselor be highly sensitive to the role of culture in understanding all individuals. Because racial and ethnic minorities suffer from two forms of oppression, their lives are doubly impacted when they identify as sexual minorities.

Sodomy Laws and the Myth of Molestation

The reality is that being gay or lesbian creates a political vulnerability. In 1960 all 50 states had some kind of sodomy law (laws that criminalize anal or oral sex between consenting adults in the privacy of their homes): These laws were selectively enforced against homosexuals. The Lambda Legal Defense and Education Fund (LLDEF), an organization deeply involved with this issue, states: "While most sodomy laws, as written, apply to everyone—regardless of marital status, gender, or sexual orientation—they are disproportionately invoked against lesbians and gay men. . . . This differential application occurs despite the facts that (a) those forms of sexuality are common among both heterosexual and gay couples and (b), conversely, a lesbian or gay couple with a sexual relationship is not necessarily violating such a law. In the minds of many, however, sodomy laws uniquely brand lesbians and gay men as 'criminals.'" In the year 2000, only 5 states (Arkansas, Kansas, Missouri, Oklahoma, and Texas) continue to have laws that criminalize sodomy between persons of the same sex; 12 other states (Alabama, Arizona, Florida, Idaho, Louisiana, Massachusetts, Minnesota, Mississippi, North Carolina, South Carolina, Utah, and Virginia) have laws on the books that criminalize sodomy between same-sex and different sex partners. In the other 33 states, sodomy is not considered a criminal activity.

Still, the existence of sodomy laws forms the basis for other beliefs that homosexuals are criminals. Those who oppose homosexuality depict gay men and lesbians as child molesters. Stemming largely from politically powerful conservative Christian organizations, their voice is sufficiently loud to prevent legal and social changes that would enable gay men and lesbians to live with more freedom and safety. Records show that 99% of child molestation takes place in the home and the perpetrator identifies as heterosexual (Child Welfare League of America, 1995; Morgan & Nerison, 1993; Jenny, Roesler, & Poyer, 1994). In spite of this, the general public remains uneasy about the presence of gay men and lesbians in career fields that involve working with children. Still, the same conservative groups continue to attack homosexuals and to claim that sexual orientation can be changed.

Laws like these and others related to employment, housing, and use of public accommodations lead the sexual minority community to participate in public actions that may influence the political process. Local and national marches, along with a growing gay and lesbian lobbying effort, attempt to influence public opinion and exert specific pressure on legislators.

UNDERSTANDING HOMOSEXUALITY

We hope that this discussion will assist mental-health professionals (like Mary at the beginning of this chapter) to develop a sensitivity to the often lonely and typically frightening experiences that gay men and lesbians have as they begin to embrace their sexual orientation and move out into a world that is more likely to greet them with disapproval and possible discrimination than to celebrate them. The debate about homosexuality in both the public and professional media has become increasingly intense, and resolution does not seem near. Several key points shape this discussion:

- What is the origin of homosexuality? Is this behavior genetically determined or is it influenced by the environment? Could it be that some men and women just choose to identify as gay or lesbian?
- Are gay men and lesbians child predators who keep their culture alive only by recruiting others?
- How did homosexuality get removed from the *DSM*? Is it possible that a mistake was made? In any event, how do I reconcile my personal understanding of homosexuality as immoral with the profession's standing that this behavior is normal? How do I prevent my often-unconscious negativity about gay men and lesbians from entering into the treatment setting?
- Can homosexuality be cured? What is the legitimacy of reparative and conversion therapies? Wouldn't it be better if everyone were heterosexual?
- Have gay and lesbian people created a *bona fide* culture? If so, what obligation do I have to learn about this culture?
- How do I provide mental-health services to a population that I know so little about and may have personal conflicts around? Is referral the correct option? If so, how do I determine those who are skilled at working with this population?
- If I become an advocate for gay and lesbian people, won't I be accused of being gay myself?

Finding answers to questions like these is not an easy task. This chapter will provide background information about some of the historical views about homosexuality and offer an update on positions taken by the mental-health professions. Along the way, these questions will be addressed. Before going any further let's take a quick look at some of the challenges in developing knowledge about sexual minorities.

Language

As the gay and lesbian community has become more visible, the term *gay* as referring to both men and women has developed political implications. Some lesbians absolutely do not define themselves as gay, insist on being identified as lesbian, and take offense at the use of the term *gay community* as descriptive of a community that includes them. Other gay women identify as gay and prefer not to be called lesbian. In the professional literature the term *lesbian women*, while redundant, seems to be used more and more frequently. In this book, *gay community* will include both gay men and lesbians. *Gay men, gays* (inclusive of males and females), *gay women, lesbians,* and *lesbian women* will appear throughout. The gay community has struggled with the proper terminology to be used to describe the entire community. Gay, Lesbian, Bisexual, and Transgendered (GLBT) has been preferred as it includes all, but GLBT is awkward and is not familiar to many. *Sexual minorities* is a term that appears more and more frequently in the literature. Not to confuse the reader but to provide variety, many of these terms will be used in this book. We hope their use will not create confusion or offense.

Research on Homosexuality

Researching and understanding sexual behavior is inherently complicated. In the area of human sexuality the conclusions of virtually all studies have been challenged because of methodological flaws. Because the essence of human sexual behavior cannot be replicated in laboratory, researchers must rely on self-reports for most of their data. While homosexuality has been a research interest for years, methodological shortcomings and other research challenges deny us the definitive understandings that would provide definitive answers to the many questions that face us. Until very recent times research on homosexuality was not popular, and it can be safely said that empirical neglect is one of the major weaknesses in the field (Barret and Robinson, 2000). Since 1970, the number of studies has expanded, and now, more often, one can find empirical as well as impressionistic studies in the literature.

Still, one weakness of the research is tied to sampling methods. Most of the studies of gay men and lesbians involve self-report instruments tendered by population samples that may or may not be representative. Partly out of fear of being exposed to unwelcome oppression, gay men and lesbians are not readily visible and must be recruited to participate in studies. Since a profile of the population as a whole does not exist, there is little data that would show that a given sample is representative of the population of sexual minorities. Possibly, the samples consist of a particular group of individuals who are eager to volunteer in order to promote a personal view about homosexuality. Or, maybe those who are willing to be research subjects reflect a narrow section of the community that have come to terms with their sexual orientation and therefore are not afraid to be visible. Finding comparison groups is also a challenge. How would a researcher know that a comparison group of nongay persons could be used reliably? Knowledge about gay men and lesbians does exist, but it is important to be wary of generalizing findings to the entire population. This methodological "softness" means that gay men and lesbians often feel vulnerable when those who condemn them demand "proof" that they are not simply immoral people choosing a deviant behavior. Like Mary, many want definite research findings before they are willing to let go of long-held beliefs about gay and lesbian people. While the findings may not be conclusive, most researchers who study the subject of human sexuality have moved toward understanding that homosexual people have the same opportunities to create successful and happy lives as do heterosexuals.

Theories About Homosexuality

Various theories have been put forward to explain homosexuality. Although Freud did not see homosexuality as pathological *per se,* he did suggest that it results from failing to develop the proper identification with the same-sex parent (Freud, 1953, 1957). Freud believed that all humans are born bisexual and move toward a sexual identity in the early years, primarily as a result of intrapersonal processing and family dynamics. Thus was created the stereotype of the domineering mother and the passive father as the determiners of their sons' homosexuality. The Kinsey studies (Kinsey, Pomeroy, & Martin, 1948, 1953) suggested that homosexuality is simply one variation of human sexuality. Kinsey and his colleagues surveyed over 10,000 persons and concluded that sexual behavior can be viewed along a continuum from exclusively heterosexual (0) to exclusively homosexual (6), and that 37% of males and 20% of females have some kind of overt homosexual experience after puberty. These researchers came to see homosexuality and bisexuality as reflections of the diversity of nature, not as deviations from normalcy. More recently, Coleman (1988, 1990) has suggested that sexual behavior is composed of many variables: lifestyle or current relationship status, self-identification of sexual orientation, comfort with current sexual orientation identity, physical sexual identity, gender identity, sex role identity, sexual orientation identity, and past, present, and idealized sexual identity. These and other developmental models will be discussed in other chapters of this book. Bisexuals and transgendered persons are also part of the sexual minority community, and their issues are covered in some of the theoretical writings about homosexuality. Although this book is focused mostly on the experiences of gay men and lesbians, Chapter 6 will give valuable background about bisexual and transgendered persons. Like their gay and lesbian brothers and sisters, their lives are deeply impacted by oppression and discrimination based largely on misinformation.

Current research efforts on sexual orientation focus on biology and genetics (Bancroft, 1990; Burr, 1993; Gooren, 1990). Genetic science is in its infancy, and it will be years before knowledge created there can be considered definitive. A growing body of literature, however, suggests that all behavior is genetically controlled (Bargh & Chartrand, 1999). After comparing the sexual orientations of monozygotic twins, the frequency of shared sexual orientation is sufficient to suggest a strong biological basis for sexual orientation (Bailey & Pillard, 1991; Whitam, Diamond, & Martin, 1993). LeVay (1991) compared the brains of gay men who had died from HIV disease with samples of brain tissue from deceased men who identified as heterosexual and found that a region in the anterior hypothalamus was smaller in the tissues obtained from the gay men, suggesting a possible biological basis to sexual orientation. As yet, he has not been successful in obtaining samples from gay men who died of other causes, so there is no conclusive evidence that homosexuality can be seen in the structure of the brain. More and more researchers, however, are beginning to attribute sexual orientation to genetics or to the result of a genetic predisposition that is enhanced by unknown environmental factors (LeVay & Hamer, 1994). From this brief historical overview, one can see that there have been numerous attempts to explain homosexuality and that most of these theories are based primarily on observations and self-reports from gay men and lesbians. The important point is that the jury is still out about why some men and women become homosexuals.

We do not know what causes homosexuality any more than we know what causes heterosexuality, but we do know a lot about the consequences of discrimination and oppression. Closeted sexual minorities often feel like misfits, worry that if they do act out their internal urges they will be rejected, and live with levels of fear and shame that can become emotionally disabling. While they may find the energy to have same-sex encounters, rarely do they have the sense of security with themselves that is essential to maintain a stable and productive life. It is only when they begin to identify themselves as gay or lesbian that they start moving toward wholeness. And, for most, it is the desire for wholeness that becomes the driving force that leads them to come to terms with their sexual orientation. Today, few serious professionals believe sexual orientation is a choice. Let's take a close look at some aspects of human sexuality to provide more context for understanding homosexuality.

Deconstructing Sexuality

At first glance, sexual orientation seems to be a static characteristic of human behavior that one assumes from a process of self-discovery. In other words, people are called gay or lesbian because they define themselves that way (Golden, 1994). However, as one looks more closely at sexuality, it is easy to see that there are many components to this complex behavior. Three primary aspects of human sexuality must be considered in order to understand homosexuality or heterosexuality. *Sexual behavior* is what one does sexually. Remember, the Kinsey studies indicated that a large percentage of people have same-sex erotic experiences as they mature. To some, sexual behavior is a mechanical activity that involves stimulating various parts of the body to create erotic energy. Men and women who live for extended periods of time in same-sex communities (armed services, penal institutions, nursing homes, and so on) are known to engage in same-sex contact. For most, this experimentation is transitory and is seen as more of a temporary necessity than as an indicator of sexual orientation. And, even in some minority communities, same-sex behavior is not seen as an indication of sexual orientation; it may just be men having sex with men, another variety of human potential. Theoretically, gender may not be the critical variable in sexual stimulation and behavior. Sexual behavior in itself does not determine sexual orientation.

Sexual orientation is the deep-seated core of one's sexual attraction toward the same sex (homosexual), the opposite sex (heterosexual) or both sexes (bisexual). For example, during adolescence, erotic feelings develop that generally lead girls to have erotic feelings about boys and boys to experience similar feelings toward girls. For most people, this is a natural (or normal) development, one stepping-stone toward the heterosexual adulthood that has been shaped for them by their parents and other social institutions. We do not know what determines sexual orientation, but, at this time, sexual orientation appears to be set at birth and to remain stable across the life span.

Sexual identity is how we name ourselves. Most children grow up being encouraged to see themselves as heterosexual. Boys are told that one day they will be married to a female and have children, and the adult heterosexual world is presented to them as if it is the place they belong. Many gay and lesbian people report knowing they were different from their early years, not always having a name for the difference, but understanding that it had to do with some kind of attraction to persons of the same gender and that such attraction was unlikely to be greeted with enthusiasm by their friends and families. Thus, there comes a time when many of these persons decide to come out, or claim a sexual identity that is more consistent with their internal experience of erotic energy.

For most people these three—sexual behavior, sexual orientation, and sexual identity—operate in tandem, constantly interacting with each other. People generally do not report an awareness of choosing a sexual identity, nor is there a tendency to expand their sexuality toward an object different from internal urges. Young adults begin to experiment with their sexual selves following this "natural" energy. And they begin to develop sexual behaviors that lead to a sexual identity. This experience is true for both heterosexuals and homosexuals. A counselor gave us the following case example.

> The client, Chris, was a 21-year-old female from a rural community who came into the office on a referral from a counselor who did not know how to help her. Wearing jeans and a shirt, her opening statement was that she was a man trapped in a woman's body and that she was coming for help so she could have surgery to correct what she called her "birth defect." She said that she had not had sex with either men or women, and that she knew she was not attracted to men at all. When exploring the ways that she determined that she was a transsexual, she stated that she had been confused about herself for years and finally saw some transsexuals on a talk show and knew at once that must be what she was. Previously she had wondered if she might be lesbian, but her father told her there were no lesbians in their family. She accepted this as fact and did convince her mother to buy her boys' clothing so she would feel more comfortable. She asked to be referred to a physician who would do the surgery. I asked if she had ever

been to a gay bar, and she replied that her family did not believe in bars and that she could definitely not go to one since that would mean she might be lesbian, something her dad had said she could not be. Her gay male friends had offered to take her, but so far she had refused. At first I worried about influencing her identity too heavily, but I knew no reputable physician would be willing to perform such major surgery on a person who had had no sexual experience. I encouraged her to meet some lesbians and watch how she responded and to meet some men who might be potential sex partners and watch her energy level. Once she did that, she came back stating that she knew she was a lesbian. When she met other lesbians, she immediately felt the kind of connection with herself that she had been seeking. The rest of her treatment focused on coming out as a lesbian and integrating that identity into her larger self-image.

Chris, not unlike many people, was trying to make sense of an internal experience that did not fit her external reality as defined by her father. She is not alone in her confusion. Many people experiment with same-sex behavior for years while identifying as heterosexual and while claiming a heterosexual orientation. Eventually some may identify themselves as gay or lesbian. Others may give up same-sex behavior and live as integrated heterosexuals. Some men, particularly in ethnic minority communities, identify as men who have sex with men. This same-sex behavior is not seen as conflicting with their heterosexual orientation. Realizing that these three dimensions combine to influence one's sexuality and that they may change across time is important, particularly when we discuss reparative therapy later in this chapter.

Homosexuality and the DSM

Prior to 1973, the *DSM* included homosexuality among the list of mental disorders. That classification was changed as a result of the efforts of many but also because of the research conducted by Dr. Evelyn Hooker (1957, 1993), a California psychologist, who had observed that her gay male clients were leading lives very similar to those of her nongay clients. She collected assessments using the Minnesota Multiphasic Personality Inventory (MMPI) from a sample of identified gay males and a comparison sample of self-identified nongay men. Next, she asked experts in MMPI interpretation to examine the profiles and to sort them by sexual orientation—heterosexual or homosexual. Her statistical analysis determined that the experts using the test profiles were not able to tell the difference between homosexual and heterosexual men. The inability of the experts to determine sexual orientation from the MMPI profiles established evidence that homosexuality *per se* was not a certifiable mental disorder. According to Hooker (1957), homosexuals had ample opportunity to live happy, well-adjusted lives and therefore could not be considered abnormal. This work encouraged many within the American Psychiatric Association to take another look at the assumption that homosexuality was pathological, and at their annual conference in 1973, the historic vote was taken to remove it as a *DSM* classification.

Obviously, taking homosexuality out of the *DSM* did not reduce the homonegativity that had been so evident within the mental-health profession. Since 1973, all other mental-health organizations have taken similar stands and have consistently worked for improved service delivery to all sexual minorities. These organizations include the American Psychological Association, the American Counseling Association, the National Association of Social Workers, the American Academy of Pediatrics, the National Education Association, and others. There is no indication that these learned societies believe they have made an error in this assessment, and it is partly due to their influence that gay men and lesbians are encouraged to come out more fully. Still, there are other social institutions that continue to oppress sexual minorities.

REPARATIVE AND CONVERSION THERAPIES

Fueled by the money and energy of conservative religious groups, a media campaign began in the summer of 1998 that extolled the lives of "ex-gays." Photographs of married couples with their children accompanied by statements reporting they had become heterosexual as a result of special treatments appeared in daily newspapers across the country. Conversion therapies (CT) have been around for years as various mainly Christian organizations respond to a behavior that they regard as sinful. Attempts to change sexual orientation typically involve Bible reading, prayer, drugs, aversion therapies, electroshock and even testicular implants. Exodus International was founded in 1976 as a nondenominational Christian fellowship that claims to have helped over 200,000 persons change their sexual orientation (Leland & Miller, 1998). Religious-based organizations like Exodus believe the causes of homosexuality are found in the family constellation. Boys with absent fathers and girls with absent mothers fail to identify with the same gender parent and continue to seek fulfillment through sexual contacts with same-sex partners.

Reparative Therapy (RT) and the National Association for Reparative Therapy for Homosexuals (NARTH) represent the work of NARTH's founder, Joseph Nicolosi (1991) who believes that men become gay because of an unsuccessful identification with their fathers. According to Nicolosi's theory, gay men seek out other men for sex as a re-enactment of their frustrated desire for intimacy with their fathers. Although condemned by the major mental-health associations, Nicolosi's work continues to receive attention primarily from the religious Right.

In spite of the persistence of groups such as NARTH and the condemnation of gay men and lesbians by conservative Christian leaders such as Jerry Falwell and Pat Robertson, the American Psychological Association (1998) passed resolutions that emphasize the tenets of informed consent, especially in regards to the treatment of sexual orientation. Informing prospective clients that there is no empirical research that indicates attempts to change sexual orientation can be successful is now seen as the most ethical and professional care. These resolutions are a direct result of the lack of scientific evidence that indicates that reparative or conversion therapy is effective. In December 1998, the American Psychiatric Association went even further and declared that there are significant negative risks involved in attempts to change sexual orientation. Finally, in the spring of 1999, the American Counseling Association passed a similar resolution condemning reparative therapy. Consumers of these treatments report they are not told the truth about this approach and that they were assailed with statements that characterized homosexuals as lonely, unhappy, and unsuccessful. The bottom line is that conversion and reparative therapies emphasize a moral or value position that is not supported by scientific research (Markowitz, 1999). In short, homosexuality is not something that needs to be "fixed."

The mental-health profession has made very clear statements about the origins of homosexuality and has likewise debunked the claims of those who believe sexual orientation can be changed. In all probability, what is being changed is sexual identity and sexual behavior. Sexual orientation seems to be immutable and constant across the life span. Some might claim that changing sexual identity and sexual behavior is appropriate, given the kind of oppression and discrimination faced by gay men and lesbians. Case reports of the many gay men and lesbians who have created heterosexual marriages attest to an inner turmoil that comes from a loss of integrity and congruence. It is easy to relate to Mary's confusion as she faced gay and lesbian clients. Without formal training in these issues, she relied on stereotypes and made assumptions that seemed logical on the surface but did not hold true to the needs of her clients. In Chapter 2 you will read about various aspects of coming out as gay or lesbian, and you will begin to understand that self-esteem is enhanced when gay persons affirm their true sexual orientation.

Is It All About Sex?

Gay and lesbian culture is very diverse and much more complex than it might appear on the surface. Sexual minorities, like other minority groups, live in at least two communities. They move about the world, mostly passing as heterosexual, for that is the assumption made about them unless they announce their minority status through some obvious statement such as dress, overt behavior, or conversation. They have learned to accommodate this world, not taking offense at being constantly bombarded by heterosexual messages and images in the media, in daily life, and even in their families. For the most part, they have adjusted to a daily life that includes being "one among many." While the decision to come out certainly is influenced by erotic desires, most gay and lesbian clients report the major impetus is an internal drive toward a greater sense of integrity. As one client put it, "I want to live as the person I am, unafraid to let others know who I love and the community that I belong to." Those who live in larger cities also have the privilege of moving into gay communities where they can find a necessary kind of support and a spirit of belongingness that is often essential to their well-being. In those enclaves, they have manners of dress, a growing body of literature and music, political and other community organizations, and a history that grounds them. The sexual aspects of their lives may only be as important as the sexual expression of the majority—a pleasurable and significant part of their lives but not the major determinant of who they are. While their culture may appear to be sexually driven, an outsider would draw a similar conclusion from observations about the heterosexual community.

Tips for Practitioners

Examine Your Prejudices   People are often heard exclaiming "I am not prejudiced!" The fact is that all of us mature in communities where prejudice is taught. The question is not "Are you prejudiced?" but rather "How do your prejudices influence your behavior?" It is essential that mental-health professionals examine carefully the often-unconscious biases that may lie just below the surface but be visible to their clients. In working with people from different cultures it might be a good idea to let them know that you may be unfamiliar with certain aspects of their communities and that you hope they will be willing to let you know if you say something offensive. Just as with Mary at the beginning of the chapter, our clients can be our best teachers. Working through prejudices is complex and can lead to much discomfort. Supervision may assist in that process.

Be Sensitive to Issues of Language   When talking about gay men and lesbians you immediately run across several language issues. Further, finding the appropriate term for a gay man's or lesbian's partner can be complex. Some use the term *lover*. Others resent that term for it focuses so much on the sexual nature of their relationship. *Partner, significant other, boy-* and *girlfriend* are terms that also may be used. Even in the professional discussions, one quickly learns that some use the term *homophobia* to describe discriminatory or oppressive attitudes toward gay men and lesbians. Others prefer terms like *homonegativity* or *homoprejudice* (Logan, 1996). (In this book we prefer *homonegativity* or *homoprejudice* rather than *homophobia*). It is always a good idea to ask your client to let you know the preferred term.

Understand the Role of Politics in the GLBT Community   Many people fail to understand the reason that sexual minorities become so involved in the political process. Some think, "Well, it's OK, but I wish they would just be quiet about it." Most minority groups in the United States have had to work for their freedom. The fact is that gay men and lesbians are often fired from jobs simply because of their sexual orientation. Some get evicted from apartments or become targets of violence. In many states, the outdated sodomy laws create a kind of legal vulnerability not experienced by other groups. The recent movement to legalize gay and lesbian marriage is just one expression of many efforts that have been made to lift oppression from this community. Be supportive in your comments about gay and lesbian political activity and consider becoming an activist to help gay men and lesbians overcome oppression (Barret, 1995, 1998).

Listen for Internalized Homonegativity   Just as the counselor may have unconscious prejudices, most gay men and lesbians also harbor deep-seated expressions of self-hate. It is not unusual to hear clients say things like "Gay relationships just don't work" or "Gay people can't keep secrets." Probing for the underlying self-condemnation can lead to helpful exploration of the client's internalized negativity. You will learn more about this in Chapter 2.

Be Aware of Various Theories About the Origins of Homosexuality   It is important to acknowledge that there is no absolute knowledge about what causes homosexuality. There are theories like and beyond those that have been discussed in this chapter. While biological and genetic sciences seem to be the most promising sources for understanding how persons become homosexual, at this time we still do not have a definitive explanation about the causes of sexual orientation. Let others know what you know about the causes of sexual orientation.

Be Conscious of the Unique Challenges Faced by Gay and Lesbian People of Color   You might expect the gay and lesbian community to be more accepting of racial and ethnic differences. Sadly, bias and discrimination on the basis of skin color or nationality is just as strong in gay communities as in the general population (Gock, 1992; Morales, 1996; Rust, 1996). Further, gay and lesbian people of color must negotiate the values and beliefs of both the majority and their minority cultures. These cultural variations can be a major source of stress for those who have dual or even triple minority status and many in this population may feel alienated from all social support.

Acknowledge the Diversity Within the Gay and Lesbian Community
Just like all communities, there is enormous diversity within the gay and lesbian community. Clients like John and Janie, in the case at the beginning of the chapter, illustrate one aspect of this diversity. While the gay and lesbian community is made up of various sub-cultures, be alert to a tendency to create groupings that disguise individual characteristics. The culture is rich and no one theme dominates. You will be more effective with your gay and lesbian clients if you are aware of the cultural richness within their community.

Assess the Client's History of Victimization   Because so many gay men and lesbians have experienced losses due to their sexual orientation, your counseling will have more impact when you ask your clients to reflect on ways their sexual orientation has "cost" them. For example, some gay and lesbians have lost contact with their nuclear families. Some have suffered job discrimination or have encountered stress as a result of anxiety over applying for employment and wondering how open to be about their sexual orientation. The fact is that being gay or lesbian does mean living with particular and unique stress. Simply coming out is a stressful event. Worrying about the potential for violence when in public places generates stress the larger population does not have to face. Enduring homonegative comments by political and religious leaders creates stress. The emphasis here is not to reinforce gay and lesbian clients as victims, but, rather, to help them understand the unique pressures they face and their need for stress-coping strategies. Helping clients learn that such stressors indicate a problem in society rather than a deficiency within themselves will enhance self-esteem enormously.

Become More Knowledgeable About Gay and Lesbian Cultures
Learning about a community that is difficult to see is complex. Clients will be glad to tell you about their culture. Most major bookstores carry a credible list of gay and lesbian books. Contact a local PFLAG chapter and attend a meeting. Many communities have gay and lesbian switchboards that will be glad to send you information about local activities. Search the Internet. (See resources at the end of the book for suggestions.) Attend a performance by a gay and lesbian cultural group. Attend a church that is gay-friendly.

Develop a List of Local Resources for Gay and Lesbian Clients   If you are not comfortable providing mental-health services to gay clients, find out those in your community who can provide this service. Get to know gay-positive clergy who are willing to talk with gay men and lesbians about their spiritual concerns. Know where the gay and lesbian meetings of Alcoholics Anonymous (AA) take place in your community. Put together a resource list you can hand to clients who are looking for ways to find the gay community.

Practice Affirmative Counseling for Gay Men and Lesbians   Examine ways that your practice might affirm the unique needs of gay men and lesbians. Does your bookcase contain books on homosexuality? Do you have gay and lesbian magazines in your office waiting room? Do you have referral lists that include agencies that serve the gay community? Have you learned enough about your local gay community to give you a more complete context for understanding your gay and lesbian clients' lives? Visit a gay or lesbian community center or go to a fund-raiser for a gay youth organization. Read gay and lesbian magazines and newspapers. Attend a political rally for candidates who support gay and lesbian issues. Attend a religious service in a church that welcomes all sexual minorities. In short, educate yourself about the community that is at your doorstep.

BIBLIOGRAPHY

Allport, G. (1954). *The nature of prejudice.* Reading, MA: Addison-Wesley.

American Psychological Association. (1998). American Psychological Association rebukes reparative therapy. *APA Online News Stand.* [on-line] Available: www.apa.org.

Bailey, J. & Pillard, R. (1991). A genetic study of male sexual orientation. *Archives of Sexual Behavior, 20*(3), 227–293.

Bancroft, J. (1990). Commentary: Biological contributions to homosexuality. In D. P. McWhirter & S. A. Sanders (Eds.), *Homosexuality/heterosexuality: Concepts of sexual orientation.* New York: Oxford.

Bargh, J. & Chartrand, T. (1999). The unbearable automaticity of being. *The American Psychologist, 54*(7), 462–479.

Barret, B. (1998). Gay and lesbian activism: A frontier in social advocacy. In C. Lee & G. Walz (Eds.), *Social action: A mandate for counselors.* Alexandria, VA: American Counseling Association.

Barret, B. & Robinson, B. (2000). *Gay fathers.* San Francisco: Jossey-Bass.

Barret, R. L. (1997). Creating change: Making an impact in the local news media. In J. Sears & W. Williams (Eds.), *Overcoming heterosexism and homophobia: Strategies that work.* New York: Columbia University Press.

Bell, A. P. & Weinberg, M. S. (1978). *Homosexualities: A study of diversity among men and women.* New York: Simon & Schuster.

Brown, L. (1997). *Two-spirited people: American Indian lesbian women and gay men.* New York: Haworth Press.

Burr, C. (1993, March). Homosexuality and biology. *The Atlantic Monthly,* 47–65.

Child Welfare League of America. (1995). *Issues in lesbian and gay adoption.* Washington, DC: Child Welfare League of America.

Coleman, E. (1988). Assessment of sexual orientation. In E. Coleman (Ed.), *Integrated identity for gay men and lesbians: Psychotherapeutic approaches for emotional well-being.* New York: Harrington Park Press.

———. (1990). Toward a synthetic understanding of sexual orientation. In D. P. McWhirter, S. A. Sanders, & J. M. Reinisch (Eds.), *Homosexuality/heterosexuality: Concepts of sexual orientation.* New York: Oxford University Press.

Dreikurs, R. (1953). *Fundamentals of Adlerian psychology.* Chicago: Alfred Adler Institute.

Freud, S. (1953). Three essays on the theory of sexuality. In J. Strachey (Ed. and Trans.), *The standard edition of the complete works of Sigmund Freud,* vol. 7. London: Hogarth Press.

———. (1957). On narcissism: An introduction. In J. Strachey (Ed. and Trans.), *The standard edition of the complete works of Sigmund Freud,* vol. 14. London: Hogarth Press.

Garnets, L. & Kimmel. D. (1991). Lesbian and gay male dimensions in the psychological study of human diversity. In J. Goodchilds (Ed.), *Psychological perspectives on human diversity in America: Master lectures.* Washington DC: American Psychological Association.

Gock, T. (1992). The challenges of being gay, Asian, and proud. In B. Berzon (Ed.), *Positively gay*. Millbrae, CA: Celestial Arts.

Golden, C. (1994). Our politics and choices: The feminist movement and sexual orientation. In B. Greene & G. Herek (Eds.), *Lesbian and gay psychology: Theory, research, and clinical applications*. Thousand Oaks, CA: Sage.

Gonsiorek, J. & Weinrich, J. (1991). The definition and scope of sexual orientation. In J. Gonsiorek & J. Weinrich (Eds.), *Homosexuality: Research implications for public policy*. Newbury Park, CA: Sage.

Gooren, L. (1990). Biomedical theories of sexual orientation: A critical examination. In D. P. McWhirter, S. A. Sanders, & J. M. Reinisch (Eds.), *Homosexuality/heterosexuality: Concepts of Sexual Orientation*. New York: Oxford University Press.

Greene, B. (1994). Ethnic minority lesbians and gay men: Mental health and treatment issues. *Journal of Consulting and Clinical Psychology, 62,* 243–251.

Hooker, Evelyn. (1957). The adjustment of the overt male homosexual. *Journal of Projective Techniques, 21,* 18–31.

———. (1993). Reflections on a 40 year exploration: A scientific view on homosexuality. *American Psychologist, 48*(4), 450–453.

Jay, K. & Young, A. (1980). *The gay report: Lesbians and gay men speak out about sexual experiences and lifestyle.* New York: Summit.

Jenny, C., Roesler, T., & Poyer, K. (1994). Are children at risk for sexual abuse by homosexuals? *Pediatrics, 94*(1), 41–44.

Kinsey, A. C., Pomeroy, W. B., & Martin, C. E. (1948). *Sexual behavior in the human male.* Philadelphia: W. B. Sanders Company.

———. (1953). *Sexual behavior in the human female.* Philadelphia: W. B. Saunders Company.

Lambda Legal Defense and Education Fund. (1999). State by state sodomy law update [on-line]. Available: http://www. lambdalegal.org/cgi-bin/pages/documents/record?record=275.

Leland, J. & Miller, M. (1998, August 17). Can gays convert? *Newsweek, 132*(7), 46–50.

LeVay, S. (1991, August). A difference in hypothalamic structure between heterosexual and homosexual men. *Science, 253,* 1034–1037.

LeVay, S. & Hamer, D. (1994). Evidence for a biological influence in male homosexuality. *Science, 270,* 44–49.

Levinson, D. (1978). *The seasons of a man's life.* New York: Ballantine Books.

Logan, C. (1996). Homophobia? No! Homoprejudice? Yes! *Journal of Homosexuality, 31*(3), 31–53.

Markowitz, L. (1999). Dangerous practice: Inside the conversion therapy controversy. *In the Family, 4*(3), 10–13.

Morales, E. (1996). Gender roles among Latino gay and bisexual men: Implications for couple and family relationships. In J. Laird & R. Greene (Eds.), *Lesbians and gays in couples and families: A handbook for therapists.* San Francisco: Jossey-Bass.

Morgan, K. S. & Nerison, R. M. (1993). Homosexuality and psychopolitics: An overview. *Psychotherapy, 30,* 133–140.

Mosak, H. H. & Dreikurs, R. (1967). The life tasks III: The fifth life task. *Journal of Individual Psychology, 5*(1), 16–22.

Nicolosi, J. (1991). *Reparative therapy of male homosexuality.* Northvale, NJ: Jason Aronson.

Rudolph, J. (1988). Counselor attitudes toward homosexuality: A review of the literature. *Journal of Counseling and Development, 67,* 165–168.

Rust, P. (1996). Managing multiple identities: Diversity among bisexual women and men. In B. Firestein (Ed.), *Bisexuality: The psychology and politics of an invisible minority*. Thousand Oaks, CA: Sage.

Whitam, F., Diamond, M., & Martin, J. (1993). Homosexual orientation in twins: A report on 61 pairs and three triplet sets. *Archives of Sexual Behavior, 22*(3), 151–170.

Zinik, G. (1985). Identity conflict or adaptive flexibility? Bisexuality reconsidered. In F. Klein & T. Wolf (Eds.), *Bisexualities: Theory and research*. New York: Haworth Press.

GAY AND LESBIAN IDENTITY DEVELOPMENT

The Case of Marion ▼

Marion is an LPC who maintains a private practice in a large metropolitan city.

Marion has had her own practice for more than seven years and feels very comfortable dealing with a wide variety of clinical issues. Her client load is primarily composed of gay and lesbian individuals and couples, but she is proud of the fact that her practice is diverse and representative of different sexual orientations, ethnic and cultural backgrounds, and religious affiliations. Marion is a lesbian and a very active member of the local gay and lesbian community. She feels very strongly about being visible and open about her sexual orientation. She believes that coming out to others was a critical and essential step toward feeling good about herself as a lesbian. Coming out to others is also a way Marion feels she can educate nongays and challenge the stereotypes and myths about gay men and lesbians. On the other hand, Marion certainly understands that there are very real and threatening challenges to becoming more visible in an oppressive society. Over the years she has watched clients agonize over whether or not to come out to friends or family members, while other clients live in terror, afraid they'll be found out and so choose to remain silent and secretive about who they are and whom they love. Still others have found that living two lives works best for them, that is, one life at night as gay or lesbian and another during the day—slipping on the cloak of heterosexuality and "passing" in the straight world. Some clients had a coming out experience that was similar to her own: She remembered that she felt different at an early age and eventually became consciously aware that she might be lesbian. After trying to date men and feeling unfulfilled, she allowed herself to explore the possibility that she was attracted to women. As a young adult she finally accepted the fact that she was indeed a lesbian, started dating women, and eventually settled down with the woman she now refers to as her life-partner. They have been together for six years. Both she and her partner were out to family and friends and living out in the suburbs as a same-sex couple. Living out to Marion and her partner means living an integrated life where their sexual orientation is just one part of who they are as women and as human beings.

After contemplating the myriad ways her clients had come to terms with being gay or lesbian, Marion decided to offer a six-week coming out/living out group. Both gay men and lesbians were invited to participate in the group. The goal of the group was to help members become more comfortable with their sexual orientation, to learn from each other about different coming out processes, and, as a result, develop strategies to cope with coming out and living out in a homoprejudiced world.

Eight people showed up for the first meeting, much to Marion's surprise and pleasure. At the initial meeting, clients introduced themselves and told their stories of coming to terms with being gay or lesbian. They shared life stories and the unique ways each had dealt with coming out as a gay or lesbian person. Special focus was placed on the first signs of feeling or being different, first awareness of being gay or lesbian, first experiences with the same-sex, and stories of coming out to others. Here are their stories:

Scott is a gay male in his mid-thirties. He has known he was different since he was 7 or 8 years old. As an adolescent he realized that he was attracted to boys but he did whatever he could to hide it from his friends. He remembers incidents of being very ashamed in the locker room when he became aroused by observing the other boys. During adolescence, Scott successfully passed all the heterosexual milestones, such as dating and the prom, but he was never completely happy. He had his first experience with another man in college: It was then that he knew unequivocally that he was gay. Since then, Scott has dated men exclusively and is currently on the cusp of a two-year anniversary with his boyfriend. Scott feels very comfortable with himself and very happy with his boyfriend and feels that it's time to tell his parents the truth. He knows they "know" but he has never told them outright. He is tired of playing the "don't ask, don't tell" game, pretending that Sean is just a friend at family gatherings and events. He's ready to tell his parents, but deep down inside he's afraid of rejection. He's afraid they'll never want to have anything to do with him again and that seems too much to bear.

Sue is a female in her mid-fifties who six months ago had an epiphany: She realized she was a lesbian. She has never been physically intimate with another woman, and until five years ago had been married to a man. Although the marriage had not been a happy one, for he was an alcoholic and abusive, she never thought she might be lesbian, she just knew she was miserable with her husband. She shared with the others in the group the excitement she felt when she realized she was lesbian. It was on that day that it all came together for her: For the first time in her life she knew who she was and it felt good. Now, she wonders, what to do with this epiphany?

Mary and Rachel are of different religious backgrounds and have been dating each other exclusively for the past year. They feel totally in love and committed to each other and, in fact, have planned to have a commitment ceremony within the next few months. Prior to dating Rachel, Mary had been in a long-term relationship with another woman. Rachel, though, has never been in a formal relationship with a woman; she had dated women but had never dated someone exclusively. Rachel was not out at work or to her family. The death of Rachel's father six months earlier had devastated her mother, and Rachel was not about to add to that grief by telling her that her only daughter was a lesbian and preparing to marry another woman. Mary had been out to her family since she was 23. She and her former partner spent holidays with her family and she felt very comfortable and accepted. Mary owns a small business and is out to her employees and customers. Usually, the issue of who was out and who wasn't did not affect the couple, but Rachel planned to spend the coming holidays with her mother. Mary felt abandoned and angry: If Rachel couldn't be with her for the holidays now, what would happen when they got married? Mary was not used to being hidden and was tempted to out Rachel herself.

Cedrick is a 45-year-old male who has been in a relationship for ten years. His partner, Rick, is from a different ethnic background and as Cedrick puts it, "the love of my life." As a dual minority, Cedrick has struggled to come out. When he was growing up, his family's focus was on ethnic pride and togetherness. No one ever talked about being gay, although they made fun of "crazy ol' Uncle Charlie," an eccentric old guy who never married, wore flamboyant clothes, and was always dramatic—he was still family, and everyone accepted and loved him. Cedrick knew from a young age that he was different. He remembers engaging in sexual activity with other boys, although no one ever talked about it. Cedrick always dated girls. His marriage to his high-school sweetheart, however, lacked passion and intimacy. Cedrick started going to gay bars a few years into the marriage; he sometimes had sex with men he met. During those sexual encounters, Cedrick felt complete and whole, connected for the first time with himself and another person. Cedrick and his wife drifted apart and divorced, and soon after, Cedrick met Rick, with whom he's been ever since. Cedrick recalls that when he told his mother and sisters he was gay, they seemed to take it well, but it's never been mentioned again. Cedrick's family has met Rick and seem to accept him as one of them, but the men's relationship has never been recognized or named. Cedrick is angry and feels discounted by this attitude of his family. He and Rick don't socialize much, and, as a mixed-race couple, they don't really feel part of the gay community. They used to go to church together but in recent years they stay home more and more. Cedrick feels isolated and angry.

Sarah is a 25-year-old female. She is college-educated, has a good job and, in general, feels good about herself. Growing up, she always had lots of dates with boys and was popular in school, but she always felt discontented. She used to have huge crushes on her teachers and camp counselors and when she started having sex with men she couldn't become aroused unless she fantasized she was with a woman. She tried to be attracted to and happy with men but it just didn't work. At age 20 she had a brief fling with a woman, which she found immensely satisfying, but she continued dating her boyfriend. At age 23 she had her first relationship with a woman: They're still together. She has told her family and her straight friends. Her family is angry and hurt with her "choice" and seems to be waiting until she "grows out of it." Her straight friends think she's a freak—or weird at best; they, too, think it's just a phase. Nobody at work knows because she just couldn't stand any more rejection. How could she feel so right yet feel so wrong in this world? The attitude of her family and friends makes life difficult, and Sarah spends a lot of time feeling guilty and confused.

Stephen is a 62-year-old male who says he feels like an adolescent. Never married, having never found anyone he wanted to settle down with, Stephen has spent his life focused on his career. After retiring last year, he's decided to start living. He quickly admits that all along he knew on some level that he was attracted to men but never acted on his feelings. Raised in a hard working, religious home, he's always been a "good boy," and would never have done anything to hurt or shame his family. But now his parents are both dead, he's retired, and "by god—I'm ready to start living." In the last few months, Stephen has been going to the bars every weekend, playing on the gay softball team, and attending the gay church. During the week, he hangs out at the bookstore, drinking coffee and meeting men. He is still amazed by all the gay books and activities he can choose from: He feels like a little kid on his birthday . . . every day is a gift, a new day to be his true self.

"Wow," thought Marion, after that session, "so many different stories and experiences, yet all of us have so much in common. Each of us has had to struggle to feel good about who we are and whom we love. I must admit, sometimes I just want to quit my job and just spend the rest of my life trying to change the world and make it okay to be gay or lesbian. Deep down inside I want all of them to come out, have positive experiences and, as a result, feel good about themselves. But I must remember it's a process every gay or lesbian must go through; it takes time and not everyone is going to evolve in the same way or in the same time frame."

Marion wanted the coming out/living out group to be a positive experience for the participants regardless of where they were in the coming out process. Accordingly, she devised the following plan for the group.

Session II   Tell the story. Describe your evolution as a gay or lesbian person. When did you first feel different? Become aware that you were gay or lesbian? Who, if anyone, have you come out to? Describe the experience(s) of coming out to others: Has it been positive, negative, or mixed?

Discuss different models of identity development and have participants map out where they are in the process and where they want to be in a month, six months, or a year.

Assignment   Begin a journal documenting your experience in the group.

Session III   Explore the effects of internal and external homo-prejudice. Explore feelings of shame, guilt, and self-hate. Grieve the loss of heterosexual privilege and its associated rituals and unbridled societal acceptance.

Assignment   List stereotypes and myths associated with gays and lesbians and counteract each one with the facts.

Session IV   Explore self-destructive behavior and thoughts (such as substance abuse, promiscuity, smoking, and overeating). Employ positive self-talk and make a commitment to love and take care of yourself.

Assignment   Attend movies and other events where gays and lesbians are portrayed in a positive light. Read books and other materials which provide accurate information and affirmation of gays and lesbians. Explore the Internet for supportive and informational websites.

Session V   Role-play various coming-out scenarios, enacting both positive and negative reactions. Explore inhibitors to coming out, such as fear of violence, rejection, and ostracism. Ascertain what is real fear versus what is a projection of one's own internalized fear and shame. Challenge members to come out in small ways and big ways when they're ready. Strategize ways to create "safe zones" or places where it's okay to be gay or lesbian. Help members to identify and utilize non-gay allies and friends.

Assignment   Encourage members to use an openly gay or lesbian service or professional. Attend a community event that is not bar or club related.

Session VI Develop a 12-month plan to feel good about being gay or lesbian. Share your plan with the other members of the group. Be open to feedback and additional suggestions.

At the end of the six-week session, each of the group members had come to terms with his/her gay or lesbian identity. All had reached self-acceptance and many had experimented, successfully, with becoming more visible to family, friends, and co-workers. Moreover, each had made a personal commitment as well as a public declaration to the other group members to live out more fully each day.

GAY AND LESBIAN IDENTITY DEVELOPMENT

To effectively work and develop a therapeutic relationship with gay and lesbian clients, it is critical for practitioners to gain an understanding and appreciation for the challenges of coming out. Coming out in this sense refers to the developmental process of acknowledging one's gay or lesbian identity first to self and then to others. It is a lifelong process that is made that much more difficult by the internal and external influence of homoprejudice. Clearly gays and lesbians are uniquely challenged by the task of trying to adopt a positive self-identity in the midst of societal oppression. Conversely, mental-health practitioners are in a unique position to facilitate this process through affirmative and empathic counseling practices.

According to Reynolds and Hanjorgiris (2000), at least four significant tasks emerge when working with clients who are grappling with sexual identity issues. The first task is to help the client with the recognition of being different from the heterosexual norm, i.e., the initial awareness of emotional and sexual feelings toward the same gender and the ensuing process of coming out to self and others. The second task is to help clients manage their sexual identity across multiple contexts such as home, work, and school. Included in this task is the additional challenge for some clients of learning how to manage multiple identities such as being African American and gay or Jewish and lesbian. A third task is to help the client identify the effects of internalized homoprejudice and how it affects the emergence of a positive gay or lesbian identity. And, finally, a fourth task is to assist the client with the continuing onslaught of societal oppression and homoprejudice.

The purpose of this chapter is to explore a number of different identity development models that typically describe the coming out experience for gay males and unique issues of lesbian identity development, which will be addressed by using a model that illustrates how lesbian women develop and evolve differently from their male counterparts. The issue of multiple identities will be explored in terms of how membership in various minority groups affects the coming out process for both gay men and lesbians. The discussion in this chapter is limited in scope to exploring gay and lesbian development. An in-depth discussion of bisexual identity development and transgender identity development can be found in Chapter 6.

Models of Identity Development

Traditional identity development models are typically characterized by an initial awareness of feeling different or having feelings toward the same sex, first sexual encounters, participation in the gay and lesbian community, self-labeling as gay or lesbian, and disclosing one's gay or lesbian identity to others. From first awareness to sexual identity integration is typically a lifelong process. Some individuals move more quickly through the stages than others do, while others become stuck and never evolve to the final stages of identity integration. Moreover, the coming out process can begin at any age throughout the life span. The reader may recall Stephen's story from the case example: He was just coming to terms with the coming out process at age 62, while Scott knew he was gay since age 7 or 8, and although he had repressed his feelings for many years, began coming to terms with his sexual orientation while he was in college. And finally, keep in mind that successful completion or movement through each stage is heavily influenced by negative societal attitudes and internalized shame. Another, more simplistic way to characterize the models is a movement from awareness, "Am I gay?" to dissonance, "Oh no, I might be gay!" to acceptance, "I'm probably gay." to the final stage of identity integration, "I'm gay and I'm okay."

The Cass Model

Cass (1979) proposed an identity development model that was intended to describe the coming out process for both gay men and lesbians. This model is particularly useful because it is not necessarily bound by a certain age or developmental stage, and can be applied at any point across the life span. The model was characterized by six stages: Stage I: Identity Confusion; Stage II: Identity Comparison; Stage III: Identity Tolerance; Stage IV: Identity Acceptance; Stage V: Identity Pride; and Stage VI: Identity Synthesis.

According to Cass (1979), at each stage there is potential for identity foreclosure, wherein the person may choose not to develop any further or the person may continue through the stages and at the end stage acquire a positive, integrated gay or lesbian identity.

Stage I: Identity Confusion The journey begins. This stage is characterized by feeling different and initial awareness that the heterosexual self-portrait doesn't fit. It is a time of great dissonance and inner turmoil. Self-acknowledgement of these feelings leads to feelings of despair, shame, and may even lead to suicidal ideation. Cedrick, Stephen, Scott, and Sarah recalled feeling different at an early age, yet none of them had any context for understanding and accepting these feelings. As a result, they tried to ignore and repress their feelings of differentness and immerse themselves in the trappings of a heterosexual world.

Stage II: Identity Comparison   To cope with the dissonance, the individual begins to rationalize or intellectualize feelings or try to bargain internally, for instance, "This is just a temporary phase" or "I only have these feelings for this particular person." The individual feels unique, like he/she is the only one in the world who feels this way. These are the four potential responses to this internal conflict.

1. Internally recognize feeling and being different yet still portray an acceptable public identity by passing as heterosexual, keeping one's gay or lesbian identity hidden or in the closet. This response requires the individual to compartmentalize his/her life, keeping a private gay and lesbian identity completely separate from other aspects of life. The individual may become hypervigilant, avoiding any reference or contact with the gay community for fear of guilt by association. The individual may even choose to compensate by becoming "super" heterosexual and promiscuous. For example, Danny, a 33-year-old client, knew for several years that he was attracted to men but was so afraid of being "different" or "found out" that he actually started dating more women, and at times dated two or three women at once just to prove he wasn't gay.
2. Accept one's homosexual behavior but reject the notion of adopting a public homosexual identity. The reader may recall Rachel's story from the case example. Rachel had been involved with Mary for over a year and even planning to have a commitment ceremony, yet she was not out at work or to her family.
3. Accept self as homosexual but reject and refuse to participate in any homosexual behavior.
4. Reject both self and behavior and actively seek to change both. The individual may seek to be healed or fixed. (Review Chapter 1 for a discussion of the dangers of reparative therapy.)

Stage III: Identity Tolerance   This stage is characterized by the realization that the individual probably is gay or lesbian and by a stronger sense of alienation or disaffiliation from the heterosexual world coupled with a desire to connect with other gay or lesbian people. Progression through this stage depends on how the individual perceives contact with the gay community. If contacts are perceived as negative or undesirable, the person may devalue the gay culture, choose to avoid future contact with the gay community, and strive to inhibit all homosexual behaviors and feelings. For example, if the first time Sue encounters the gay community is at a gay pride march, where everyone around her happens to be wearing leather and drinking heavily, she may decide that she unequivocally doesn't fit in and decide to avoid any future contact with gays and lesbians.

If, however, contacts are perceived as positive, gay and lesbian people become more important and significant, leading to positive self-esteem and a greater commitment to adopting a gay and lesbian identity.

Stage IV: Identity Acceptance   This stage is characterized by continued and more frequent contact with the greater gay community. Individuals begin to develop friendships with other gay and lesbian people and, as a result, move from identity tolerance to acceptance. They may still choose to "pass" as a heterosexual if necessary and avoid or limit contacts with people who are perceived as unaccepting or judgmental. It is during this stage that the individual begins to selectively disclose his/her identity to significant heterosexuals.

Stage V: Identity Pride   Individuals at this stage immerse themselves in the gay community, feeling a strong sense of identification with the gay community, and a heightened awareness that the internalized feelings of dissonance, shame, and guilt are directly related to societal oppression and prejudice. Anger and outrage at society and the notion of heterosexual privilege typify this stage. The world is divided into two camps, heterosexuals who are discredited and insignificant and homosexuals who are credible and significant. At this stage, some individuals are propelled toward social activism and seek membership in organizations such as ACT-UP or the Lesbian Avengers (examples of radical political action groups). This stage is also characterized by an increased disclosure of identity.

Stage VI: Identity Synthesis   At this stage, anger and righteous indignation soften somewhat, and individuals begin to let go of the "us vs. them" attitude and recognize that some heterosexuals are credible and can be trusted. They remain cognizant of societal oppression yet spend less energy on anger and outrage. At this stage, gay and lesbian individuals develop a sense of pride and begin to integrate their lesbian and gay identity into the tapestry of a personal mosaic. Marion, the counselor in the case example, is a good example of someone who has synthesized her lesbian identity. Marion is out to her friends and family and she and her partner live openly in the suburbs of a large metropolitan city. Being lesbian is just one part of who she is as a woman and as a human being.

The Troiden Model

Troiden's (1989) model has an underlying assumption that the process begins prior to puberty and that evolution implies progression through the stages in accordance with chronological age. This model is useful for working with clients who have felt "different" from an early age. In addition, this model includes suggested coping strategies one might use to deal with societal oppression and homoprejudice.

Stage I: Sensitization   According to Troiden (1989), this stage occurs before puberty and is characterized by a sense of feeling "different." Differences are typically manifested in gender-neutral or gender-atypical behavior; for example, girls may be interested in sports and boys may be interested in dance or cooking. Individuals report feeling marginalized and alienated from their peer group at a young age.

Stage II: Confusion   Post-puberty, the individual may become increasingly aware of homosexual thoughts and feelings, and may even experience both homosexual and heterosexual arousal. It is during this stage that the individual becomes aware of the societal stigma that surrounds homosexuality. As a result, these stereotypes and misconceptions are internalized. Lack of accurate information and lack of contact with other gay people who can model healthy, integrated lives leaves many gay and lesbian youth plagued by feelings of dissonance, guilt, shame, and a deep sense of isolation. To cope with these feelings individuals engage in a complex process of rationalization: "I won't act on it." "That isn't me." "I'm not anything like that. I'll prove it's not me." "I won't get involved with anyone" or "I'll rid the world of homosexuality." Alternatively, the client may choose to avoid dealing with the issue by trying to inhibit and deny same-sex feelings by saying, "I can get over this." The individual may choose to avoid all contact or reference to homosexuality ("I don't want to know anything about it") or even limit exposure to the opposite sex for fear of being exposed and found lacking in heterosexual desire. The individual may choose to make excuses for his feelings or behavior: "I was drunk" or "It was an accident" or "I was just experimenting."

To progress to the next stage, the individual begins to accept the feelings, fantasies, and behaviors as homosexual. Doing so releases the individual to seek out accurate information and contact with the gay community. Connection with the gay community affords him/her the opportunity to understand that being gay or lesbian is a valid sexual orientation.

Stage III: Identity Assumption   This stage typically begins in late adolescence, at a time when the individual begins to assume or try out a gay identity. It is characterized by more contact with the gay community, sexual experimentation, and exploration. Possible responses at this stage include the following:

1. The individual succumbs to homoprejudice and societal oppression and tries to avoid same-sex behavior while haunted by desire: This response leads to shame and self-hatred.

2. The individual may choose to "pass" or lead a double life, portraying her/himself as a heterosexual to family, friends, and co-workers while living a secret gay life.
3. The individual may choose to immerse her/himself in the gay community and to avoid or severely limit contact with the nongay world.

To progress to the next stage the individual begins to accept a gay self-identity.

Stage IV: Commitment   Self-acceptance and comfort with a gay identity characterize this stage. Commitment to a gay identity has both internal and external dimensions.

> Internal Dimension: Being gay becomes a valid and satisfactory self-identity resulting in the fusion of sexuality, emotionality, and spirituality into a whole—a state of well-being.
> External Dimension: The individual enters into same-sex love relationships and is more comfortable with self-disclosure.

Individuals at this stage manage oppression in at least three ways:

1. *Cover:* Acknowledge gay or lesbian identity if asked, but try to keep it hidden and minimize its importance to ensure being viewed as a respectable person by nongays.
2. *Blend:* Ensure that one is gender-appropriate and conventional while neither disclosing or denying sexual identity. Individuals who choose this option consider a gay identity irrelevant and keep it cloaked in secrecy.
3. *Live with pride:* Seek to dispel the stereotypes about gay people. Work toward eliminating societal homoprejudice.

The Coleman Model
Coleman's (1987) developmental model differs from the first two models because it characterizes identity development by the way the individual forms romantic attachments and relationships.

Stage I: Pre–Coming Out   The individual becomes conscious of same-sex feelings. These feelings are immediately followed by strong defenses against acknowledgement of those feelings. Individuals are cognizant of feeling different but don't understand the full meaning of these feelings.

Stage II: Coming Out   The individual begins to acknowledge the presence of same-sex thoughts or fantasies. This acknowledgement is coupled with confusion. He/she may choose to disclose to one or two trusted people for validation or even make contacts with gay or lesbian people but avoids telling close friends or family who are presumably heterosexual.

Stage III: Exploration   The individual begins to experiment with adopting a gay identity. This stage is characterized by increased contact with gay and lesbian individuals. Some move through this stage at adolescence; others do not, experiencing "developmental lag" and may not have this opportunity to experience gay adolescence until much later in life.

Recall the case of Stephen. Sixty-two years old and experiencing life and love for the first time! Stephen is a perfect illustration of someone who did not experience his gay adolescence until he was much older. He currently is experiencing many aspects of the gay world and trying to find his place in the community that may not always make sense to him. For example, after years of being in the closet, Stephen feels very uncomfortable with younger men who are very flamboyant and refer to themselves as "queer." Stephen is offended by this term and prefers to define himself as a "homosexual." Astutely, Marion recognized that Stephen hails from an era when openness about one's sexual orientation was completely unacceptable. Stephen's discomfort with the term *queer* and self-identification as a "homosexual" is not necessarily a reflection of his internalized homoprejudice but rather an implication of his socialization. Marion validated his experience of "gay adolescence" by giving him permission to play and explore and by helping him find a place in the community where he feels comfortable and accepted. Moreover, Marion recognized Stephen's discomfort with contemporary terms and slang and always referred to Stephen as homosexual.

Stage IV: First Relationship   Following a period of experimentation, the individual may require a more stable and committed relationship which combines emotional and physical attraction. According to Coleman (1987), first relationships often do not last because tasks of coming out and exploration stages have not been completed.

Stage V: Integration   During this stage, public and private identities merge into an integrated identity that is continuous, ongoing, and lasts the rest of the person's life. Relationships are characterized by less possessiveness, honesty, and trust and are usually more successful than a first relationship.

LESBIAN IDENTITY DEVELOPMENT

Separating lesbian identity development from gay male development is a relatively new concept because lesbians have been typically subsumed under the rubric of gays and not seen as unique. Existing identity development models have been criticized for being stage-sequential and linear in progression and based primarily on the retrospective accounts of white, middle-aged males, failing to recognize the more fluid and relationship-oriented aspects of lesbian identity development. According to McCarn and Fassinger (1996), these models also fail to recognize the effects of multiple minority statuses and multiple oppressive environments. In response, the authors proposed a dual lesbian identity developmental model which tracks individual or personal identity development and relationship identity development or how one relates to the reference group. For example, a lesbian couple may live in a rural environment and have little or no contact with the gay community yet still feel positive and healthy as lesbians.

This new model of lesbian identity development was derived from existing models of gay and lesbian identity development and information gleaned from the gender, sociopolitical, and diversity literature. Borrowed from the feminist literature was the notion of sexual repression and the tendency of women to develop and come out in the context of a relationship. Women face a struggle when trying to incorporate the sexual identity that men traditionally do not, that is, women are taught that sexual desire is dangerous and inappropriate, and furthermore, that the object of their sexual desire, a woman, is inferior. Moreover, women tend to come out later in life in the context of a relationship as opposed to an independent process of articulating and acting on sexual desire or feelings. In Box 2.1 you will find a summary of McCarn & Fassinger's (1996) model of lesbian identity development.

This model is useful for mental-health practitioners as they help facilitate the coming out process of lesbian women. Clearly, lesbians can be in different phases of the identity development process simultaneously. For example, in the case study, Sue described her recent discovery of her lesbian identity as an epiphany. Since divorcing her husband, she had become involved in the women's movement and even came across a number of lesbian women, but it had never crossed her mind that she was lesbian. To facilitate her coming out process, Marion may encourage her to become involved in the lesbian community while at the same encouraging her to explore what it means to be lesbian. Remember Rachel and Mary who were struggling with being incongruent in their coming out processes? Teaching them this model may give each a better understanding of the other's developmental process. Mary may need to be more patient with Rachel's reluctance to coming out, particularly in the wake of her father's death. For example, Rachel's grief may be exacerbated by the distance she created between herself and her parents as a way of staying hidden about her sexual orientation. Rachel may need to do some individual work around grieving the loss of her father and to process the guilt related to not meeting her family's expectations of heterosexuality. Finally, remember Sarah and her experience of coming out? She came out in a relationship with another woman and is currently struggling with feelings of guilt and confusion. She is acutely aware of her strong emotional and sexual attraction to women but she has no experience with the gay community. In this case, Marion could encourage Sarah to connect with the gay and lesbian community in order to find support and validation for her sexual identity.

BOX
2.1

Lesbian Identity Development Model

Individual Development	Group Identity Development

Awareness

1. Aware of being different.

1. Aware of sexual orientations other than just heterosexual.

"I feel pulled toward women in ways I don't understand."
"I had no idea there were lesbian/gay people out there."

Exploration

2. Experience strong feelings toward another woman, may not be erotic, may include different affectional targets, "a crush."

2. Active pursuit of knowledge about lesbians, may not self-identify, trying to ascertain, "do I fit in?"

"The way I feel makes me want to be sexual with other women."
"Getting to know gay and lesbian people is scary and exciting."

Deepening Commitment

3. Recognize sexual desire for women, develop sexual clarity and commitment to fulfillment as a sexual being. Who I'm intimate with and my identity begin to intertwine. Grieve loss of heterosexuality.

3. Deepening commitment to lesbian identity, culture. Active rejection of heterosexual norms and parameters. Place high value on lesbians. Feel anger and frustration with societal oppression.

"I clearly feel more intimate sexually and emotionally with women than men."
"Sometimes I have been mistreated because of my lesbianism."

Identity Integration

4. **Internalization/Integration** of identify, self-acceptance, and self-love as a lesbian woman.

4. **Identity** as member of a group, feeling secure, fulfilled, and able to maintain lesbian identity across contexts.

"I am deeply fulfilled in my relationships with women."
"I feel comfortable with my lesbianism no matter where I am or who I am with."

(Source: *Adapted from McCarn and Fassinger, 1996.*)

Cultural Differences
and the Coming Out Process

Mental-health practitioners must also be aware of the stress associated with the compounding effect of oppression that is associated with being a member of multiple minority groups, that is, female, lesbian and African American, Asian and gay, and so forth (Reynolds & Pope, 1991; Greene, 1994, 1997; Smith, 1997; Fukuyama & Ferguson, 2000). For an ethnic minority the fear associated with the coming out process can be greatly exacerbated, for being gay or lesbian may cause rejection and ostracism from the cultural/ethnic group, a place where there has been relative safety and an ingrained sense of identity.

It is important to be aware of each group's historical prejudice toward homosexuals, and the specific stereotypes and myths held by each group toward gays and lesbians. Expectations of strict adherence to gender roles and responsibilities may also thwart the coming out process, for being gay or lesbian is perceived as contradictory or a violation of those roles and therefore unacceptable. In addition, many minority groups traditionally have strong ties to organized religion and maintain strong fundamental religious beliefs against homosexuality (Greene, 1997).

It is also critical to recognize the importance of the family system. Homosexuality may not be addressed or discussed but gay or lesbian children may still be considered part of the family. For gay or lesbian ethnic minorities, the emphasis may not be on saying the words and literally "coming out to family" but rather the recognition that the family is "accepting" by incorporating the same-sex partner as one of their own (Smith, 1997). In the case of Cedrick, it is validating and reinforcing for his family to accept Rick as part of the family at various get-togethers, and at the same time, Cedrick is angry and hurt that his sexual orientation remains a subject of taboo. For additional support, Marion might encourage Cedrick and Rick to join a gay mixed-ethnic support group where they can find support and validation for their relationship, ethnicity, and sexual orientation.

The stress associated with managing identities cannot be overestimated. Mental-health practitioners need to understand that ethnic minorities may make choices about identification, choosing at times to honor ethnic or religious group membership over identification with his/her sexual orientation. Or members of different minority groups may choose not to be active in the gay community and instead may choose to be active in political causes for racial or religious equality. This type of choice is not necessarily indicative of dysfunction or denial of sexual orientation; rather, it is a way to innovatively juggle diverse interests and identities.

THE NOTION OF LIVING OUT

Studies clearly indicate that disclosing one's gay or lesbian identity increases self-esteem, self-worth, and overall psychological adjustment (Berzon, 1988; Cass, 1979: Coleman, 1987; Dank, 1971). In fact, achieving a positive gay or lesbian identity appears to be contingent upon disclosing one's sexual orientation to significant nongay others (McDonald, 1982). This notion has been criticized because it implies that healthy identity integration is only achieved through universal disclosure. This said, it must be noted that every theory of identity development culminates in one way or another with living out—the integration of one's gay or lesbian identity into his/her life. Obviously, it is not the only measure of successful identity development, as it does not account for choosing not to come out or to stay invisible in the face of threatening and hostile environments (McCarn & Fassinger, 1996). Nor does it account for the choices associated with managing multiple identities and oppressions. Yet, no one can deny the critical importance of personal authenticity and identity synthesis. Moreover, living out or being visible as a gay or lesbian person is undoubtedly one of the most effective educational tools, as we know that greater visibility leads to greater acceptance. Visibility shatters myths, fears, and stereotypes about gay and lesbian people as nongays realize that they do know gay people and are forced to reexamine their beliefs and attitudes.

This is not, however, a call for every gay or lesbian client to come out to everyone, all the time, under any circumstances. In a homoprejudiced world this would be irresponsible and ill-advised. Poorly timed or unplanned disclosures about one's sexual orientation can result in job loss, verbal or physical abuse, and personal rejection. On the other hand, it's important to help the client sort out whether his or her fears around coming out are real or perceived. For example, some clients shudder at the thought of coming out to their families but upon doing so, find acceptance and love. The reader may recall the case of Scott. Scott is tired of hiding who he is and who he loves from his parents, yet he is deeply afraid of their rejection. Using the group process, Marion can help Scott feel more confident about who he is, as well as help him work through his fears and prepare to come out to his family. It is true that some clients have come out to family members and have been figuratively or literally disowned. This type of rejection is deeply painful and overwhelming. Yet, even when the response is negative, being authentic and honest about one's sexual orientation is ultimately more satisfying and self-fulfilling than living in the shadows of a lie. Encouraging clients to come out and live out does not in any way mean to underestimate the challenges associated with being visible. Being visible is risky and often fraught with intense fear and anxiety; however, as thousands of gay men and lesbians can testify, the experience of living out and coming out to relatives, friends, and co-workers has been positive, immensely satisfying, and incredibly freeing.

The truth is that denial and silence about who gay and lesbian people really are thwart growth and healthy identity development (Berzon, 1988). It must be emphasized that coming out is a choice, a choice gay and lesbian people make on a daily basis. Living out, however, is a goal comparable to attaining self-actualization as a sexual minority, that is, "being who I am, all of the time, with everybody." Living out is absolutely necessary for a portion of the gay and lesbian population in order to effect social change, and is a long-term goal for others who feel more restricted and threatened by oppression.

The notion of living out suggests that coming out and being out and living our lives authentically is a greater, healthier goal than hiding and denying who we are and whom we love. Living out is the inalienable right to participate fully in the global community.

Box 2.2 provides a summary of issues that you and your client may want to consider as he/she prepares to come out.

Helping a Client Come Out

As a mental-health practitioner you are likely to find yourself in a position to help your clients navigate the coming out process. Berzon (1988) has devised a series of questions to help practitioners facilitate the likelihood of a positive experience.

Who? Determine to whom the client is planning on coming out. Explore the ramifications, potential outcomes, and pitfalls.

What? Help the client decide what to say when he or she comes out. For example, prepare a written statement or role-play various scenarios.

Why? Before disclosing, encourage client to explore why he/she is disclosing at this particular time. Prepare your client for potential questions he/she might be asked:
- Are you sure you're gay?
- How long have you been gay?
- Have you tried to change?
- Have you tried to be involved with a person of the opposite sex? Did something go wrong?
- Do you think you'll always be gay?
- What is your gay life like?
- Don't you want children?
- Do you hate men or women?

Where? Help your client decide where he or she will disclose, whether it's in a letter, over the phone, or, preferably, in a quiet, private place.

When? Encourage your client not to disclose during an event or holiday. An important occasion, let it have the full attention it deserves.

BOX

2.2   *Coming Out*

Some Suggestions for Coming Out to Parents, Relatives and Nongay Friends.

- Be clear about your own feelings about being gay or lesbian. If you are still experiencing a lot of guilt or depression, seek professional help and surround yourself with support. If you are comfortable with being gay or lesbian, those to whom you come out will often sense that fact and perhaps be more open to acceptance.
- Timing can be very important in coming out. Be aware of the health, mood, priorities, and problems of those with whom you would like to share your sexual identity. The midlife crises of parents, the relationship problems of friends, the business concerns of employers and countless other factors over which you have no control could have a profound effect on how receptive the individual is to your disclosure.
- Avoid coming out during an argument or using it as a weapon to hurt someone. Avoid giving the impression that your parents or friends should feel guilty for having 'caused' your sexual orientation—they didn't.
- Be prepared that your revelation may surprise, anger, or upset other people at first. Try not to react angrily or defensively. Try to let people be honest about their initial feelings, even if they are negative. Remember that the initial reaction is not likely to be the long-term one. Ultimately, the individuals who have really faced and dealt with their homoprejudice may be far more supportive than those who give an immediate but superficial expression of support.
- Emphasize that you are still the same person. You were gay or lesbian yesterday and will be tomorrow. If you were loving and responsible yesterday, likewise you will be loving and responsible tomorrow.
- Keep lines of communication open with people after you come out to them—even if their response is negative. Respond to their questions and remember that they are probably in the process of reexamining the myths and stereotypes about gay and lesbian people that we have all received from society. We hope you've taken the time to analyze and dispel this misinformation and will give them the time to do the same.
- Encourage your parents or friends to whom you have come out to meet some of your lesbian or gay friends. This can be a great way to normalize homosexuality and dispel the common myth that gay and lesbian people lead lonely lives.

Coming Out (continued)

- Remember that it probably took you a very long time to come to terms with your own sexuality and even longer to decide to share the fact with others. When you come out to a nongay person, be prepared to give them time to adjust and to comprehend the new information about you. Don't expect immediate acceptance. Look for ongoing, caring dialogue.
- If someone to whom you have come out rejects you, try not lose sight of your own self-worth. Remember that your coming out was a gift of sharing an important part of yourself, which that person has chosen to reject. If rejection does come, consider whether the relationship was really worthwhile. Is any relationship so important that it must be carried on in an atmosphere of dishonesty and hiding? Was the person really your friend or simply the friend of someone he or she imagined you to be?
- Remember that the decision to come out is yours. You can usually choose when, where, how, and to whom you wish to come out.

(Source: *Adapted from "Coming Out to Your Parents," by Tom Sauerman and PFLAG of Philadelphia. Copyright © 1995 Tom Sauerman and PFLAG of Philadelphia. Adapted with permission.*)

In addition, PFLAG suggests that you prepare your client for potential reactions of friends and family to his/her disclosure:

1. Shock
2. Denial—Some friends and family members may try to deny that it's true and avoid reference to the information.
3. Guilt—Some family members may react with a sense of responsibility for your sexual orientation or feel to blame.
4. Coping with the information—Eventually, friends and family members will respond in these ways:
   React with ongoing hostility and anger
   Continue to love and care about the person while making it clear that they would rather not discuss the topic any further
   Continue to love and care about the person and learn how to be actively supportive and part of the person's life
5. Acceptance—Friends and family members will continue to love and care about the person and will recognize and understand that the person's sexual orientation is a part of his/her personality. They may even speak out against oppression and discrimination against gays and lesbians.
   (*Adapted from a PFLAG pamphlet*)

Tips for Practitioners

Be Aware of Your Own Internalized Homoprejudice   Explore your own biases toward sexual minorities. If you are gay or lesbian, be cognizant of projecting your own coming out experience onto the process of your clients.

Be Prepared to Assist Your Clients With the Coming Out Process   Validate feelings and experiences. Be aware of identity development models. Apply these models with caution, being careful to explore whether a given model fits the client versus trying to make the client fit the model (Reynolds & Hanjorgiris, 2000). Remember that the coming out process can begin at any age. Be sensitive to the historical and sociopolitical circumstances that may influence the coming out process for older gay and lesbian clients.

Be Aware of the Effects of Homoprejudice   Be careful to use appropriate, affirmative, and nonheterosexist language, creating an atmosphere for clients to disclose and explore their sexual orientation: We have heard too many mental-health practitioners proclaim that they have never worked with a gay or lesbian client. Remember, the responsibility is yours, as the practitioner, to create an affirming therapeutic environment where clients feel safe to self-disclose. If you've been practicing for any length of time, it is likely that you have worked with a gay or lesbian client. The question is, "How have you either created barriers or built bridges with your sexual minority clients?" Another concern we've heard from counselors is the fear of being labeled gay or lesbian if they publicize or admit to working with sexual minority clients. This fear is deeply rooted in internalized homoprejudice, indicating a belief that there is something shameful or inherently wrong with being gay or lesbian. Unchecked, this type of insidious prejudice can influence your ability to work effectively and empathically with sexual-minority clients. You are ethically obligated to either resolve these issues or refer your client to another practitioner who is able to provide affirmative therapy.

Provide Support and Serve as a Resource to Your Gay and Lesbian Clients   Help to bridge the gap between the individual and the community by serving as a case manager and helping clients access resources.

Assist With Identity Management and Integration   Be prepared to deal with issues of religion, ethnicity, and gender. Be sensitive to multiple identities and to how a client copes with oppression across the various aspects of his/her life. Be sensitive to choices clients make regarding the decision to come out or stay invisible. At the same time, challenge your client to come out in whatever way he/she can and begin to integrate his/her identity in all aspects of his/her life.

Actively Address and Combat Societal Oppression Serve as an advocate and adopt the role of a social activist. Attend events in the gay and lesbian community. Present at local and national conferences regarding the issues associated with sexual minorities.

BIBLIOGRAPHY

Berzon, B. (1988). *Permanent partners: Building gay and lesbian relationships that last.* New York: Plume.

Cass, V. C. (1979). Homosexual identity formation: A theoretical model. *Journal of Homosexuality, 4*(3), 219–235.

Coleman, E. (1987). Assessment of sexual orientation. *Journal of Homosexuality, 14*(1/2), 9–24.

Dank, B. M. (1971). Coming out in the gay world. *Psychiatry, 34,* 180–197.

Fukuyama, M. A. & Ferguson, A. D. (2000). Lesbian, gay, and bisexual people of color: Understanding cultural complexity and managing multiple oppressions. In R. M. Perez, K. A. Debord, & K. J. Bieschke (Eds.), *Handbook of counseling and therapy with lesbians, gays, and bisexuals.* Washington, DC: American Psychological Association Press.

Greene, B. (1994). Lesbian women of color: Triple jeopardy. In L. Comas-Diaz & B. Greene (Eds.), *Women of color: Integrating ethnic and gender identities in psychotherapy.* New York: Guilford Press.

———. (1997). Ethnic minority lesbians and gay men: Mental health and treatment issues. In B. Greene (Ed.), *Ethnic and cultural diversity among lesbians and gay men.* New York: Guilford Press.

McCarn, S. R. & Fassinger, R. E. (1996). Revisioning sexual minority identity formation: A new model of lesbian identity and its implications for counseling and research. *The Counseling Psychologist, 24*(3), 508–534.

McDonald, G. J. (1982). Individual differences in the coming out process for gay men: Implications for theoretical models. *The Journal of Homosexuality, 8*(1), 47–60.

Reynolds, A. L. & Hanjorgiris, W. F. (2000). Coming out: Lesbian, gay and bisexual identity development. In R. M. Perez, K. A. Debord, & K. J. Bieschke (Eds.), *Handbook of counseling and therapy with lesbians, gays, and bisexuals.* Washington, DC: American Psychological Association Press.

Reynolds, A. L. & Pope, R. L. (1991). The complexities of diversity: exploring multiple oppressions. *Journal of Counseling and Development, 70,* 174–180.

Smith, A. (1997). Cultural diversity and the coming out process: Implications for clinical practice. In B. Greene (Ed.), *Ethnic and cultural diversity among lesbians and gay men.* Thousand Oaks, CA: Sage.

Troiden, R. R. (1989). The formation of homosexual identities. *The Journal of Homosexuality, 17*(1/2), 43–73.

COUNSELING LESBIANS

The Case of Jessie

Jessie has been a counselor at the Empowerment agency for the past six years. Empowerment was established ten years ago by a group of gay and lesbian mental-health professionals as an oasis for sexual minorities who were seeking nonjudgmental, affirmative mental-health services. Jessie, a feminist, considered using her knowledge and skills to work with gays and lesbians as a logical career choice, and she jumped at the chance to do her internship at Empowerment. Her roommate in college had been a lesbian, and they had enjoyed attending meetings and activities of women's groups. She loved her training experience at Empowerment and decided to stay on after she completed her master's degree. Jessie is heterosexual, is married, and has two children. She keeps a picture of her husband and children on her desk. For Jessie, working with sexual minorities has been both fulfilling and extremely challenging. In many ways she feels a strong sense of sisterhood, particularly with her lesbian clients, yet as a heterosexual, she sometimes feels like an outsider or an impostor.

Over the years, Jessie has counseled many lesbian clients, and they have been, by far, her most rewarding and challenging cases. For example, Denise has been her client for several years. Denise had been to other therapists in town, mostly "straight," but had never felt comfortable with any of them. Denise specifically came to Empowerment because it was a gay and lesbian agency, a place where she felt she would be safe and accepted for who she was. Denise had grown up on a farm in the Midwest as the only girl of five children who were forced to work on the farm as soon as they were old enough, and life revolved around school and work, work and school. Both of Denise's parents were alcoholics. Once the chores were done for the day, both parents would start drinking until they fell into bed and passed out. Most nights were filled with loud arguments and slamming doors, and the children learned to stay out of the way—especially Denise. It was her job to try to keep the peace, keep everyone happy, be a "good girl," and not make any trouble. She was being such a "good girl" making sure not to upset or make anyone mad that she never told anyone that her uncle was sexually abusing her on a regular basis. Denise had been working for several years on dealing with the effects of the abuse. She had begun to accept that the abuse was not her fault, but she was still struggling to find her voice and learning how to draw healthy boundaries. With Jessie's help, she had mustered the courage to share the "secret"—to tell her family about the abuse—and begin the process of healing.

Repeatedly, Denise faced situations where she would not assert herself. This was true in business, in relationships, and with her family. For example, it took her years to come out to her family as a lesbian even though she had known she was a lesbian since she had been a little girl. Unfortunately, her family didn't handle her revelation about her sexual orientation very well. To this day they firmly believe that the abuse made her queer and that if she would "just find the right man," she would "give up this crazy man-hating lesbian phase." "And you know," Denise said, "I really have tried to please them and make myself straight for them—I dated man after man after man, and nothing ever worked; I am a lesbian and that's that and believe me, my uncle didn't make me that way. In fact, I believe I was born this way." Denise was tired of always trying to please everyone. She didn't know how to say no, and she didn't know how to deal with her emotions, especially her anger. For example, her last relationship was fraught with conflict. Denise and her partner argued all the time—her partner would get angry and start yelling, and Denise would have to calm her down. Three years later the relationship ended after her partner had an affair. During the entire relationship with her partner, Denise never got angry; she kept all her emotions inside. When the relationship abruptly ended, Denise knew she had to work on herself before she could be involved with another woman.

Jessie was reminded, when she first started working with Denise, of all the myths and stereotypes about lesbians, particularly the one about incest turning girls into man-hating lesbians. "If that were true," Jessie mused, "there would be many more lesbians, wouldn't there? Given that the clinical data indicate that one in three women has experienced some type of sexual trauma, there should be many more lesbians than heterosexual women!" She was also concerned that Denise, given her prior experiences with less-than-understanding and nonempathic therapists, might not trust her because she was heterosexual. One day, Denise asked if the picture on Jessie's desk was of her husband and children.

Much to Jessie's surprise, her being married didn't seem to be an issue for Denise, and Jessie was once again reminded of the power of authenticity. In the words of her favorite professor from graduate school, "You gotta be real. . . ." Jessie worked with Denise to help her establish boundaries, to learn how to assert herself with others, and to help her learn how to express anger. Because of her parents' behavior, Denise had a skewed view of anger, believing that it could be manifested only in drunken rages. Jessie spent a great deal of time working with Denise to help her first to identify feelings of anger and then to express those feelings in appropriate ways.

In addition, to help Denise as she recovered from the effects of sexual abuse, Jessie encouraged her to attend a female incest survivors' support group. She also provided her with a list of books designed to help her develop a sense of self and a self in relation to others.

Another challenging case for Jessie was that of Jill. Jill was a successful, middle-aged lesbian whose six-year relationship seemed on the brink of ending. Jill was absolutely devastated. Her partner was the love of her life, and Jill wasn't going to give up without a fight. She knew there had been problems in the relationship but thought it would never actually end. One of the biggest areas of conflict had been in the bedroom. Over the years they had stopped having sex, but they never talked about it. Jill described herself as very sexual, and she didn't understand why they weren't having sex anymore. "I mean, you should have seen us at the beginning of the relationship; we barely came up for air and water, and, then, over the years, it happened—the dreaded lesbian bed death." Jill laughed when she said this, although she started to sob, "I don't want to lose her. What can I do?" Jill stated that she and her partner wanted to come to couples counseling, but she also knew she had a lot of work to do on her own. Intuitively, she realized that she was so afraid of losing her partner that she was smothering her. Jessie agreed to work with Jill individually, and she also agreed to see Jill and her partner together.

Couples sessions quickly illuminated some of the reasons for the lack of sexual intimacy. Stacy, Jill's partner, felt overwhelmed by Jill. She felt that they had become one and she had lost herself somewhere along the way. "People don't even refer to us as individuals anymore; we're just one long name—Stacy and Jill—I feel like I'm suffocating." Stacy shared that she wanted more time alone and time away from Jill to spend with her own friends. Regarding sex, Stacy said she always felt pressured by Jill. It felt as though Jill was always asking for sex at the wrong time; she never just let it "naturally unfold." Requests for time apart felt very threatening to Jill, and, in fact, Stacy's desire to spend time away seemed to be a punishment, as if she were being abandoned.

Working with Jill individually revealed that Jill had felt abandoned as a child because her mother had been killed in a car accident when Jill was six. Stacy's request for time alone was very threatening to Jill and made her cling more tightly. She expressed her core fear by saying, "What if she went away and never came back?" Jessie helped Jill identify and understand her feelings of fear. Part of that work was to empower and validate Jill's fear and, at the same time, help her realize that Stacy was her partner, not her mother. She couldn't be abandoned as an adult in the same way she had been abandoned as a child. Jessie helped Jill and Stacy begin to balance the need for autonomy and the need for togetherness.

Jessie had encountered this difficulty before with her lesbian clients. Partners would become so enmeshed with each other that the individual could feel lost and trapped. Jessie remembered a former supervisor telling her that this was actually an inherent flaw in lesbian relationships: Women would engulf each other and eventually have to break up in order to reestablish their own identities. Jessie disagreed. This emotional connection and deep involvement with each other were actually strengths. Although sometimes it could be overwhelming, a close-knit relationship could also be a rich source of strength in an oppressive society that negated and discriminated against same-sex couples. In many cases, the bedroom would be the arena in which the struggle for autonomy would be acted out. To address this issue, Jessie would typically draw a Venn diagram, i.e., two circles that overlap to varying degrees in order to illustrate the two separate individuals and their overlap as a couple. In addition, Jessie consistently affirmed Jill and Stacy as a couple and validated their commitment to the relationship. At the same time, she encouraged each to have time alone and time away from each other. She also helped them work through the issues of sexual intimacy. Jill needed to stop pursuing Stacy and trust that Stacy would initiate sex. Jessie also helped them communicate better about sex—to ask for what they wanted, and to experiment and have fun.

Jill and Stacy worked very hard on rebuilding their relationship and were very excited about their upcoming commitment ceremony. Jill, after completing individual and couples therapy, verbalized that she would love to have Jessie attend their wedding. Jessie politely declined, stating that she made it a rule never to socialize with her clients. Jill was obviously hurt by her answer, and Jessie hoped that Jill didn't think she wasn't attending because she was not lesbian. Following this rule wasn't very difficult for Jessie, but she wondered how her friends who were lesbian therapists managed both to work and live in the lesbian community.

Issues in Counseling Lesbians

Lesbians seek counseling for many of the same reasons that heterosexual women do. Lesbians also struggle with problems such as anxiety, depression, low self-esteem, eating disorders, substance abuse, and the devastating effects of incest and sexual trauma. Like heterosexual women, lesbians are also impacted by the effects of sexism. Different from heterosexual women but similar to their gay male counterparts, lesbians grapple in a therapeutic context with issues that are often exacerbated by the ongoing onslaught of societal homoprejudice. Put simply, lesbians are doubly challenged by the effects of sexism and homoprejudice.

Counselors are therefore challenged to empower and affirm lesbian clients both as women and as lesbians, recognizing the effects of homoprejudice and sexism while collaborating closely with clients to navigate and attain the agreed-upon goals of therapy.

Images

Who are lesbians? What images come to mind when you hear the word *lesbian* or picture yourself counseling a lesbian? These are important questions to answer because lesbians have often been rendered invisible, ignored and disenfranchised from both the heterosexual and the gay communities. Stereotypical images of lesbians range from those of mysterious witches to emasculating bullies and masculine "mommas" to "dykes on bikes." Be prepared and willing to separate the folklore from the reality because there are lesbian representatives from all of these, and some lesbians who represent none of these, images. Lesbians are chefs, business executives, professors, separatists, "earth mothers," electricians, and women of color. They can be old, young, or disabled. Lesbians play sports, wear makeup and skirts, have long hair and short hair, cut the lawn, and lead Fortune 500 companies. They typically aren't men-haters and didn't become lesbian because they couldn't get a man. One doesn't necessarily "play" the husband to the other's role as "wife" in a couple, and they don't all secretly want to become men. These stereotypical notions, sometimes referred to as "butch" and "femme," respectively, are primarily a reflection of lesbian choices to expand restrictive gender boundaries rather than of assigned roles in a relationship.

Note that many of the stereotypical images of lesbians are deeply entrenched in sexism, stemming from the erroneous notion that the mere existence of lesbianism is an act of resistance against men. Lesbians are a diverse group of women who love women, and women who have sex with other women, and they are in need of affirmative and effective counseling services.

The purpose of this chapter is to provide an overview of the issues associated with counseling lesbians as well as to offer techniques and strategies to enhance the counseling relationship.

The Relationship Between Lesbianism and Feminism

Coming out and accepting a positive self-identity as a lesbian is a lifelong process. This process is made even more complex by the struggle to manage dual and triple minority memberships, e.g., female and lesbian; or female, lesbian, and African American or Latina (Greene, 1994). An in-depth discussion of the lesbian identity development process was presented in Chapter 2. Highlighted in that discussion was the critical influence of the women's community and the feminist culture on lesbian identity development. For example, many lesbians find that the diversity within the women's community is an even greater source of solace and solidarity than the overall gay community. Other women identify as a feminist first and lesbian second, signifying their commitment to feminism and the principles of empowerment and equality for all women.

Before we proceed, we present one brief note on the relationship between feminism and lesbianism. Be aware that the issue of "choosing" to label oneself as a lesbian may be raised when working with feminist clients. In Chapter 1 we discussed the scientific evidence that supports the notion of a homosexual orientation, refuting the idea that it is simply a choice, and thereby rejecting the idea that clients could just make a different choice and be heterosexual. Nevertheless, it is important to understand that there are some feminist women who have "chosen" to label themselves as lesbian in order to feel empowered in a male-dominated society. In our work we have encountered a few women who are deeply ensconced in the feminist movement and "choose" to identify as lesbian for sociopolitical reasons, as a way to completely reject patriarchal expectations and heterosexual norms. However, a political choice does not involve the same challenges or tasks required of someone who is working through the issues of adopting a positive lesbian sexual identity that includes an ongoing struggle to combat the effects of internalized and externalized homoprejudice (McCarn & Fassinger, 1996).

The Coming Out Process

In a homoprejudiced society, coming out as a lesbian can be extremely challenging and often frightening and isolating. Some women have always known they were "different," and coming out as a lesbian is a relatively smooth process. For example, in the case presented, Denise had known she was a lesbian since she was a little girl. She was always a "tomboy," played sports, and preferred to hang out with her girlfriends rather than flirt or interact with boys. She recalls trying to make herself "straight" by dating men to please her parents, but she knew she was a lesbian. In Denise's case, coming out to herself was the easy part; coming out to her family and others was an entirely different issue! Other lesbians remember painfully and reluctantly shifting from a heterosexual identity to a more authentic identity as a lesbian. At some point, they share with us that they became consciously aware of considering the possibility of becoming romantically involved with women, perhaps because of involvement with the women's movement or friendships with other lesbians. Suddenly they understood why relationships with men never worked or were always unfulfilling. Being with a woman felt right in a way that being with a man never did, yet accepting a different sexual orientation can be frightening and overwhelming, and many lesbians try to repress and ignore these feelings. The truth is, unfortunately, that as a result of overwhelming internalized homoprejudice, some women may choose to live their lives in the closet, either abstinent or in the societally approved safety of heterosexual relationships.

For example, a seemingly heterosexual client once shared that the love of her life had been a woman. They had met in college and had become intimately involved. The client easily imagined that they could have been lovers and even life-partners if only life had been different. She stated that it was never **really** a possibility that she would have ended up with a woman. She knew she was "supposed" to get married and have children; being with a woman would have been much too hard, and her family would never have accepted it. Tragically, she succumbed to homoprejudice and lives her life trapped in heterosexuality, unfulfilled and unhappy with who she is and who she loves.

Mental-health practitioners must realize how hard it is to be true to one's homosexual orientation, for the effects of cultural homoprejudice are enormous. Clearly, the process of accepting a lesbian sexual orientation or coming out to oneself, when heterosexuality is the norm, is often frightening and seemingly insurmountable for some clients. Be prepared to listen empathically, educate clients about different sexual orientations, and normalize feelings of attraction toward members of the same sex. Be patient with your client as she struggles with the coming out process. Allow her time to grieve the loss of heterosexuality while helping her celebrate her emerging, authentic self. The following set of questions is useful in assisting clients who are struggling to come to terms with a lesbian identity.

> Which gender(s) is prominent in her sexual fantasies? To which gender(s) does she find herself sexually attracted? With which gender does the client find herself falling in love? What are her emotional preferences? With which gender has the client had sexual experiences, and what has been the quality of those experiences? Probably the most important question is, How does the client self-identify? (Golden, 1994)

Increased contact with the lesbian community can help promote a sense of self-esteem and a positive self-identity (Browning, Reynolds, & Dworkin, 1991). Make sure that you are aware of lesbian-friendly resources in the community.

Find out about places where lesbians gather and meet each other, and share this information with your clients. For many lesbian clients, the idea of socializing in a bar setting is completely unappealing even though it may provide an opportunity to meet other women like themselves. You may find that some women are more comfortable being involved in support groups, women's festivals, book clubs, informational workshops, or other group activities.

Mental-health practitioners need to be cognizant that some women trying to cope with the prospect of accepting a lesbian identity and the coming out process may exhibit emotional upheaval, depression, stress, anger, and even thoughts of suicide. Finding an empathic and affirming therapist is essential. For example, Angie came to therapy because she was furious that she might be lesbian. In listening to her personal history, her counselor learned that Angie had always felt "different," not necessarily because she thought she was a lesbian but because she just "felt different" and never fit in anywhere. Most of her life, she dated men and identified as a heterosexual, but she never felt fulfilled or happy. Almost by happenstance, she became involved with a woman, and for the first time in her life she felt connected. She and her partner were extremely compatible sexually, emotionally, and spiritually, and she felt happy. Then she felt rage. Here I go again. . . . Why do I always have to be different? Why do I have to be with a woman? Why do I have to be lesbian? Jessie empathically listened to Angie's feelings of anger and confusion, validated her experience, and normalized her feelings and reactions. In addition, she referred her to a women's coming out support group where Angie learned that she really wasn't different from other lesbians. Many of the members experienced the same feelings of anger, confusion, and loss as they grappled with the process of coming out and living out.

Coming out as a lesbian to family and friends can be an extremely daunting task. Some lesbians choose to live extremely closeted lives for fear of losing jobs, family support, and love and friends. These fears are real, and while it is our job as therapists to challenge our clients to live authentically and help sort out real fears versus perceived fears, we must also be respectful of the decision to maintain "selective outness" or choices about who and when to come out. This type of support and affirmation is particularly important when working with dual and triple minorities. The decision to come out to others, even though it may give a sense of freedom and be essential to one's self-esteem, requires careful forethought and planning. Coming out to family can dredge up old wounds and patterns of dysfunction—the person may be vilified, rejected, or even ignored. Friends may be "accepting" on the surface but refuse to talk openly about what it means to be a lesbian. Counselors can help a client work through the decision to come out to others by exploring the cost/benefit ratio as well as her goals, motivations, and expectations. Refer clients who are struggling with this decision to local support groups, such as PFLAG, to other affirmative resources that might exist in the gay and lesbian community, such as coming out groups, or even to a supportive hot line. Review Chapter 2 for strategies and techniques to assist clients with the coming out process.

What's in a Name?

The challenges and choices associated with how to label oneself can vary among lesbians. This decision is often a product of how comfortable a lesbian is with her sexual orientation as well as other factors such as age, cultural background, geographical location, and so on. Some women really don't like the "L" word and prefer to call themselves queer or dyke. Some women may refuse to adopt any type of label (Clunis & Green, 2000). Older women may prefer to identify as gay or use code words, such as this is my *friend* or *roommate*. Younger women are typically more comfortable with the term *lesbian* or even terms such as *queer* or *dyke* (Clunis & Green, 2000). How your client self-labels may give you information about how comfortable she is with her sexual orientation. For example, early on in the coming out process, some women are more comfortable identifying as gay, and then, over the years as they become more comfortable with their sexual orientation, they may choose to identify as lesbian. Other women, from the very beginning of the coming out process, are very comfortable self-identifying as lesbian. These women usually prefer to identify as lesbian versus gay because the term *gay* generally refers to men. For others, the term *lesbian* makes them uncomfortable, and they may always choose to self-identify as gay women. Some women prefer the implied power of the term *dyke,* embracing a name that has traditionally been used by others to be hurtful and derogatory. Other minority groups have also reembraced these negative names. Older lesbians may refer to themselves as *butch* or *femme,* terms that are reflective of a past era when gays and lesbians were virtually invisible and acceptable only if they adopted characteristics similar to those of their heterosexual counterparts.

Given the various ways that lesbians self-identify, it is absolutely essential that counselors actively listen and avoid prematurely or carelessly imposing labels on their female clients. Be prepared to educate a client about these different labels, and encourage her to label herself in a way that is comfortable for her yet congruent with her sexual orientation. Listen carefully to how the client self-identifies, and affirm her experience, encouraging the evolution of her unique story and coming out process.

Relationships

As noted in Chapter 2, women are different from their gay counterparts in that they are more likely to come out as lesbian in the context of a relationship; therefore, practitioners are quite likely either to work with lesbian clients in a relationship who are struggling with sexual identity issues or to have the opportunity to work with the couple itself. The old joke about lesbians bringing a U-Haul on the second date (see Chapter 5) actually rings true more often than not. Be aware that societal sanctioning of intense, emotional bonds may actually push women to become involved in a relationship before they are ready and before they have had time to work through the tasks of accepting a positive lesbian identity (Slater, 1995). This intense meshing together can often invoke what is fondly referred to within the lesbian community as *Dyke-U-Drama,* a term that describes the emotionally intense, roller-coaster, high-drama coupling and uncoupling of lesbian women. This tendency to become involved quickly has both positive and negative ramifications. Often this abrupt coupling and uncoupling can wreak havoc on a relationship; in addition, issues related to creating and building a relationship can thwart and stifle individual growth. Counselors who are sensitive to this tendency of lesbians to form relationships quickly will encourage clients to move slowly and date rather than to settle down immediately in a committed relationship. This may mean literally teaching clients "Dating Skills 101." For example, have clients list characteristics of potential partners and role-play asking a woman out on a date. Encourage them to talk to lesbians in long-term relationships to discover the joys and challenges associated with settling down with a partner. Paradoxically, forming couples quickly can help emerging lesbians have positive experiences with same-sex relationships and therefore provide a new context that actively contradicts societal taboos and stereotypes. In fact, positive and meaningful same-sex relationships may actually contribute significantly to individual growth and healthy development in closeted or geographically isolated couples (Slater, 1995). Chapter 5 presents a more detailed discussion of the issues in counseling lesbian couples.

Fusion

As noted earlier, a relationship between women tends to be emotionally intense and tightly entwined. This type of relationship can be described as *fused,* a term that has traditionally been used to signify an unhealthy relationship, one that is overburdened with emotion and lacking clear boundaries (Nichols & Schwartz, 1998). Fusion indicates a state of merging together, an intense emotional connection that causes the individual to lose sense of her separate self. Moving away from pejorative descriptions, Ossana (2000) defines fusion as a relationship in which the boundaries between female partners are blurred and a premium is placed on emotional intimacy and togetherness. As noted earlier, emotional intimacy and togetherness between two women can be a source of strength because it fosters deep trust and a sense of safety and allows the couple to bond together and meet the challenge of ongoing homoprejudice and oppression. Fusion or merger is a problem only when it's inflexibly too high or too low (Slater, 1995).

Too much fusion occurs when the individual begins to lose a sense of her separate self and partners become merged to the point where they may even begin to limit contact with the outside world. At this point, sexual intimacy and physical connection can become much too threatening because all other aspects of life are merged. As presented in the case of Jill and Stacy, Stacy felt overwhelmed by the relationship. She felt she had lost herself, and, in her opinion, the only way to find herself again was to end the relationship. Jessie helped the women address the issue of fusion by working with Jill individually and helping her to understand and resolve her fears of abandonment. By doing so, she helped Jill feel less threatened by Stacy's request for time alone. Jessie also helped Stacy ask constructively for what she needed rather than try to reclaim her autonomy by being destructive—starting fights, withholding sex, shutting down, or even breaking up. In the case, Jessie used a Venn diagram to illustrate the independence and interrelatedness of the couple. She encouraged the women to spend time together as well as time apart.

When overly fused, even seemingly small differences between partners can feel extremely threatening. Differences may seem to be a threat to the emotional cocoon of the relationship and therefore something that should be avoided at all costs. Differences may occur in terms of identity development, level of outness, life experiences, or even personality. For example, Sue and Mary have been together for the past five years. Mary has known she was a lesbian since she was very young. Sue, on the other hand, came out five years ago when she met Mary. Mary is very comfortable with her own sexual orientation and is out to her family, friends, and co-workers. Sue is not so comfortable with her sexual orientation, although she is very clear about loving Mary and wanting to spend the rest of her life with Mary by her side. Mary is very supportive of Sue's reluctance to come out, except during holidays. Mary is tired of spending holidays alone with her family while Sue spends time with her own family. This year, Mary has insisted that they spend the holidays together, either in their own home or with one of their families. This mandate has really upset Sue, making her scared and angry. The couple has started to argue all the time. In working with Mary and Sue, the therapist was quickly able to see that their differences were mainly based on different degrees of outness. The therapist worked closely with Sue to help her explore and understand her sexual orientation as well as to address her real and perceived fears about coming out. The therapist also helped Mary understand Sue's ongoing struggle, encouraging her to be patient and understanding. Eventually, Sue was ready to take some steps toward coming out more fully, and the therapist helped the couple develop a plan of action that included how to deal with potential reactions, how and when to come out, and how to prepare for the future as a lesbian couple.

Sexual Intimacy

One of the most common challenges faced by lesbian clients is learning how to be sexual and remain sexual within the context of a lesbian relationship. What is lesbian sexuality, and is it unique from any other form of sexuality and sexual expression? Loulan (1984) describes lesbian sex as "anything two lesbians do together." Lesbian sexuality itself is unlimited and may include masturbation, tribadism (sexually rubbing together), oral sex, toys, vibrators, and sadomasochistic activities (Caster, 1993). Lesbians have sex with longtime partners, new lovers, or groups of friends, or they may masturbate alone. Lesbians may have long, languorous sessions of heart-melting, soulful sex or loud, sweaty sex that wakes the neighbors (Newman, 1999). Women have been having sex with other women throughout history across every society and culture. Therefore, the question remains, "Is lesbian sex different from any other type of sex or intimacy?"

In a review of the available literature, Schreurs (1993) found that in general, lesbians meet the cultural stereotypes for all women in that they are indeed more interested in romance and relationships than men are. In fact, lesbians are more similar to heterosexual women than to gay men in terms of their preferences for emotional intimacy and monogamy. In general, lesbians reported that they were satisfied with their sex lives, just as gay and heterosexual couples say they are. Furthermore, lesbians have a higher rate of orgasm than their heterosexual counterparts, and the most common sexual behaviors with a partner include mutual masturbation and manual-genital and oral-genital stimulation. As happens with heterosexual couples, lack of communication, conflicts about sex, and an unequal power balance led to dissatisfaction with the relationship. Techniques and strategies effectively used with heterosexual women to address these issues are likely to be useful with lesbian couples. These strategies might include learning how to communicate with a partner, to resolve conflicts, and to recognize and articulate needs and desires. On the surface, at least, lesbians appear to be similar to heterosexual women because they prefer and derive satisfaction from a relationship.

However, there are two popular yet divergent views about lesbian sex. As noted, one view maintains that lesbian sex is highly satisfying, usually orgasmic, emotionally fulfilling, and gratifying. The other view maintains that lesbians have low sexual desire and that female couples are destined to experience the dreaded "lesbian bed death." Studies do indicate that lesbians may indeed have sex less frequently than heterosexual couples or gay male couples; however, they appear to spend much more time in each sexual encounter (Ossana, 2000). Lesbians seem to spend more time cuddling, passionately kissing, and holding each other. In truth, the notion of lesbian bed death may actually be mitigated by society in that deep emotional bonds with other women are socially sanctioned as long as they are nonsexual (Berzon, 1997). Lesbian couples are doubly constrained because women are taught to repress sexual desire and sexual relationships between women that exclude men are generally forbidden. Lesbian bed death or lack of sexual intimacy may simply be the result of programmed reluctance to initiate sex to keep from appearing sexually aggressive or immoral; or, as discussed previously, partners may withhold sex as a means to gain independence and escape merger. In any case, sensitive counselors can facilitate frank discussions about sexuality and the effects of sexism and homo-prejudice and therefore provide the framework for renewed and improved sexual intimacy.

When working with issues related to intimacy and sexuality, one cannot overestimate the impact of homoprejudice. Adopting a positive lesbian self-identity in the face of society's onslaught of negativity and oppression is daunting and likely to have a profound effect on one's ability to be sexual and intimate with another woman. Society teaches all of us that lesbians and lesbian sexuality are immoral, disgusting, and perverted, which can have a devastating effect on clients who are trying to come to terms with a nonheterosexual orientation. Given the pervasiveness of societal oppression, issues of comfort with sexual orientation, level of visibility, or degree of outness are important to consider when working with lesbian clients who are struggling with sexual intimacy issues. Lacking the privileges that heterosexual couples usually take for granted, such as the being intimate in public or legal sanctioning of relationships, can have a profound effect on intimacy and sexual expression. For example, public displays of affection between lesbian partners are generally looked upon with disdain, and couples are forced to be unnatural, making no contact in public situations, or to resort to furtive hand-holding or other signs of affection when they think no one will see them. This cultural mandate to hide one's affection for a same-sex partner surely and insidiously seeps into the bedroom, as it is difficult to switch back and forth from silence and shame to unfettered sexual celebration. In our work, we are proactive about affirming gay and lesbian relationships and are honored when couples we work with feel safe enough to sit closely together, hold hands, or even kiss and embrace. All too often in society, sexual minorities are forced to avoid physical contact and intimacy, and my office is at least one place where they can be free and open about who they are and whom they love.

In recent years there has been a shift in the lesbian community toward a more open sexual scene akin to the gay men's culture (Esterberg, 1996). Women-made pornography, magazines, go-go clubs, and other more frank expressions of sexuality have challenged the previously held myths about the nature of lesbian sexuality. Younger lesbians appear to be much more comfortable with themselves sexually and more open with public displays of affection and other types of intimacy. Clearly, this new openness is a reflection of society's gradual and tentative shift to more tolerant attitudes and perceptions of homosexuality, as evidenced by the state of Vermont's revolutionary decision to afford civil rights to same-sex couples.

Mental-health practitioners working with lesbian clients must be willing to address issues related to sex and sexuality. Not doing so is a disservice to your client and perhaps indicative of your own internalized homoprejudice. Frank discussions about sexual practices may be uncomfortable for both you and your client. Be aware of your comfort level with sex-related issues, and assess and address any biases you may have toward lesbian sexuality. For example, Cheryl liked to be vaginally penetrated but was afraid to admit it to her partner because she didn't want to be disloyal or hurtful, fearing that her partner would think she wanted a man. Filled with fear and shame, Cheryl reluctantly talked about this issue with her therapist. Fortunately, her therapist was comfortable with her own sexuality and not at all uncomfortable when clients talked about sex during counseling sessions. First, she validated Cheryl's desire to be penetrated and had her role-play talking to her partner about her feelings. The therapist also referred Cheryl to a feminist-owned sex-toy store and encouraged her to explore the possibilities of incorporating nonrepresentational dildos into her lovemaking with her partner.

Increasing Sexual Intimacy

When working with clients who are struggling with issues related to intimacy, counselors will find it useful to teach women how to give and receive sensual and sexual pleasure, and how to learn to say what does and does not give them pleasure. Open communication is absolutely essential and may require practice and coaching from the counselor. For some women, open communication about sex will be very difficult, and it may take time for them to understand and articulate their sexual needs. Take time to explore the effects of internalized homoprejudice as well as the additional effects of sexism and heterosexism. Have the clients write down negative sexual messages and, with the counselor's help, refute them with positive counterstatements. Help your clients recognize and avoid habitual practices in which one person is *always* the initiator and the other is always passive; suggest that they take turns being the initiator. Encourage your clients to explore feelings and attitudes toward being the "sexual aggressor"; address negative self-talk and societal prohibitions. Also, encourage your clients to avoid saying "no" for unimportant reasons. If they don't have time or energy for long, languorous lovemaking, teach them how to compromise or how to discover ways, even when they are not as interested in lovemaking, to satisfy their partners. Challenge clients to avoid using sex to punish or hurt their partners. If they're hurt or angry, ask them to risk talking about it to resolve the situation. Above all, teach and encourage your clients to have fun in the bedroom. Have them vary the places they have sex and experiment with fantasy, costumes, sex toys, or a vibrator (Tessina, 2000).

Sexual Abuse

The high incidence of sexual trauma and incest against women can also serve as an obstruction to sex and intimacy. According to a survey conducted by Loulan (1987), 38% of lesbians have experienced sexual abuse by a family member or stranger before the age of 18. Although this high percentage is similar to the rates of sexual abuse in heterosexual women, which disputes the notion that women become lesbian as a result of sexual abuse or sexual assault, there is a high probability in lesbian couples that not just one partner but both have experienced sexual abuse (Brown, 1995). In the case example of Denise discussed earlier, Denise was very comfortable with her sexual orientation and knew that her history of sexual abuse did not make her choose to be a lesbian; however, Denise knew she had to work through the issues related to her past before she could have a successful relationship. The counselor understood this and was able to validate and support Denise through the recovery process. In a relationship, the impact of issues related to sexual abuse can have a devastating effect on intimacy and sexuality. Each partner may be at a different stage of recovery or have different needs. One or both may experience flashbacks of the abuse during sex or avoid sex altogether, which may anger, frustrate, or even trigger a flashback for the other (Browning, Reynolds, & Dworkin, 1991). Mental-health practitioners need to be prepared to address the myriad effects of sexual abuse and perhaps to assist both partners as they begin to negotiate the lifelong process of recovery.

Lesbians of Color

Lesbian women of color are uniquely challenged by the tasks of managing multiple oppressions or "triple jeopardy," the combined effects of racism, sexism, and homoprejudice (Greene, 1994). A culturally sensitive counselor must apply the templates of culture and ethnicity when working with lesbian clients. Be willing to explore the importance of procreation; the nature and impact of traditional gender-role stereotypes; the importance of family and community; the nature, degree, and intensity of religious values and beliefs; and attitudes toward sexual minorities (Greene, 1997). It is important, though, to avoid generalizations since there is great diversity within groups from different cultures and races.

Lesbians of color may struggle and resist the idea of coming out to their families and cultural community. Many feel a strong sense of safety in the cultural group and live in fear of being labeled a lesbian and perhaps losing such an important source of identity and emotional support (Smith, 1997). In fact, some clients may choose to remain closeted rather than risk ostracism. Counselors need to understand and affirm clients who move between cultural identity and sexual identity and recognize that this vacillation is not necessarily indicative of a thwarted developmental process.

However, many of those who do come out are faced with discrimination from the gay and lesbian community. They, in turn, feel marginalized by both communities, never truly part of any group, but alone and isolated. Accordingly, counselors who are sensitive to this issue will validate their clients' feelings and refer them to various support groups specifically designed for lesbians of color. Many of these groups are available in larger communities and through the Internet.

According to Greene (1994), lesbians of color may actually have the advantage over their white counterparts because they have had to cope with multiple levels of oppression throughout their entire life. Problems occur if these coping mechanisms were maladaptive or self-destructive and therefore exacerbated by the pressure of adopting a lesbian identity.

Interracial Couples

Counselors may find that lesbians of color in interracial couples are more prepared to deal with racism and prejudice than their white partners are (Greene, 1994). A white partner unfamiliar with racism may overreact or be surprised and become overly protective and hypersensitive to external oppression. Both externalized and internalized racism may serve as a source of conflict for interracial couples. Both partners may have trouble dealing with the effects of racism and may not know how to explore the issues in the context of the relationship. Culturally sensitive counselors are aware of these challenges and are thus able to create a safe and therapeutic forum where these issues can be addressed. At the same time, the counselor must be aware that racism does not account for all problems and may be inappropriately blamed for existing relationship issues (Greene, 1994).

Substance Abuse

Research shows that lesbians tend to drink more than their heterosexual counterparts (Bux, 1996). This may be the result of the effects of multiple oppressions and the tendency of the overall gay community to socialize in bars or club settings. Many lesbians may find themselves abusing drugs and alcohol as ways to numb the feelings of guilt and shame associated with having a "different" sexual orientation.

In the process of recovery, lesbians may be uniquely challenged by the following issues (Browning, Reynolds, & Dworkin, 1991).

1. Many lesbians in recovery struggle with the decision about whether or not to come out to potentially hostile and prejudiced staff in a chemical-dependency treatment program. On the other hand, remaining hidden and closeted fuels shame and guilt and inhibits the recovery process. Be aware that there are a number of treatment facilities available nationwide specifically designed to meet the needs of recovering sexual minorities.
2. Another consideration is the extent to which a lesbian's partner or social support network will be involved in her recovery process. Given that lesbians are more likely to operate in a relationship, partner and peer support may be critical to her success.
3. Many lesbians in recovery find it difficult to accept the traditional male-dominated AA models and therefore never connect with an important

source of support. Counselors can help lesbian clients in recovery locate meetings that are specifically for women or even meetings that are specifically designed for the overall gay community.

Domestic Violence

Traditionally, there has been reluctance to admit that domestic violence between lesbians occurs. We generally perceive women and lesbian relationships as happy, healthy, and violence-free (Coleman, 1996). Studies indicate that domestic violence between women is comparable in prevalence and severity to that of heterosexual relationships. However, because it is rarely talked about or even reported, it is still not taken very seriously by mental-health practitioners. Domestic violence between women is characterized by the need to dominate and control and likely develops from an overall sense of powerlessness fueled by homoprejudice, sexism, social isolation, and low self-esteem.

When seeking help, lesbians may encounter at least four significant challenges (Browning, Reynolds, & Dworkin, 1991). The first, and perhaps the most formidable, challenge is the culturally pervasive denial that domestic violence occurs between women. Second, the victim may have trouble identifying battering as abuse because she may have reacted violently in self-defense; therefore, she may inaccurately perceive violence as mutual aggression. Third, the victim often resists reporting incidents of domestic violence because of lack of sensitivity and understanding by service providers. Fourth, women's shelters fail to deal with domestic violence between women openly and sensitively.

Clearly, education and sensitivity are sorely needed. Counselors need to understand that domestic violence between women does indeed occur and must be prepared to address all aspects of the situation, including finding appropriate and affirming safe spaces for the victims and lesbian-friendly treatment options for the perpetrators.

Counselor–Client Relationship

As illustrated in the case study, heterosexual therapists may struggle with feeling that they are considered outsiders or untrustworthy because of their sexual orientation. In the case example, Jessie struggled with feeling like an impostor because she was heterosexual. However, lesbian mental-health providers are urged to consider the unique challenges of living and working in the gay community. Gartrell (1994) suggests that strategies must be developed to cope with such issues as self-disclosure, informal contact with clients in a social setting, and the maintenance of personal privacy. Discussion of personal problems with a client is inappropriate with lesbian clients just as it is with other clients; however, answering questions honestly regarding sexual orientation and relationship status may be useful to a client who is looking for affirmation and connection with a therapist. Contact with clients in the community may be unavoidable, and the parameters for these encounters should be addressed frankly with the client. Many clinicians use the "just say hi" approach (Gartrell, 1994): The therapist does not say hello unless the client does, and judiciously avoids intimate gatherings where clients may be present. Other therapists chafe at the idea of being a social recluse or limited by their profession and choose to participate actively in the lesbian community at all levels, carefully maintaining confidentiality when faced with a client.

Tips for Practitioners

Explore and Challenge Your Own Homoprejudice Explore your own internalized stereotypes and biases toward lesbians. Include in that self-analysis an exploration of any preconceived notions or prejudice you may have toward feminism and the women's community.

Connect Lesbian Clients With the Feminist Community Given the oppression and fear associated with dual and triple minority membership, lesbians and lesbians of color can often feel disenfranchised, disempowered, and ignored by all relevant communities. A useful and affirming resource can be the feminist community. Gain an understanding and appreciation of the feminist movement in your community. Have a list of feminist books and other materials available in your office. Be aware of resources in the community, such as women's support groups, music festivals, arts/crafts shows, book clubs, and other social networks.

Understand and Appreciate How Difficult It Is to Accept a Homosexual Orientation Some clients will have trouble identifying as lesbian; others will have trouble identifying as gay or nonheterosexual. Avoid prematurely imposing labels, and allow the client to self-identify. At the same time, provide accurate and affirmative information regarding homosexual, bisexual, and heterosexual orientations. Empathically facilitate the coming out process, both as the client moves toward self-acceptance and as she begins to become more visible to others. Be aware that aging may trigger a new coming out process for lesbian clients. For example, the death of a life-partner who has always been euphemistically referred to as a "friend" may force your client to come out to family and friends, or, alternatively, she may withdraw completely, feeling isolated and afraid (Deevey, 1990). Older lesbians may need assistance finding peer-related support groups and social functions. There are resources available on the Internet, such as the Gay and Lesbian Association of Retired Persons (GLARP) or Seniors Active in a Gay Environment (SAGE).

Be Prepared to Teach Dating Skills to Lesbian Clients   Societal sanctioning of female same-sex friendships and relationships may push some
clients to become involved in relationships before they've had time to date
and get to know potential partners. Avoid discounting or dismissing client
concerns because they may seem too emotional or dramatic; instead, pa-
tiently and empathically help your client work through her feelings. Be willing to address issues of fusion, and avoid prejudging close lesbian relationships as unhealthy. For example, in the lesbian community former lovers
commonly become close friends and establish new ways of relating to each
other. Some of our lesbian clients have taken these former relationships and
knit together families of choice, a circle of friends and ex-lovers who share
holidays and other special events. Needless to say, this new way of relating to
each other can be confusing and emotionally stressful. Be prepared to help
your clients devise ways to maintain autonomy while building relationships
and friendships.

Be Able to Talk About Sex and Sexuality   Become familiar and comfortable with lesbian sexuality and its expression. Explore your own feelings and
attitudes toward sex and sensuality. In addition, be familiar with and ready to
address the multiple effects of sexual abuse and trauma.

Be Culturally Sensitive   Seek to understand the effects of racism and sexism. Be willing to explore your own myths and biases regarding lesbian women
of color. What are your images? stereotypes? Be sensitive to the realities of
multiple oppressions. Be aware of your own cultural baggage. If you are a
white therapist, be aware of the effects of privilege and the potential to feel
guilty for having membership in the dominant culture. Explore how these dynamics might have a detrimental effect on the counseling relationship. If you
are a counselor of color, avoid collusion or the assumption that your clients of
color share your feelings and attitudes, for this assumption may be inaccurate
and harmful to the therapeutic relationship (Greene, 1997).

Be Aware of Treatment Programs for Lesbians in Recovery   Be aware
of lesbian-friendly AA programs and treatment facilities. Because substance
abuse can be a symptom of internalized homoprejudice, be willing to explore
why the client is abusing alcohol or drugs and avoid prematurely labeling
clients as chemically dependent.

*Recognize That Domestic Violence Does Occur in Lesbian Relation-
ships*   Be prepared to offer appropriate and affirming resources. Make sure
you keep an up-to-date list of lesbian-friendly shelters and other sources of
support. Avoid minimizing battering or blaming the victim; domestic violence
between women does occur, and counselors must be prepared to take immediate and empathic action.

Develop Strategies to Set Boundaries With Clients Decide how you want to handle contact with current or former clients outside the therapeutic milieu. Find a strategy that is comfortable and works for you. Living and working in the gay and lesbian community can be challenging, and mental-health practitioners are encouraged to set healthy and realistic boundaries.

BIBLIOGRAPHY

Berzon, B. (1997). *The intimacy dance: A guide to long-term success in gay and lesbian re-lationships*. New York: Plume.

Brown, L. S. (1995). Therapy with same-sex couples: An introduction. In N. S. Jacobson & A. S. Gurman (Eds.), *Clinical handbook of couples therapy*. New York: Guilford Press.

Browning, C., Reynolds, A. L., & Dworkin, S. H. (1991). Affirmative psychotherapy for lesbian women. *The Counseling Psychologist, 19*(2), 177–196.

Bux, D. A. (1996). The epidemiology of problem drinking in gay men and lesbians: A criti-cal review. *Clinical Psychology Review, 16*(4), 277–298.

Caster, W. (1993). *The lesbian sex book*. Los Angeles, CA: Alyson Publications.

Clunis, D. M. & Green, G. (2000). *Lesbian couples: A guide to creating healthy relation-ships*. Seattle, WA: Seal Press.

Coleman, V. E. (1996). Lesbian battering: The relationship between personality and the perpetration of violence. In L. K. Hamberger & C. Renzetti (Eds.), *Domestic partner abuse*. New York: Springer Publishing.

Deevey, S. (1990). Older lesbian women: An invisible minority. *Journal of Gerontological Nursing, 16*, 35–39.

Esterberg, K. G. (1996). Gay cultures, gay communities: The social organization of les-bians, gay men, and bisexuals. In R. Williams & K. M. Cohen (Eds.), *The lives of les-bians, gays and bisexuals: Children to adults*. Fort Worth, TX: Harcourt Brace.

Gartrell, N. K. (1994). Boundaries in lesbian therapist-client relationships. In B. Greene & G. M. Herek (Eds.), *Lesbian and gay psychology: Theory, research and clinical appli-cations*. Thousand Oaks, CA: Sage.

Golden, C. (1994). Our politics and choices: The feminist movement and sexual orienta-tion. In B. Greene & G. M. Herek (Eds.), *Lesbian and gay psychology: Theory, re-search and clinical applications*. Thousand Oaks, CA: Sage.

Greene, B. (1994). Lesbian women of color: Triple jeopardy. In L. Comas-Diaz & B. Greene (Eds.), *Women of color: Integrating ethnic and gender identities in psycho-therapy*. New York: Guilford Press.

————. (1997). Ethnic minority lesbians and gay men: Mental health and treatment is-sues. In B. Greene (Ed.), *Ethnic and cultural diversity among lesbians and gay men*. New York: Guilford Press.

Loulan, J. (1984). *Lesbian sex*. San Francisco: Spinsters Ink.

————. (1987). *Lesbian passion: Loving ourselves and each other*. San Francisco: Spinsters/ Auntlute.

McCarn, S. R. & Fassinger, R. E. (1996). Revisioning sexual minority identity formation: A new model of lesbian identity and its implications for counseling and research. *The Counseling Psychologist, 24*(3), 508–534.

Newman, F. (1999). *The whole lesbian sex book: A passionate guide for all of us.* San Francisco: Cleis Press.

Nichols, M. P. & Schwartz, R. C. (1998). *Family therapy: Concepts and methods.* Needham Heights, MA: Allyn and Bacon.

Ossana, S. M. (2000). Relationship and couples counseling. In R. M. Perez, K. A. Debord, & K. J. Bieschke (Eds.), *Handbook of counseling and therapy with lesbians, gays, and bisexuals.* Washington, DC: American Psychological Association Press.

Schreurs, K. M. G. (1993). Sexuality in lesbian couples: The importance of gender. *Annual Review of Sex Research, 4,* 49–66.

Slater, S. (1995). *The lesbian family life cycle.* New York: Free Press.

Smith, A. (1997). Cultural diversity and the coming-out process: Implications for clinical practice. In B. Greene (Ed.), *Ethnic and cultural diversity among lesbians and gay men.* New York: Guilford Press.

Tessina, T. B. (2000). Fanning the flames. *Girlfriends, 6*(7), 29.

COUNSELING GAY MEN

The Case of Leon

Leon is a 40-year-old out gay counselor working in an urban Southern community. His private practice consists of both gay and nongay clients, and his particular areas of expertise are couples counseling, grief and loss, and coming out issues. An advocate for the civil rights of all persons, Leon has worked diligently and publicly on behalf of his gay and lesbian community. Read his description of his work with Jeff, a 30-year-old gay male who has been coming out for the past three months.

Jeff became a client in my practice about two weeks after he had decided to come out. He had seen some gay-centered articles I had written for our local paper and thought I might be able to help him. When he first came in, he was an emotional wreck, crying all the time, not able to concentrate on work, and terrified that his family was going to find out and reject him. Initially very empathic, I affirmed his courage in claiming his integrity, and I sat as he wept. He had thought things were going to be easier once he came out, but once he had begun to meet gay people he had become even more depressed. In that initial session he said something like, "This is more difficult than I had imagined. I have known I was attracted to men since I was tiny, so that is no surprise. What scares me is that I want to have sex with men, but I keep feeling like I am doing something wrong, something I am not supposed to be doing. I have only had sex with one man, and that was very awkward: I had to get drunk in order to accomplish that, and I don't want to get into that habit. I had a date last week with a guy I am very attracted to, and I got so anxious I had to cancel the date. We've talked on the phone since then and are going to have dinner soon, but just as friends. I can't handle being with him wondering if we are going to have sex or not."

In that same session I assessed his level of distress and recommended he consider antidepressants. He was shocked at this and muttered something about being "crazy" so I backed off but went over the ways antidepressants work. He had not been able to tell his family practice physician he is gay, and he definitely was not so "messed up" that he needed a psychiatrist. I mentioned a couple of gay family practice physicians in our community who might be willing to help him. At first he was stunned that there were gay physicians who were willing to be visible, but when I reminded him that he might have felt that way about me if he hadn't read my newspaper pieces, he decided that he would take the two names. Exposing him to more role models was one of my first objectives.

Also in the initial session he spoke about his fears of telling his family he is gay. His dad had been dead for about five years, and his mom was an invalid. He, his sisters, and his brother took turns taking care of her. This burden was more than they could handle, and he could not even consider adding to their worries by telling them he is gay. He felt conflicted about lying to them. The family had always been close, and he felt they would understand and support him. As we explored his emotions, he wept over a conversation he had with his dad before he died. "Dad and I were talking, and he asked me if I was gay. I got so angry and told him no and not ever to ask something like that about me again. Six months later he was dead, and I feel so bad that I could not tell him why I was afraid to talk about it with him. I wish I had not let him down so. We both knew I was lying, and all I did was tell him I did not trust him to talk about it." Probing his fear, Jeff came to realize that at the time he was struggling with himself and that he was just too afraid to talk about it with anyone. I suggested that he write a letter to his dad telling him everything and asking for his support. He gave me a funny look when I said that, but soon he started talking about what he might say. The conversation about his family ended with my asking how he might feel if one of his sisters or his brother died before he could tell them. He said his oldest sister had hinted around and that he had just ignored her. He figured she knew but was afraid to ask.

He told me more about his friendships. He had been referred to me by one of my former students who was also gay. He also talked about his best friend, a woman who had been a client of mine as she was coming out. This suggested that he had good reference points in the gay community and that I did not need to shift into the case management approach I often use when someone is coming out but knows no one who is gay or lesbian. For example, at the same time I was seeing Jeff, I was also counseling a 45-year-old married man with two daughters who was trying to figure out how to come out. Over the years I have learned that I sometimes have to be more a case manager than a psychotherapist. The gay community is relatively invisible here, and too often people who are coming out think the only way to find other gay men is by going to the bars. I suggested that he get in touch with our local gay and lesbian switchboard and ask for the welcoming information packet that is sent to people new to our community. I also referred him to a gay parents support group that met each week. With a former client's permission, I referred him to another gay man who had also been married with children and who had really struggled to find gay men like himself. In my training I did not learn that taking that kind of initiative was appropriate, but I sure have seen how effective it can be. There are times when I am exploring and sorting through life experiences with gay clients, and there are many other times when I am teaching about the gay and lesbian community and helping clients look beyond the stereotype of what they think it is like.

Just as being a case manager has been challenging, another issue that has been difficult is that I often find myself at social events attended by my clients. There has been more than one occasion when I have gone to a dinner party and found a client sitting across the table. Sometimes I try to ask casually who else might be invited, but I can't always do that. When I do happen to see a client at a social event, I try to be as relaxed as possible, leave the event early, and make sure the client and I talk about it in the next session. I haven't been able to figure out any other way to manage this, and so far I have kept the boundaries clear. I routinely tell my clients that if I happen to meet them in the community, I will not speak until they greet me first, and I assure them there will be no offense if they decide they are not comfortable greeting me. Seeing clients in their own environments often gives me insight that I would not otherwise have. For instance, I have often met a client's potential boyfriend or ex-lover and once, even his parents. Sometimes knowing these people helps me understand my client more fully and other times it confuses my understanding of the client.

Jeff was able to come out to his family after our first session. Fortunately, he was right about their acceptance, or at least, mostly right. His sister-in-law told him that she loves him but that she hoped he would keep his sexuality separate from the family. In other words, she did not want him bringing friends or boyfriends around his nieces and nephews. He was upset with her attitude and eventually let her know that he was not willing to pretend he was not gay when he was around the family. He learned early that coming out is just the first step in teaching his family about his life. Often the teaching is the most difficult step, and some clients never take these necessary steps. Naturally, I have had other clients whose families rejected them when they came out. Overcoming that pain is a big task for anyone, and there have been many times when the client had to give up his family in order to get on with his life.

Realizing that family rejection really makes a statement about the family's intolerance rather than about the gay son can help clients in this situation move on.

Watching these men re-create themselves is a wonderful privilege. Forming a new self-identity is difficult for anyone but is especially hard when the community is unknown and threatening. I have been moved many times by the courage of men who are trying to learn how to be themselves in a world that can be intolerant and biased against them. I read in a journal that being gay might be more an asset than a liability. Some gay youth push themselves harder to succeed and actually separate from their families at earlier ages than their nongay peers. Certainly, being gay involves a lot of adventure. I remember the first time I realized that I liked being gay. I was so surprised to feel that being gay had added to the richness of my life. After many years of struggling with my sexual orientation, I was very excited to realize I was proud of who I am. That's what I hope will happen for each of my clients. The potential is there if one can get beyond the external and internal oppression that seems to come along with having a minority sexual orientation.

ISSUES IN COUNSELING GAY MEN

Leon represents the kind of counselor who practices gay affirmative psychotherapy. While Jeff's situation is complex, there are elements in his presentation that are typical for gay men. More often than for lesbians, gay men must encounter the strong prohibition against daily life tasks such as living together, parenting together, and so on. While it may be acceptable for two women to live together, two men being roommates is often not accepted. Men like Jeff face coming out issues almost everywhere they turn. Given the emphasis on the acquisition of masculine behaviors, men find their male image challenged as they express their interest in cooking, gardening, or living with another man. Creating intimate relationships in the absence of role models or even going on vacation with groups of men may generate uneasiness in some clients. One gay man told us: "Shortly after I came out, I went to a New Year's party at the beach. On January 1, several of us decided to take a walk. As we approached the beach, I saw all of these families and children, and I began to worry that they were going to know that we were a group of gay men. I felt very uncomfortable being so openly gay then. One seven-year-old studied us for a long time, and I could see that he was trying to figure it out. Suddenly he shouted, 'Hey Mom! It's a bachelor party!' Then I began to relax." In this chapter you will read about many of the issues that gay men often present in counseling. Most of them hinge on some aspect of coming out, and some of them may mirror the issues presented by lesbians (Garnets et al., 1991).

The preceding chapters have presented the context in which sexual minorities form their lives. This chapter will give you some tools that will help in counseling gay men, although counseling gay men is not terribly different from counseling any other person with similar issues. However, because both internal and external oppression stifles ego development, and because most nongay counselors know so little about gay communities, there are important issues that need illumination. One anxiety that can interfere, particularly for nongay mental-health professionals who may not be familiar with gay clients, is the fear of offending the client by asking questions that reveal a lack of knowledge or perhaps embarrass the client. McHenry and Johnson (1993) warn counselors to be wary of unconscious collusions with self-hate, such as not responding when a client makes a negative comment like "All gay relationships are troubled" or not congratulating a client who has recently moved in with her/his lover. There certainly can be overt or subtle negative inferences in the counselor's response. Mary, in Chapter 1, really had very little understanding of the situations her clients faced. She had to be careful to avoid giving offense. The best way to manage this anxiety is to make the client aware of the discomfort and ask him to let you know if any response or comment is offensive.

This chapter contains several counseling techniques that have been useful in our work over the past 20 years and also draws from the work of others. These ideas can be useful in counseling relationships and might stimulate curiosity and creativity that lead to other more effective approaches. Arranged somewhat in the order they should be used, they represent common issues and responses when working with gay men.

Coming Out Issues

For many counselors, the initial contact with gay men involves issues related to coming out. Although clients often come to treatment with complaints about depression, suicide, or a crisis (Meyer & Dean, 1998), the real impetus for counseling is their struggle with questions about their sexual orientation. This can occur at any point in adult life. Some men come out in adolescence or young adulthood; others may wait until their old age to come to terms with their feelings of same-sex attraction (Beard & Glickauf-Hughes, 1994; Grace, 1992). Because they have internalized so much negativity about themselves, they may present with extreme amounts of stress caused from facing oppressive attitudes and potential discrimination or rejection (Franke & Leary, 1991). The following techniques will help the counselor determine what can be done to facilitate the coming out process.

Listen

As with all counseling issues, the initial task involves listening carefully as the client speaks. Ask questions when the subject seems vague. Probe gently and respectfully at all times. Suspending judgmental tendencies will be necessary for counselors who are not comfortable with gay and lesbian clients. If judgmental attitudes persist, referral is the appropriate response.

Take Initiative

Many gay men seek out mental-health professionals when beginning to come out. For some, simply telling another person that they are gay is a challenge; talking about it makes it become more "real." Gay men coming out may approach the counselor warily, not wanting to risk rejection just as they are hoping to explore a part of themselves that has been troubled. Sometimes they use language that only subtly hints at issues related to sexual orientation. "I have not dated in several years." "I feel as if there is something wrong with me." Some come for treatment because of depression, anxiety, substance abuse, or even a relationship crisis (Meyer & Dean, 1998). Consider Jay's comments:

> I am here because I have a drinking problem. I started drinking heavily when I was in the 10th grade, and, at 23, I'm still at it. I dropped out of high school after the 11th grade, mostly because I was having too much fun drinking. I've tried to quit several times, but I get so lonely and don't know what to do with myself. About the only time I can really relax and have sex is when I am drunk.

A counselor working with Jay might spend lots of time getting a history of his substance use and maybe refer him for treatment. A better approach would be to explore the reasons alcohol is necessary to have sex. Responding to the latter exploration, Jay told haltingly about his fear of his sexual energy. And when the counselor probed further into Jay's experience of sexual energy, he became silent. He only spoke up when asked if he was worried about his sexual orientation. At that point, Jay was able to talk in depth about his attraction to men. As he began to feel more comfortable with the idea that he was gay, he stopped drinking completely and began to face the tasks of integrating his sexual orientation into his life.

The counselor who is patient and respectful, like Leon in the case at the beginning of this chapter, will carefully help the client begin to feel more safe. Recently, one of my clients talked about not meeting people and being lonely. At the age of 35, he said he had never had a girlfriend and wanted to learn how to go out with women. We could have spent several sessions on this topic, but when asked, "Are there any concerns about your sexual orientation?" he began to cry and stammered out that he thought he was gay.

Be Prepared to Educate

Gay men come for counseling with different levels of knowledge about their sexuality and about the gay community. It is not rare to see a client who has no gay friends and knows virtually nothing about gay community activities. Working with this kind of client means the counselor will need to shift back and forth from being a counselor to being a case manager. For instance, it is not uncommon for gay men to come to counseling to get information they do not know how to obtain elsewhere. Knowledge about gay community events can be invaluable. Being able to give the telephone number of the nearest gay and lesbian switchboard will enable the client to gather some information on his own. Naturally, gay bars are gathering places in most communities. Although bars can be enormously useful as places to meet others, they represent a particular aspect of gay culture that may not be attractive or even safe for some men who are just coming out, particularly those with substance abuse issues. Some counselors find that being in the role of guide for men who are coming out violates the counseling models they learned in graduate school. Realizing that the client may be completely overwhelmed and that the counselor is the safest source of information enables the counseling to be more effective.

Be Sensitive to Diversity

The gay community seems to be monolithic, but it is enormously diverse (Diggs, 1993). Be conscious that most of the research on gay men has used samples that are primarily white and that in some minority communities, men who have sex with men may not identify as gay (Peterson, 1992). Their sexual behavior with men may be viewed simply as an expression of sexual interest that has nothing to do with their sexual orientation (Greene, 1994). Men who face dual oppressions find themselves on very different terrain from that of white men who are gay (Atkinson & Hackett, 1995; Reynolds & Pope, 1991). Native American culture views homosexuality from a different perspective than does the majority culture (LaFromboise, Trimble, & Mohatt, 1993; Tafoya, 1992). Asking clients how their culture views homosexuality will help the counselor increase credibility with minority clients.

What About the Client Who Is Not Sure?

Helping a client who is unsure about his sexual orientation is not such a difficult task if the client is ready to take action. A beginning assignment could be to have the client walk through a crowd of people (such as at a shopping mall or any other public place where men and women would be walking around). Have the client observe himself as he approaches others. Does he look more often at males or at females? If a couple is walking toward him, is he more likely to be paying attention to the man or to the woman? Have the client go to a romantic movie and observe the sources of his sexual arousal. He might purchase a magazine such as *Playboy* or *Playgirl* and look at the nude bodies, paying particular attention to which ones create a greater awareness of sexual energy for him. Visiting a gay bar is another way for him to monitor his reaction to sexually charged atmospheres where men are present. In each of these instances, it is important for the client to be as relaxed as possible and to understand that all observations are tentative. Giving oneself labels too impulsively can complicate treatment. The absence of a strong response toward persons of both genders may not mean anything other than that anxiety is interfering. If the client reports similar levels of sexual arousal from both men and women, it is possible that he is bisexual. Direct sexual encounters with men and women usually resolve what questions may remain.

Anticipate Thoughts of Suicide

Coming out is not just about information. For many the emotional turmoil can be bewildering. Fear of one's own sexuality can be immobilizing. Consider the situation Bob faced as he counseled Philip. Philip began with the following statement.

> I have known I was gay since I was very young, and I have hated myself for it. Many times I have thought about killing myself. I know my life will be ruined if I come out, but I just can't stand lying any longer. I am so lonely, and I'm tired. When I think about telling my parents, I feel awful. They will be angry, hurt, and disappointed in me. I'm sure my brother and sister will not let me be around their kids. I expect I will be alone at Christmas and other holidays, and I'm not sure how I will be able to keep my sexuality a secret at work. If anyone there found out, I would really be lost! I just can't figure out what to do. I go home alone at the end of each day and don't want to go out. My life is pretty miserable. I went out to a gay bar last weekend, but once I got to the bar, I ended up just sitting in my car. I was too afraid to go in. I don't drink anyway, and I worry about someone I know seeing me there. What am I going to do? Life seems like punishment that will not end until I can die.

Before Philip would be able to take any steps toward meeting other gay men, he needed to explore his feelings. Establishing a relationship with a counselor who was accepting and understanding would be his first step toward affirming himself as a gay man.

Joe, who was married, stated the following:

> I am so depressed. I have worried about being gay for so many years, but I was not like the gay people I had seen on TV, so I just pushed that thought aside. Still, those feelings don't go away. My wife and I had our first child six months ago. I had wanted to be a father and was excited to hold my daughter for the first time. Later, mom asked why I so rarely interacted with the baby. I hadn't been aware of this. I guess they thought it was just a male thing. You know, babies are women's stuff. As I thought about it though, I realized that I was not holding her because I do not want her to love me. She is going to grow up hating me because I am gay. About the only way out for me is to try to find a way not to be so afraid of being gay. Maybe if I can do that, she will understand one day. My whole family can see that I am depressed. I know if I tell them, I will be tossed out. They will never want to see me again, that's for sure. I sometimes think the only way out is death. My life is pretty awful right now, and I haven't even told anyone other than you about this.

Working with this client demanded very careful attention to his need to understand and face his emotions and his need for more information about what it means to be gay. The most helpful thing the counselor did was to contact a former client who had been married and who agreed to meet with Joe and tell his own story. After this meeting, Joe began to realize he was not alone in facing the potential loss of his family. Not only had he met someone who could be a resource for him, but he had also made a friend who was happy to introduce Joe to other gay men who were also fathers. His suicidal thoughts faded as he began to find a way to be himself.

Selective Outness

As clients come out, the counselor will begin to understand various ways that gay men selectively let others know who they are. One feature that distinguishes gays and lesbians from other minorities is the ability to "pass." Because sexual orientation is not immediately visible and because the general presumption is of heterosexuality, gay men may remain closeted in some aspects of their lives. They may not tell co-workers or family members but let everyone else know. They may make references to "de-fagging" their homes when family members come to visit. Some invent fictitious friends and lovers so they feel comfortable talking about their personal lives with those who don't know. Naturally, the energy involved in maintaining these stories can be a source of conflict. Shannon said, "When I talk to my parents, I speak of Joe as Jo and remember to change the references to she and her rather than he and his. This can get very complicated at times. But so far, they have not suspected and it helps them to know that I have an active dating life." Eventually, many clients tire of this subterfuge and begin to make plans to come out fully.

BEYOND COMING OUT

One other aspect of coming out deserves attention. Some men think that once they have told their family, friends, and co-workers, their coming out tasks are done. Telling others is just the first step. Providing information that helps friends and family understand what it means to be gay can be useful if the support systems are willing to face their own discomfort. Encouraging attendance at a PFLAG meeting may also be useful. The teaching aspect of coming out is frequently missed. Clients often make comments such as, "Well, I told them and now we don't have to talk about that again." Educating others about the diversity and complexity of the gay community will help them understand that it's not just about sex and will enable those potential sources of support to grow as well. Letting others in as the client's gay life evolves can be important (Preston, 1992).

Delayed Adolescence

It is not unusual for gay men to report emotional confusion as they come out. Chapter 1 discussed the Adlerian life tasks (society, work, sex, self, and spirituality) that were worked on at various times across the life span. Learning about sexual relationships during those years is eased by careful supervision and gradual maturity. The man who is coming out after age 25 is likely to go through experiences that seem more appropriate for an adolescent. Falling in love quickly, spending long periods of time pursuing sexual relationships, hanging out in bars, or simply being distracted by thoughts about sex or dating is generally associated with boys who are 15 or 16. To have this experience when one is 30 or 40, or even 50, can be both exciting and confusing. Gay men coming out will frequently refer to this experience as inappropriate or maybe even embarrassing. The counselor can help normalize what is going on by discussing that a developmental period was skipped while the client moved through an adolescence that did not include same-sex relationship-building skills. While this may not dispel all the anxiety, it can give the client a construct for understanding what is happening. Counselors who are not familiar with this aspect of coming out may be shocked at the amount of energy that is poured into sexual pursuits. Carefully monitoring internal reactions to client presentations is essential when sexual activities are being discussed.

Coping Strategies

As gay men come out more fully, one is apt to see the reappearance of the coping strategies used during their childhood and adolescence as they struggled with the fear and shame of being gay. The gay sexual orientation has likely been compartmentalized and protected by layers of fear and shame. Figure 4.1 illustrates how this compartment might look. One consequence of keeping sexual orientation in a compartment is that letting others get close (intimacy) is likely to raise anxiety that is dealt with by isolation. In the safety of the compartment, one is alone but also relatively invulnerable.

I like to draw this figure when I am sitting with a client who seems to be struggling with trying to find out how to be more comfortable being gay in front of others. It is not unusual to have a recently out gay man talk about his euphoria when he walks into a gay bar. What he is doing is opening his compartment and letting others see some of the gay part he has kept hidden. I have also found it not surprising that many gay men struggle with establishing intimacy with other gay men. Long-held prohibitions against letting others into the gay compartment are not easily dispelled. Retreating into isolation feels safe, but in reality, that coping strategy is counterproductive. The reflective client will recognize feelings of fear, and the counselor will be able to refer back to this fig-

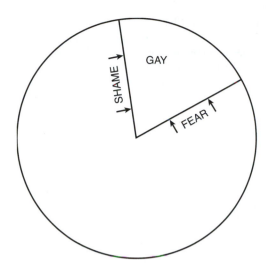

FIGURE **4.1**

Compartmentalization of sexual orientation.

ure to assist in cognitive understanding. Many gay men continue to use isolation as a coping strategy when faced with the opportunity for intimacy. Exploring the anxiety that often accompanies intimacy, especially in light of the tendency to compartmentalize, can help them understand themselves more fully and may enable them to become more comfortable with intimate relationships.

How far should the counselor go in encouraging gay male clients to live out? Rather than assigning sexual orientation to a compartment, a gay man can make being gay the backdrop against which a life is constructed. Of course, this is only possible when the client makes the decision to be fully out. As discussed in Chapter 2, those who live out have been found to have higher self-esteem than those who stay in the closet. Opening the compartment to others can be very frightening and often does involve the loss of some relationships. Over the years I have observed that gay men do better once they are totally out. They report more happiness and satisfaction with their lives, seem to have stronger support systems, and enjoy lives free of the fear that is generated when one is trying to keep a secret. Naturally, there are some who, because of employment considerations, will not be able to be totally out. Schoolteachers and child-care workers may face loss of employment if their sexual orientation becomes known. It is not the counselor's role to establish living out as a goal. However, it is the counselor's responsibility to encourage the client to examine his fears. Sometimes the fears associated with coming out stem more from a perceived threat than an actual threat.

Overcoming shame and fear is a necessary step in the coming out process. These emotions may emerge frequently as the client encounters new situations. Understanding that they arise as a result of opening the compartment more fully can be a source of encouragement. Dan's comments represent this well:

> Coming out has been much harder than I thought. I have lots of gay friends and have even dated a couple of guys. I like being gay and feel so relieved that I do not have to hide any longer. But I am having trouble giving myself permission to be sexual. When I am in situations where there is an opportunity to have sex, I just shut down and pretty soon I couldn't have sex even if I wanted to. I've thought a lot about this and realize that gay sex has always been bound in that compartment. Letting a person close to that part of me is scary.

The counselor working with Dan can help him by encouraging him to tell his potential sex partners about his anxiety and to give him permission to let the sexual moments extend as far as they might. In other words, be active in sexual situations without the expectation that orgasm will occur. Finding a willing partner who is sensitive to Dan's plight can be an enormous assist. This is what Dan said two weeks later:

> I did what you suggested. My boyfriend wanted to have sex with me, and I immediately felt anxious. Then I told him I was willing but that I did not need to have an orgasm and would prefer just to go slowly and let myself enjoy being with him as long as the anxiety was not distracting me. We started off just like that, and I really got into it. As a matter of fact, I never got anxious at all, and we both had a great time!

Another proven technique that can be very helpful for many gay men is to explore the ideal self/real self disparity. Writing *Ideal Self* above *Real Self* on a piece of paper can help some clients add more detail to what might be an abstract concept. Some will continue to see their ideal self as heterosexual. When the ideal self becomes gay (like the real self), the client has made significant progress toward accepting a positive gay identity. Another application of this technique is to write the criticisms the ideal self expresses toward the real self. Developing ways for the client to intervene in the critical internal dialogue can lead to an enhanced sense of well-being.

RELATIONSHIP AND DATING ISSUES

Perhaps the most common issue discussed by gay men in counseling revolves around intimacy, dating, and relationships. Being single in a world of couples has its unique challenges regardless of one's sexual orientation. Some gay men believe their gayness is affirmed primarily by being in a loving relationship with another man. While couples do tend to hang out together, in virtually every community there are many activities and organizations that welcome both single gay men and gay couples. Once again, knowing about a gay bowling league, a gay chorus, or gay political groups will enable the counselor to educate the client. Scasta (1998) estimates that the chances of a gay man finding an appropriate mate are 8 in 100,000,000. From his statistical analysis he suggests that in the United States there are only 22 men who would make a suitable partner for an individual gay client.

For gay men, intimacy can be complicated by various factors: unrealistic expectations (Scasta, 1998), internalized homophobia (Meyer & Dean, 1998), developmental issues, and low self-esteem and shame, as well as addictive behavior and co-dependency (Alexander, 1997). In our clinical work we have found that single gay men frequently present with depression and anxiety tied to relationship status. Often lacking the skills necessary to build intimate relationships, many gay men suffer with fears of being alone as they age and view their single status as an additional stigma (Isay, 1989). There are no easy solutions to the dilemma of loneliness. Certainly, as the client develops a relationship with the counselor, intimacy begins to grow. The counselor should have knowledge of places and activities where gay men can meet and get to know each other, environments that are not infused with sexual energy. Using the client–counselor relationship as an example of intimacy development can be very powerful but also requires caution lest the client lose his boundaries and develop romantic attachments to the male counselor. Rejection by the counselor for whatever reason can be very damaging to gay men with relationship difficulties.

Fear of abandonment underlies the struggle with intimacy for many gay men. Primarily because of internalized homophobia (Meyer & Dean, 1998), some gay male clients will need to examine the negative attitudes they have developed about themselves before they will be able to establish close relationships with others. In their longitudinal study, Meyer and Dean found a direct relationship between levels of outness and self-esteem. Men who were explicitly out to others, routinely read the gay press, were members of a gay group (such as a political or athletic group), or were coupled had higher levels of self-esteem than those who did not participate in these activities. In the same study these researchers found that men with higher levels of internalized homophobia were two to three times as likely to seek mental-health services for help with depression, guilt, suicidal thoughts, and AIDS-related traumatic stress.

The alert counselor will recognize statements that indicate internalized homophobia and challenge the assumptions on which they are based. It is not unusual to hear gay men say things like "gay men cannot be monogamous," "you just can't trust gay men," "he's just like all other gay men," or "you know how gay men can be." The negative implications of statements like these need to be identified and explored. At the same time, helping the client recognize his anxiety about abandonment and its possible connection to beliefs and fears about potential rejection purely because of sexual orientation can lead to the development of more risk taking in building intimate relationships. In Box 4.1, several issues related to dysfunctional relationship styles and intimacy are explored.

Chapter 5 contains more information about gay and lesbian relationships. Gay men often face serious challenges as they seek contact with other gay men. Even friendships can be complicated by the sexual energy that can be present between two men. Understanding that struggles with intimacy often result

BOX

4.1

Issues of Intimacy for Gay Men

In his work on intimacy and gay men, Scasta (1998) identified some characteristics of dysfunctional styles of relationship building. The list below has been adapted from his work.

Dysfunctional Relationship Styles

1. **One-Night Stand Intimacy.** The kind of intimacy experienced in one-night stands undermines finding more fulfilling and long-lasting relationships. The counselor and client might agree that the client postpone sex until the relationship has had time to develop.
2. **Shyness.** Shyness is lethal. Assertiveness training or social skills training can help overcome this deficit.
3. **Seeking the Sexual God Desired by All.** Selecting the most desirable man as a potential partner can be a setup for failure. Some men who are extremely attractive may not be willing to stay around to resolve complex issues. They may seem to be good catches, but they can easily wander since there are so many attracted to them.
4. **Being Attracted Only to Someone Younger, but Mature.** Clients may need help in recognizing "red flags" that make some men potentially dangerous as partners. Many younger men have not developed comfort with their sexual orientation and do not have the ability to make a commitment. Helping the client identify the personal qualities that will make a good mate is one way to help him deal with the power and attractiveness that youth may hold.
5. **Seeking Perfection.** The fear of making a mistake leads many to fear commitment. Personal ads often sound like descriptions of objects rather than of human beings. Unrealistic expectations are best explored through the use of reality therapy.
6. **Repetition Compulsion.** Repeatedly selecting the same type of potential partner can be an effective means of blocking intimacy. Teaching the client to see the "red flags" that indicate potential trouble and then to move cautiously may enable him to avoid future hurts. The unconscious dynamics that lead a client to become repeatedly involved in hurtful relationships may be traced to early childhood experiences and expectations.
7. **Forcing a Relationship to Work.** Some men find themselves in relationships that have lost their energy, but they persist in trying to force the relationship to work. This may happen because of fear of being alone, or fear of encountering the sometimes-harsh dating scene.

Issues of Intimacy for Gay Men (continued)

>   Helping the client recognize when a relationship cannot work and take appropriate steps may be the first step toward his successfully finding a partner.
> 8. **Giving In to Peer Pressure.** Some men carefully grade potential mates based on feedback from peers. Finding a partner who meets certain "community standards" in terms of body type, financial success, or hair color often is a recipe for troubled relating. Help the client both to identify desirable qualities and to manage pressure from peers who may not have similar values.
>
> (Source: *Adapted from Scasta, 1998.*)

from compartmentalization and fear of rejection caused by oppression will enable the counselor to respond sensitively to clients.

Sex

The sexual environment in which gay men live can be shocking at first glance. Gay men probably do have more sex partners than nongay persons do. Gay men seem more casual about sex and may be quicker to take advantage of a sexual moment than their nongay peers. Pornography and explicit sexuality have a more open presence in the gay world. In large cities there are sex clubs, bathhouses, and even bars where men engage in sex publicly. In most cities there are parks or public bathrooms where men go to have sex. Writing about this aspect of the gay male experience is difficult because the topic is complex and value laden. Gay male sexual activity is also a prime target for religious leaders and politicians who are apt to use this part of gay male culture as the single defining characteristic of all gay men. Counselors need to know that the erotic energy that exists in some aspects of the gay community is very high, and that some clients can get caught up in sexual activities that are potentially harmful. It is important to remember that many sexual behaviors are not inherently pathological, and some of the more bizarre activities do represent aspects of responses to oppression.

Gay men may find themselves exploring sexual venues that help them develop a deeper understanding of themselves. Because of the constancy of oppression stemming from their sexual energy, some men defiantly expre sexual energy by hypermasculine dress or activities or find themsel to sexual interactions that involve power or dominance. The reaso this behavior vary. Some professionals believe that gay boys gro vironment where they feel like failed men. Denied access to the of their masculinity because of their lack of sexual interest in women, they seek reassurance of their maleness by an overinvolvement in sexual expression. Others may simply be reacting to the reality that being gay has cost them something important, so they are going to take advantage of every sexual opportunity that comes along. Whatever the reasons, overt sexuality is commonplace in the gay male community. Attitudes toward overt sexual activity, pornography, and multiple sex partners underlie a level of promiscuity that can be troubling to both the client and the counselor.

There are no easy techniques to help clients who want to talk about these activities. As in most groups, the diversity within the gay male culture is broad. Becoming involved in the sexual subculture may be a normal part of adult male development. Listening to clients talk about the leather community, sadomasochism (S&M), or other aspects of gay eroticism may not always be comfortable for one who is not familiar with the gay sex scene. Some men take part in these activities regularly, and some experiment with them but eventually abandon them. Others shy away from them and perhaps condemn them as unhealthy expressions of gay sexuality. Because sexual feelings may have been deeply oppressed, many men express a curiosity and adventurous attitude as they explore some of these expressions of being gay.

It is not necessary that every counselor be knowledgeable about this aspect of the gay male culture. The client is the best teacher. Those clients who need to talk about it will do so, and they will be able to teach the counselor about aspects of their experiences that are unfamiliar to the counselor. Asking for information from a client who understands the gay world better than the counselor is a smart way to increase effectiveness. When does such sexual activity become a problem? Like other addictions or compulsive behaviors, becoming caught up in the search for sexual "highs" can place the client at increased risk of sexually transmitted diseases and may lead to the use of alcohol and other drugs (Cabaj, 1995). Fundamentally, these activities become a problem when they put the client's health at risk or when they begin to dominate the individual's life. The key criterion in defining sexual compulsivity is control—if the behavior is out of control, it is a problem. Individual treatment and referral to a local meeting of Sex Addicts Anonymous (SAA), which uses a 12-step approach, is the best course of action (Hendrickson, 1995).

Safe Sex and HIV

Educating the client about safe sex and exploring the client's adherence to safe-sex practices is a fundamental aspect of counseling gay men. Although the knowledge about how to prevent HIV is widespread, gay men continue to contract HIV disease, indicating ongoing unsafe sexual activity. Prior to the availability of combination drug therapy in the treatment of HIV disease, the infection rate was fairly stable. In recent years, however, increasing numbers of young gay men are testing positive. Once seen as an "old man's" disease, many young gay men believe they are not at risk as long as they have sex with other young gay men. The street term that has developed around this activity is *barebacking*. Both young and older gay men may take the risk of having sex without protection because they now believe that current treatments for HIV infection will enable them to live long lives.

In smaller communities, HIV is not commonly discussed. Rarely does the topic come up in casual conversation, and the rapid decline in deaths has led to a climate in which HIV no longer plays a central role. Clients who fail to adhere to safe sex practices may not feel comfortable talking about their behavior because discussing it demands admitting the behavior is taking place and may lead to increased anxiety or avoidance of sexual interactions completely. Bob Remian, a psychologist and HIV researcher in New York City, was astounded when over 600 gay men showed up for a presentation on helping gay men recover from relapsing into unsafe sex (Remian, 1997).

Another aspect of gay male culture that places some men at risk is the so-called circuit party. Circuit parties are held in various parts of the country and typically involve a weekend of heavy substance use and recreational sex. A source of concern to many in the gay and nongay community, these parties are seen by many as glamorous events attended by large numbers of attractive and available men. Clients who attend these parties are likely to find themselves in situations involving risk, and counselors are advised to initiate frank discussions about their clients' plans to adhere to safe sex practices.

Counseling newly diagnosed HIV-positive gay men presents unique challenges to mental-health practitioners. A growing body of literature explores the issues involved in HIV-related psychotherapy (Anderson & Barret, 2001; Winiarski, 1996; Kain, 1996; Rabkin, Remian, & Wilson, 1994). Counselors working with gay men will inevitably encounter clients who have HIV disease. Dealing with the double stigma of being both gay and HIV-positive is a challenging hurdle for many gay men. For others, HIV seems to be quickly incorporated into their daily routines and does not demand the kind of focus it did when HIV led to AIDS and to certain death. Counseling HIV-positive gay men brings up a number of issues, such as shame, anger, grief over the loss of health, confusion about how to manage safe-sex negotiation, and life planning that incorporates the realities of HIV treatment. Chapter 10 provides further information about safe-sex practices, negotiating temptations to lapse into unsafe sex, sexually transmitted diseases, and HIV and substance abuse.

Tips for Practitioners

Gay male clients can offer an enormously challenging and rewarding clinical experience. Providing a safe place for these men to explore aspects of themselves that may never have been brought to the surface and watching as they take steps to integrate their sexual orientation allow the counselor to be part of a rich exploration that may involve significant suffering but also to support and celebrate as clients begin to create a new life. Participating in the liberation of these men from the oppressions that hold them back can be extremely exciting and gratifying. Special knowledge and skills enable this clinical experience to move more smoothly, but the client can also be an excellent and patient teacher to the counselor who is respectful and open to learning.

Resources   Virtually every community has numerous resources that can provide valuable assistance to gay men. A counselor with knowledge of these resources has enhanced credibility, and clients may find that they are able to progress more quickly once they know places where they can make contact with other gay men. Most cities have a congregation of the Metropolitan Community Church, which is predominantly gay and lesbian. There will also be mainstream religious organizations that welcome gay men. You will find many resources once you start looking. If you experience trouble, there may be a lesbian and gay switchboard (usually listed in the "G" section of the phone book). The local HIV/AIDS organization will also know of other resources in your community.

Learn About HIV Disease   Knowledge of HIV disease is necessary in counseling gay men. Although statistics suggest otherwise, HIV continues to be seen by many as a gay disease. It is a fact of life in the gay community, and all gay men should be seen as at risk. Learn about the progression of this disease and its treatment, and how to talk about safe sex with all clients. When a client is discussing a recent sexual encounter or a new relationship with you, exploring the dynamics of the safe-sex negotiation should be almost routine. You may have to initiate discussions about relapses into unsafe sex. Such initiatives many be essential, especially if the client regularly abuses alcohol or other drugs.

Older Gay Men   Like the larger culture in which we live, gay male communities are infused with an obsession about youth and beauty. Men who pass the age of 50 and are still single may present with increasing anxiety about being alone in their old age (Kimmel, 1992). It is not rare for a single gay male under the age of 30 to present with concerns that time is running out, believing that he must find a partner before turning 30 or it will be too late.

Many of the "old and gay" generation report that when they are out socially, younger men do not acknowledge their presence. Others retreat to their homes and may be very isolated and lonely. Resources in most communities that serve older gay men may be scarce, but larger cities usually have organizations like Prime Timers, a social group for gay men over the age of 40, or other less-structured opportunities available for older gay men. Just as aging baby boomers are beginning to demand more services, it is probable that gay men will likewise seek communities that assist them as they age. Retirement communities designed for gay men and lesbians may not exist now, but it is increasingly common to hear gay men in their 40s and 50s wonder when they can expect such specialized services.

Substance Abuse The level of substance use in the gay community is very high. Fueled by internal homonegativity and the easy availability of bars as gathering places, many gay men develop serious substance abuse problems. A complication in treatment can be the absence of gay-friendly treatment centers or AA meetings. In most large cities the local AA organization will sponsor gay-only meetings. In larger cities there most likely is a large gay and lesbian recovery community that understands the pervasiveness of the bar culture. There are several national treatment centers that serve the gay community exclusively. Often substance use is a coping strategy that allows some gay men to have sex with men (I was drunk and did not know what I was doing) without having to acknowledge they are gay. Excessive drinking or drugging may also be seen as a way to fit in or belong by a client who has experienced and feared rejection (Krus, 1991). When you routinely ask about substance use, you are communicating awareness that this issue can be complex for gay men.

Family Issues Family issues will come up in treatment. The issues range from coming out to the discomfort of not coming out. Some men may need to divorce their families because of excessive criticism and rejection. Others may need to learn how to educate and incorporate their families into their gay community. David, a client who had been treated for depression with electroconvulsive therapy (ECT) and was also in and out of treatment centers for substance abuse, finally told his parents he did not want to see them anymore. "I told them that they needed help, and that I would no longer interact with them until they showed they could acknowledge me as their gay son and welcome me and my partner to family gatherings. This was hard for me to do, but, I am happier than I have ever been. I am not depressed and have no desire to drink or do drugs." Withholding your own impulse to urge clients to heal their relationships with their families until you know more about their particular situation is a good guideline.

Abuse While sexual abuse does not appear more frequently in the gay community than in the community at large, there are fewer agencies that reach out to gay men who have been abused (Genius, Thomlison, & Bagley, 1991). Learn about community resources for those recovering from family violence. If there is no group for gay men who have been sexually abused (the treatment of choice), start one. Be aware that because of internalized self-hate, some gay men see themselves as not having much or any self-worth and may accept abusive relationships matter-of-factly. In those instances, it may be necessary to help the client explore his experience and affirm him as a person of value before tackling the abuse issues. Be sure to help the client examine how safe his situation is and to have a plan to get help when he feels threatened. Some gay men also have become victims of violence when they are in public. Helping clients assess their degree of risk for violent hate crimes can be an essential act for clients who are considering public gay rights stands (Herek, 1991; Herek & Berrill, 1991).

Domestic Violence   Some gay couples, like their straight counterparts, find themselves in relationships that involve physical violence. Unfortunately, few resources exist for them, and, in some cases, the appeal of S&M practices may lead them to believe that the violence is just an extension of their sexual energy. Even law enforcement officials may not be much help, and few shelters exist that will take in gay men who need a refuge. Helping your client who is a victim of violence develop an escape plan or find a safe place to stay can be a first step toward a decision not to tolerate this destructive behavior. This is a cycle that is difficult for many to break, and careful and empathic listening may often appear to lead nowhere. Becoming a community activist for the creation of shelters and other services for battered men may enable the counselor to make a significant contribution toward the amelioration of this issue.

Codependence   In recent years the codependence movement has not been highly visible, and there have been some charges that codependency is not a real phenomenon. Some gay men desperately hang on to friendships or romantic relationships that are unhealthy and destructive primarily because they fear being alone. Some move quickly from relationship to relationship without experiencing much time to explore their identity as a single gay man. You can help by encouraging clients to explore how their gay selves may have been desperately lonely during the years in the closet. This can lead to an understanding of the tendency to cling to relationships that should have ended long ago.

Reparative Therapy   Some gay men will come for counseling wanting to change their sexual orientation (Haldeman, 1994). As discussed in Chapter 1, the so-called reparative or conversion therapies have no research base to support their effectiveness. You are advised to tell your clients that you do not believe this treatment will work and then extend an invitation to examine the forces that are encouraging them to consider a treatment that has not been

proven effective. One client told us, "I was so relieved when you said reparative therapy had not been proven effective. I came in asking for that because
my minister told me to. Once you let me know that you believed sexual orientation was not chosen, I was able to begin the coming out process from a
hopeful and affirming place."

Transference/Countertransference Issues Gay men, like many other
clients, often tend to idolize their counselors. You may find yourself struggling with your own needs to affirm and heal clients who have experienced
excessive rejection. A client who has been brutally rejected by his parents
when he came out to them may awaken a nurturing parent in the counselor,
who, in turn, might seek to make up for this abusive parenting. Gay men face
many daunting situations and certainly can present with intense levels of suffering resulting from negative social attitudes rather than from any deficiency
on their part. When a client overtly or subtly expresses feelings that may indicate transference, you must explore those feelings in the safety of the professional relationship. If you develop excessive involvement with the client, supervision is essential and referral may be necessary.

Counselors like Leon in the case example at the beginning of this chapter
are presently working in most communities and are usually happy to provide
assistance in the form of supervision or mentoring for mental-health professionals who are unfamiliar with counseling gay clients. Their experiences can
provide a rich collection of approaches that will enhance the ability of a counselor new to this work. Finding them may take a little time and patience, but
the payoff in terms of increased client insight and progress will be invaluable.

BIBLIOGRAPHY

Alexander, C. J. (1997). *Growth and intimacy for gay men: A workbook.* New York:
    Herrington Park Press.
Anderson, J. & Barret, B. (2001). *Ethical issues in HIV-related psychotherapy.* Washington
    DC: American Psychological Association.
Atkinson, D. & Hackett, C. (1995). *Counseling diverse populations.* Dubuque, IA: William
    C. Brown.
Beard, J. & Glickauf-Hughes, C. (1994). Gay identity and sense of self: Rethinking male
    homosexuality. *Journal of Gay and Lesbian Psychotherapy,* 2(2), 21–37.
Cabaj, R. P. (1995). Sexual orientation and the addictions. *Journal of Gay and Lesbian
    Psychotherapy,* 2(3), 97–117.
Diggs, M. (1993). Surveying the intersection: Pathology, secrecy, and the discourses of
    racial and sexual identity. *Journal of Homosexuality,* 26(2–3), 1–19.
Franke, R. & Leary, M. (1991). Disclosure of sexual orientation by lesbians and gay men:
    A comparison of private and public processes. *Journal of Social and Clinical Psychol-
    ogy,* 10(3), 262–269.

Garnets, L., Hancock, K., Cochran, S., Goodchilds, J., & Peplau, L. (1991). Issues in psychotherapy with lesbians and gay men: A survey of psychologists. *American Psychologist, 46*(9), 964–972.

Genius, M., Thomlison, B., & Bagley, C. (1991). Male victims of child sexual abuse: A brief overview of pertinent findings. *Journal of Child and Youth Care, Fall,* 1–6.

Grace, J. (1992). Affirming gay and lesbian adulthood. In N. J. Woodman (Ed.), *Lesbian and gay lifestyles: A guide for counseling and education.* New York: Irvington.

Greene, B. (1994). Ethnic minority lesbians and gay men: Mental health and treatment issues. *Journal of Consulting and Clinical Psychology, 62,* 243–251.

Haldeman, D. C. (1994). The practice and ethics of sexual orientation conversion therapy for gay men and lesbians: A scientific examination. In J. C. Gonsiorek & J. D. Weinrich (Eds.), *Homosexuality: Research implications for public policy.* Newbury Park, CA: Sage.

Hendrickson, R. (1995). Sexual addiction in a gay man: A brief treatment approach. *The Journal of Gay and Lesbian Psychotherapy, 2*(3), 85–95.

Herek, G. M. (1991). Stigma, prejudice and violence against lesbians and gay men. In J. C. Gonsiorek & J. D. Weinrich (Eds.), *Homosexuality: Research implications for public policy.* Newbury Park, CA: Sage.

Herek, G. M., & Berrill, K. T. (Eds.). (1991). *Hate crimes: Confronting violence against lesbians and gay men.* 2d ed. Newbury Park, CA: Sage.

Isay, R. A. (1989). *Being homosexual: Gay men and their development.* New York: Avon.

Kain, C. (1996). *Positive HIV affirmative counseling.* Alexandria, VA: American Counseling Association.

Kimmel, D. (1992). The families of older gay men and lesbians. *Generations, 16,* 37–38.

Krus, R. J. (1991). Sobriety, friends, and gay men. *Archives of Psychiatric Nursing, 5*(3), 171–177.

LaFromboise, T., Trimble, J., & Mohatt, C. (1993). Counseling intervention and the American Indian tradition: An integrative approach. *The Counseling Psychologist, 18*(4), 628–654.

McHenry, S. & Johnson, J. (1993). Homophobia in the therapist and gay or lesbian client: Conscious and unconscious collusions in self-hate. *Psychotherapy, 30*(1), 141–151.

Meyer, I. & Dean, L. (1998). Internalized homophobia, intimacy, and sexual behavior among gay and bisexual men. In G. M. Herek (Ed.), *Stigma and sexual orientation: Understanding prejudice against lesbians, gay men, and bisexuals.* Thousand Oaks CA: Sage.

Peterson, J. L. (1992). Black men and their same-sex desires and behaviors. In C. H. Herdt (Ed.), *Gay culture in America: Essays from the field.* Boston: Beacon.

Preston, J. (1992). The importance of telling our stories. In B. Berzon (Ed.), *Positively gay: New approaches to gay and lesbian life.* Berkeley, CA: Celestial Arts.

Rabkin, J., Remian, R., & Wilson, C. (1994). *Good doctors/good patients: Partners in HIV treatment.* New York: NCM Publishers.

Remian, R. (1997). Personal communication, April.

Reynolds, A. L. & Pope, R. L. (1991). The complexity of diversity: Exploring multiple oppressions. *Journal of Counseling and Development, 70*(1), 174–180.

Scasta, David. (1998). Moving from coming out to intimacy. *Journal of Gay and Lesbian Psychotherapy, 2*(4), 99–111.

Tafoya, T. (1992). Native gay and lesbian issues: The two spirited. In B. Berzon (Ed.), *Positively gay.* Berkeley, CA: Celestial Press.

Winiarski, M. (1996). *HIV mental health into the 21st century.* New York: New York University Press.

COUNSELING GAY AND LESBIAN COUPLES

The Case of Susan ▼

Susan is a counselor in an agency that provides services to children and families. She has been licensed for five years and is seen as a very strong counselor who often takes on clients with more complex situations. In the past year her agency has seen an increase in the number of gay and lesbian couples seeking help, and she has grown in her confidence about working with them. Still, there are some patterns she sees that confuse her, and she seeks consultation with Clara, a lesbian psychologist.

I think I do a pretty good job with lesbian and gay couples. At first I thought sexual orientation was not a key factor in relationship counseling. I assumed that couples are couples regardless of whether they are gay or straight. However, I've begun to see some major differences. For example, one gay male couple I worked with had been together for 15 years, yet they had never spent a Thanksgiving or Christmas holiday together. One partner was out to his family, but the other was not, so holidays were spent apart. When one set of parents came to visit, the couple had to restructure their home as if they were roommates. They jokingly called it "de-gaying the house," but I could tell that having to do that put pressure on the relationship. We frequently talked about their different levels of outness but never really made much progress until Robert told Tom he was not going to spend Christmas without Tom. Tom made up an excuse to his family, and because they accepted it, he realized that he did not have to go home every holiday.

Since many marriages today do not last, I am sometimes amazed that gay and lesbian couples manage to stay together. There is such variety in the ways they merge their lives. Unlike most straight couples, gay couples seem to have to negotiate everything. Who is going to cook or do the dishes, how are joint bills going to be paid, how is the "extra" money to be spent, and who gets to make that decision? Of course, straight couples also deal with these questions, but with the absence of role models, most gay relationships apparently begin without any assumptions to guide them. For instance, potential male and female roles are at least outlined for straight couples, but gay and lesbian couples have to work out not only the complicated problems but even the daily chores.

One of the lesbian couples I worked with was in an unusual situation. Their social network was quite confusing because most of the couples had been together in different configurations over the years. Mary Ann and Debbie came to see me after they had been together five months. As I listened to them, I found myself struggling to understand. Their best friends consisted of three other couples, and over the years each person had been in at least a short-term relationship with each of the others, as in a square dance where the caller gives a signal and the couples separate and then reconfigure. I had the sense that once each new relationship was in place, the boundaries between the couples were clear. They didn't drift back into sexual relationships with ex-partners, but they obviously knew a lot about each other! I know this is not typical of all gay and lesbian relationships, but I sometimes struggle to understand a gay couple's situation. Once I clearly see the structure of their lives, I think I can help them communicate better and even offer a safe place where they can talk about things they are afraid to bring up when they are alone together.

Boyce and Paul are a good example of this. They came in because they had stopped having sex with each other. They had met ten years ago when Boyce was 42 and Paul was 28 and moved in with each other after the first date. Neither of them had had a steady relationship before they got together. For over ten years they had lived as a couple, but many aspects of their lives were still separated. For example, Boyce bought a house without consulting Paul, and they moved in with the understanding that Paul would pay one-quarter of the house payment. Each had his own car, and they had come up with a system of paying the joint bills that seemed equal, but almost every month they argued about who had paid the most. On the surface this looked like a dilemma that would be easy to solve, but once we started discussing it, I began to realize how complicated it was. Paul made less money than Boyce, and he worried about what would happen to him if Boyce were to die. Boyce's family did not understand or support their relationship. If anything were to happen to Boyce, Paul thought Boyce's family would probably kick him out of the house since they regarded him as just a roommate. Boyce was reluctant to merge their finances or to make a will because he was not sure he could trust Paul. After several sessions I learned that Paul was having

an affair and that Boyce also had sexual encounters outside the relationship. Neither of them wanted to be monogamous, and they had agreed
that casual sex outside the relationship was acceptable as long as it did
not lead to emotional entanglements. When Paul began to see Bob on
a regular basis, Boyce didn't say anything, but he did not like it. Over
the years they had gradually quit having sex with each other. It took us
a while to sort through all these issues. Both of them were afraid of intimacy and commitment; once they began to understand that, we were
able to move forward.

I have been seeing a lesbian couple for six weeks. Margaret is an
attorney who left her husband when she fell in love with Greta. Their affair started shortly after Greta became Margaret's paralegal assistant.
Now they have been living together for two years, but there is a lot of
tension between them. Greta continues to work for Margaret, and Greta
has decided that she would like to have a baby. When they first got together, they had talked about children, but Margaret had not really taken
it seriously. The problem is not that she does not want Greta to get pregnant. Her objections have to do with Greta leaving her job and Margaret
having to find someone new to help her. They also must confront the legal problems that accompany parenthood; I'm not an attorney and don't
feel right about trying to help them sort out legal difficulties. Margaret
seems to be worrying about her parental rights. What will happen if she
and Greta should ever separate? Would she lose access to their child?
Since this state does not allow gay people to adopt, the legal issues are
very complex. The couple communicates well, and they seem to respect
each other enormously. However, this conflict may destroy the relationship, and I can't seem to come up with anything that might help them.

I don't think the real issue concerns the legal questions. Margaret
seems afraid of taking on this more serious commitment. This couple
seems to be a good match. They have a lot of mutual friends and have
merged nearly all aspects of their lives. They put all of their incomes into
one bank account and rarely argue about who does the family chores.
Both their families are in and out of their lives and seem to support the
relationship. Their sex life gets dull at times, but that's pretty normal for
a couple. Nevertheless, the question of whether or not to have a baby
has pushed the relationship to a different level. Greta is adamant in saying that she is going to get pregnant and have at least one baby even if
she has to leave Margaret to do it. I think they have merged too completely. Being with them is almost like being with one person. They drive
to work together and spend every evening together. They don't seem to
have any individual privacy in their lives, any separate friends, or even
interests that would take them apart from each other. I think the problem
about having a baby is that it forces them to differentiate. Greta will be

staying at home, so Margaret will not have her along at work. I am going to see what will happen if I frame the issue this way. Maybe then they can talk about their relationship more easily. I know some straight couples have similar issues, but I see much more of this kind of struggle with my lesbian couple clients.

CHALLENGES FACING GAY AND LESBIAN COUPLES

Mental-health professionals who have not had experience working with gay and lesbian couples are likely to assume that the process mirrors heterosexual relationship counseling. In fact, there are many factors that contribute to the unique situations gay and lesbian couples face (Peplau, Veniegas, & Campbell, 1996). Forming an intimate relationship in environments characterized by oppression means that both partners are likely to be dealing with some internalized homonegativity as well as experiencing fears of how the external world, made up of family members, friends, and co-workers, will respond to them (Atkinson, 1998). The absence of role models causes sexual minority couples either to try to adapt the relationship model created by nongay persons or to come up with their own notion of how their relationships will look and work (Sanders, 2000). Further, these couples inevitably encounter the negative stereotypes and myths that are often used to describe their relationships. Comments and beliefs such as "gay relationships don't last," "gay and lesbian relationships are inherently sick," or "the biggest problem facing gay and lesbian relationships is who will wear the pants in the family" reveal a lack of understanding of these unique relationships. Common issues presented by gay and lesbian couples in counseling include identifying as a gay or lesbian couple to family, work colleagues, and health-care professionals; different levels of outness; and issues from the effect of gender socialization in same-sex couples (Cabaj & Klinger, 1996; Slater, 1995).

Researchers estimate that the number of gay men and lesbians in relationships varies between 40 and 60% for men and 45 and 80% for lesbians, and report that many of these relationships will be lifelong (Blumstein & Schwartz, 1983; McWhirter & Mattison, 1984). Gay and lesbian relationships do not differ from heterosexual relationships in terms of relationship satisfaction and perceived levels of love (Peplau & Cochran, 1990). Further, these relationships show normative changes over time, just like those of nongay persons (Klinger, 1996; Kurdek, 1995). Does this mean that counseling gay and lesbian couples mimics relationship counseling of nongay couples? The answer to that question is not yet clear, for gay relationships face challenges that are unlike those of heterosexual people. Kurdek (1994) explores the lack of theory that illuminates gay male and lesbian relationships. His longitudinal studies are in the early stages of addressing this lack and consistently reveal that gay male and lesbian relationships do not differ significantly from those of heterosexuals.

Still, it is important to remember that the context in which gay and lesbian relationships occur is quite different from that faced by nongay persons. Counselors working with gay couples will need to understand aspects of this context to be able to provide effective treatment. For example, gay and lesbian couples often struggle to determine their anniversary. Did the relationship begin at the first date, first kiss, first sexual intercourse, or the day when they moved in together? Most heterosexual couples do not have trouble marking their anniversary, but this can become a point of contention for gay and lesbian couples. The following discussion presents other challenges gay and lesbian couples face as they create relationships and families.

Oppression

In virtually every chapter of this book, the role of oppression in creating barriers to successful lives has been explored. Unfortunately, once again that experience plays a fundamental role in the ways gay men and lesbians forge their relationships. There is a special challenge in creating and being public about a relationship that is denounced by many. Fear of negative sanctions and consequences if they are too open about their relationship can become a significant wedge that undermines the couple's stability. Like Robert and Tom in the case example, couples who have varying degrees of outness to their families face unique stress. Some couples cut themselves off from the mainstream by isolating themselves in gay and lesbian ghettos where they feel more free. Others attempt to merge their relationships into their larger lives but inevitably face the question of bringing their partners to the office Christmas party or high school class reunion. Still others spend most of their time together and rarely let others be close to them.

The current debate about legalizing gay and lesbian marriage reflects the kind of oppression these couples face each day. Some see access to marriage as a constitutional right and push for changes in state and federal laws. Others firmly believe that extending marriage benefits to gay and lesbian persons will tear the fabric that holds our social organizations together. As state legislatures and court systems face challenges from gay organizations, the level of the debate escalates. Fear and oppression (perhaps as well as an attempt to satisfy the politically conservative right wing) may be factors in the passage of the Defense of Marriage Act by the U.S. Congress. This law protects the right of individual states not to honor gay and lesbian marriages that might become legal in other states or countries. However, in 2000, Vermont passed laws that recognized gay

and lesbian relationships and granted them the equivalent rights and responsibilities extended to married couples but avoided using the term *marriage* when
describing these relationships.

A similar kind of oppression can be seen in the debate about employers extending domestic partner benefits to unmarried but cohabiting couples. A court
order was necessary to require Atlanta city officials to implement domestic
partnership legislation that had been passed by the city council. Even though
the number of municipalities, state governments, and private businesses that
provide domestic partner benefits steadily grows, legislation about these benefits is not even proposed in many communities. These highly politicized debates create an atmosphere where many gay and lesbian couples feel vulnerable as they live together publicly. Stress from the negative attitudes expressed
in this public debate can lead some in the gay community to erosive levels of
cynicism about the viability of their relationships.

Finally, until recently, the public has considered gay and lesbian relationships to lack the kind of stability attributed to traditional heterosexual relationships. This negative attitude may also be present within the minds of gay
and lesbian persons as they form relationships. When Eric Marcus (1998), a
gay man and former CBS newscaster, told others he was writing a book about
long-term (nine years or longer) gay and lesbian relationships, he was met with
cynical comments such as, "That'll be a short book," "*Reader's Digest* won't
need to condense it," and "You're writing a pamphlet?" rather than more encouraging statements (p. xiii). These comments were made primarily by his gay
and lesbian friends. Challenging the notion that gay and lesbian relationships
cannot be long-lasting or rich attacks a stereotype that many are reluctant to
give up.

Lack of Visible Role Models

Most people learn about primary relationships from watching their parents
and other significant adults. As they mature, gay and lesbian couples rarely experience up close models for their relationship. Only in the very recent past
have gay and lesbian couples been depicted in the media, and in the last decade, gay men and lesbians have been more visible in real life than ever before.
While gay couples are common in most communities, a primary model for gay
and lesbian relationships has not emerged. The nontraditional nature of many
gay and lesbian relationships creates a unique kind of vulnerability, particularly
for those who feel sensitive about the negative stereotype suggesting that gay
and lesbian relationships are inherently unsuccessful. Some couples create relationships that might suit the two people involved but that seem outrageous to
those not comfortable with straying far from the heterosexual marriage model.

The absence of accepted models for gay and lesbian relationships means
that couples have the opportunity to be creative as they describe the relation-

ship they believe will work for them (Hart, 1996). Turning this challenge into an asset, Marcus (1998) writes: "Without a set road map or clear expectations — their own or those of friends, family, or society — the couples I spoke with were free to do what they wanted and to make their own discoveries. But certainly those who never imagined that gay people could even have relationships would have benefited from the knowledge that it is indeed possible. And a general road map to relationship life might have helped more than a few of the couples avoid some of the early problems they faced — although with sound instincts and a healthy dose of resilience they got through their courtship with a clearer understanding of their partners and of the kind of life they wanted together" (p. 26).

Absence of Extended Support

Most heterosexual relationships are created in an atmosphere of support from family and friends. A couple begins to date and gradually becomes known within their social and family support system. Over time the system identifies the two as a couple and routinely expands to include both at all gatherings. Employers extend available benefits to married couples and have even become increasingly supportive of dual-career couples. There are certain defined rites of passage, such as engagement, marriage, and parenting, that are anticipated and celebrated in most straight relationships. Conversely, gay and lesbian relationships are challenged by the internal homonegativity that may be present at the same or differing levels within the couple as well as by overt resistance from extended social and family support systems. Myron told us, "I just got tired of my family ignoring my partner at every holiday. They expected me to be present but never would even ask if we had plans together, and they certainly never invited Les. It was as if they wanted to pretend he did not exist and that I was not gay. When we bought a house together, I thought they were going to disown me. They used that occasion to tell me that they would never enter our home and that Les was not welcome in theirs. I haven't seen them for six years now and sometimes that hurts. But I am better off not having to face their anger and rejection."

Dual-Career Issues

One aspect of coming out is that most gay and lesbian people, like other single persons, come to terms with the likelihood that they will not have children to support them when they age and die. This awareness leads them to focus on their career and to place primary emphasis on the security careers provide. The specter of growing old alone and without sufficient resources motivates many gay and lesbian persons to place work at the top of the list of their life responsibilities. Sometimes that can mean that the relationship comes second or that intense negotiation may be needed when a career crisis occurs. Marty and

Dana had been together for five years and had what looked like a very strong relationship. However, when Dana was offered a promotion that required moving to a large city 400 miles from their home, cracks began to appear. Dana had worked hard to earn these new responsibilities and wanted to enjoy the prestige of being a manager along with a significant increase in income and career potential. When she told her boss she was not sure she was going to accept, the boss responded with, "Why, I thought that as a single woman this change would be ideal for you. You would be living in a larger city where you would meet more eligible men than you meet here." Dana tried to talk with Marty but did not get a lot of sympathy. Marty's position was clear as she stated, "I like my work here and cannot see moving, knowing I am unlikely to be able to replicate the future I know is ahead of me in my job." Although this situation does not appear to differ from that faced by many dual-career couples, without a marriage contract, the presence of children, or understanding support in the workplace, the couple's commitment is being tested at deep levels. Unless Marty and Dana have learned to communicate well, there is a good chance that Dana will choose her job over the relationship. Workplace issues, even those as simple as who to take to the office party, place unique stresses on gay and lesbian couples.

Tension Between Autonomy and Intimacy

The absence of the traditional models of intimacy and interdependence combines with the autonomy that gay men and lesbians develop as they form their lives to make intimacy a challenge (Schreurs & Buunks, 1996). Chapter 4 described compartmentalization, the coping strategy of isolation used by many gay men as they develop. This compartmentalization can be seen in some of the tension surrounding intimacy. Marty and Dana illustrate this struggle well. Does being in an intimate relationship mean that autonomous decisions about career and other life events now must be negotiated? If that is so, some individuals may conclude that romance would be preferable to intimacy.

Counselors faced with gay and lesbian relationships that suffer from a lack of intimacy are apt to be bewildered by what looks like serial monogamy. Couples often form relationships before they have had a chance to get to know each other and then fall apart because of the real differences between the partners. A case example will illuminate this dilemma. Mark and Manuel met in a bar while Mark was on a business trip. Almost immediately they became involved in an intense romantic passion, and within a month Manuel had moved 700 miles and set up housekeeping with Mark. A few months later the couple found themselves in trouble. Mark was not a person who spent a lot of time in bars, but Manuel conducted most of his social life in that setting. Manuel was fastidious about saving money and watched every cent he spent while Mark rarely looked at his bank balance and had several thousand dollars of credit card debt. Mark resented Manuel's attempts to "control" his finances, and

Manuel was frustrated over their "boring" social life. As their arguments escalated, the passion waned, and they came for help to see if the relationship had any future. While familiar with the rubric "Sex first, relationship later," they had not realized that neither of them knew much about intimacy, even though they both agreed that is what they wanted. Other couples may find themselves in arguments that become so heated that violence results (Reilly & Lynch, 1990; Renzetti, 1992). Such strong expressions of anger are clearly dangerous and need special attention.

Intimacy rarely comes easily. Taking the time to get to know each other, and learning to negotiate, listen, and compromise are qualities that might not be readily apparent. Given the number of gay men and lesbians who need but do not seek mental-health services, the odds of finding an appropriate partner can be low. Often, the anxiety about being single can drive gay men and lesbians prematurely into relationships that have little chance of success (Cole, 1999).

Challenges like these would present hurdles to any relationship, and in many ways it is surprising that gay and lesbian relationships are stable at all. It is becoming increasingly common to see these couples celebrating 10, 20, or 30 years together. Their endurance makes a strong statement about their ability to maneuver creatively through these challenges. The counselor needs to understand these hurdles to be effective in working with gay and lesbian couples. Most of these have to do with the context in which the relationships are formed. Each is significant and needs careful attention.

ISSUES IN GAY AND LESBIAN RELATIONSHIP COUNSELING

The counseling process involved in working with gay and lesbian couples may look very similar to all relationship counseling, but there are several specific issues that are unique. Most couples enter a relationship with an assumption about monogamy or may have both marriage and children as part of their life plans. Gay men and lesbians do not have these assumptions placed on them. Being free from these kinds of expectations can be liberating, but developing the necessary communication skills to negotiate through issues like these demands special skills. For the counselor, dropping heterosexist assumptions and affirming new dyadic potentials is essential (Hart, 1996). There can be a tendency not to take these relationships seriously or to approach the couple with the negative stereotype of instability. Likewise, an understanding of the legal issues facing gay and lesbian couples may illuminate important underlying issues (Clifford, Curry, & Leonard, 1996). Effective counselors will understand that even though the issues might be different from those encountered by heterosexual couples, the possibility for growth and increased intimacy between individuals is the same (Hawkins, 1992).

Monogamy/Nonmonogamy

Many gay and lesbian couples find the issue of monogamy to be one of the first pitfalls in relationship establishment. Because many of these relationships are established quickly, couples may not have taken the time or risk to explore the issue of monogamy thoroughly. For example, Freida has been in several long-term relationships, none of which has been monogamous. Her new partner, Mickey, on the other hand, believes that monogamy is essential for relationship stability. Their relationship was founded with an awareness of their differences on this issue, but each assumed the other would come to adopt the other's point of view. Mickey requested counseling when she learned that Freida had been involved in several brief sexual encounters. Freida's position was that these relationships were just about sex and that her love for Mickey was not threatened or in any danger. Extrarelationship affairs, such as these, lead many gay couples into counseling. Kurdek (1988) surveyed 65 gay and 47 lesbian couples and found that all of the lesbian couples and 53.3% of the gay male couples practiced monogamy. A survey ($n = 2500$) of gay men conducted by *Advocate,* a popular gay and lesbian magazine, reported that of the 87% of gay males who stated they seek a long-term commitment, 71% wanted these relationships to be monogamous, but only 52% had been sexually exclusive with their present or past partners.

There are no easy techniques to help couples negotiate the issue of monogamy nor are there patterns that might serve as models. Some couples agree to nonmonogamy with the understanding that neither wants to know what the other is doing. Some agree to have sex with others only when it occurs in the context of their own relationship. Others go as a couple to sex clubs or other places where sex is readily available. Men who have been socialized to value sexual variety may develop the ability to honor their emotional commitments without seeing outside sexual experiences as a threat (Peplau & Cochran, 1990). Differences in beliefs about monogamy can serve as a springboard to greater intimacy and trust. Greg was stunned when Vic, his partner of 13 years, said that he was going to practice monogamy because he wanted their relationship to become more of a sexual cornerstone in his life. Vic said this without any expectation that Greg would make a similar commitment, and, at first, Greg felt threatened by this change in their relationship and withheld sex completely. Vic took no offense and continued to let Greg know how much he loved him and how important his commitment was. Eventually, Greg requested counseling so they could learn how to communicate about this issue more successfully, and two years later, he was able to affirm their relationship by making a similar commitment. Another client, Ric, spent five years convincing his partner, Jim, that sex outside the relationship might be an advantage. Reluctantly, Jim agreed to go to a sex club with Ric, and they both found that mutual outside sexual activity did, in fact, stimulate their relationship. Both of these couples were able to affirm their relationships through careful listening to and trusting of each other.

Roles and Gender

As it is for monogamous couples, assigning domestic roles and responsibilities is an essential negotiating point for gay and lesbian couples (Peplau, 1991, 1996). Without the relationship models discussed earlier, virtually every task must be assigned. Once again, the assignment of these tasks rarely falls along the lines of what might be taken on by a "wife" or "husband" but typically is the result of personal preferences. Single gay men and lesbians create households without the expectation that tasks are going to be assigned on the basis of gender. Therefore, they enter relationships with little firm expectation of who will do the laundry, pay the bills, or take care of the car. Of course, some relationships do mimic traditional heterosexual alliances, but generally the couple will make decisions about who wants to do what and then assign the undesirable tasks somewhat equally. Unlike in heterosexual relationship counseling, we have rarely encountered gay or lesbian couples who find themselves arguing over differing standards in terms of cleanliness, promptness, and so on.

There are also few gender-driven guidelines over the distribution of money. Some couples stay together for 20 years and still keep their money separate. Some make major investment decisions independently, and others merge all finances almost immediately. The vast majority of gay and lesbian relationships can be characterized as dual career, in which neither partner expects to be taken care of financially. In situations where there is significant income disparity, the more typical issue seems to be a struggle for autonomy. The partner who has the lower income often is unwilling to let the more affluent partner pay more than one-half of their joint expenses. Excessive fears about dependency may create unique relationship stresses.

Commitment and Marriage

The discussion about the legitimacy of same-sex unions is not a recent phenomenon (Boswell, 1994). As noted in the discussion about monogamy, the definition of *commitment* may vary between gay and lesbian partners. Similarly, there are varying attitudes about the importance of rituals that celebrate the relationship. Some couples create a private and personal ritual that might involve the exchange of tokens, such as rings, and others want a more public ceremony attended by friends and, perhaps, family. Some persons resist taking on any of the heterosexual models of coupling and recoil at the idea of a ceremony to celebrate their relationship. Strong objections to symbolic rituals that suggest commitment either may be philosophical or could suggest underlying homonegative

BOX
5.1

Husband of the Bride's Father

I am a gay man. I am an Episcopal priest. I am in a 13-year relationship. I am the husband of the bride's father. What an odd place for me to find myself.

Last weekend my partner, John, and I traveled to Atlanta to celebrate his daughter's wedding. Some months ago her fiancé had asked for her hand in marriage, an act which I thought was rather archaic until I realized that he was from Virginia, the "old South," and valued many of the traditions we had fled years ago. Once engaged, the bride and groom planned and replanned the wedding of their dreams—church, white dress and veil, flowers, reception, friends and family, a most traditional wedding in the best of Atlanta style.

Over the years, John has kept a warm and wonderful relationship with all five of his children. He has stayed in close contact with his brothers. With them, children and brothers, we have established a wonderful, nontraditional family, in the best sense of the word. However, the days before our trip to Atlanta were filled with anxiety for me. How would we be received by John's ex-wife? How would John's children respond to us in Atlanta? Would there be tensions with John's brothers and their families? How would the groom and his family accept a gay in-law couple? What of John's friends still in Atlanta and left behind some 13 years ago when John came out—would they be warm or distant? How would I be received in the Episcopal Church where the marriage was to take place? So many fears!

So what am I to say concerning one of the happiest weekends of our life together? First, that as a couple we experienced it together side by side, hosting a dinner party for the other parents, being warmly received by John's former wife, greeting her family, meeting John's sons' girlfriends, touching one another while vows were exchanged. It was a couple experience—two men deeply in love sharing a family event.

Second, gay men and women and gay couples are no longer seen as living on the edge. They are usually accepted as any other mainstream individual or couple. There we were in Atlanta, having our picture taken with the bride and groom, talking to old friends about their gay friends, and being invited for dinner because that "old gang of John's" missed seeing him regularly. I was laughing with the bride's mother's college roommates, discussing church policy with the priest, and sharing tears of joy with one of John's other children—so normal and everyday, and yet so rewarding after all of the years. To know that people love us and accept us as straight or gay. To know that the nontraditional is becoming traditional. That the world

Coming Out (continued)

is not straight or gay, black or white, tall or short. The world is this wonderful diversity of people—the bride's family, the groom's family, the young guests and the old, the new friends and those of a lifetime, the liberals and the conservatives, the gays and the straights. This world is that collection of people who gathered for the wedding and through the love of the bride and groom felt love for each other. At least for that moment the world was warm and one, which is a goal for us all.

Last, I am reminded that John and I cannot be married in the church, nor is our relationship protected by law. Perhaps it may never be. But I am equally sure that the love we have for each other is stronger than both the church or the state. That the love that binds us together is of God, whoever or whatever he/she may be. That just as John's daughter and her husband said their vows in the sanctity of the church at their wedding, so John and I say ours in the sanctity of our daily living.

I wish the new bride and her husband much happiness, just as John and I have found much happiness in our relationship. It is wonderful to be a couple—gay or straight. The feelings are the same!

—*John Templeton*

thoughts ("As a homosexual I am not worthy of the kinds of celebrations others take for granted. After all, my family will not attend, and I don't want to spend the day feeling sad that they are rejecting us"). In dealing with internalized oppression, developing an awareness that external rejection is a statement more about the family member's problem than about the gay or lesbian person can lead to a greater sense of freedom and expanded choices. John Templeton comments in Box 5.1 on the way his partner's daughter's wedding created anxiety and then relief for him.

Routine exploration of the couple's sex life may have to be initiated by the counselor. Talking about sexual intimacy may be difficult for some but will be easier if the counselor is familiar with the language and sexual creativity that is possible when people of the same gender are being sexual with each other. Once again, there are no preconceived roles for the partners to play as they have sex. Often the partners do not discuss such intimate aspects of their relationship with others. The counselor may need to bring up the subject and use the clients as teachers when the material seems confusing. For those couples dealing with HIV disease, learning to communicate feelings about sexual activity (especially about the limits imposed by the HIV infection) can lead to potentially painful, but significant, intimacy.

After being together for seven years, Jess and Troy came for counseling when Troy was returning to work after two years off because of disability caused by HIV disease. Most of the counseling focused on Troy's fears and new sense of independence as he rejoined the workforce. After several weeks of counseling, a routine question about their sex life led to important disclosures. Jess, who was HIV-negative, began to express his anger at Troy, who had become infected during a time when both of them had agreed to be monogamous. Jess showed his suppressed resentment along with anger about the limitations Troy's HIV status had placed on their sex life: "I get so tired of having to keep your HIV status in mind when we are having sex, and I dream about the days when we could have sex without having to worry. I love you and do not want you to leave, but I also want you to know that you are not the only one who has had to struggle with the consequences of your being infected. I want you to go back to work, but at the same time I worry that you will get involved with someone else once you are out meeting new people. You are the most important person in my life, and I am afraid that you will go back to work and not need me any longer." These few sentences provided glimpses into several important issues that they were able to work through as Troy started back to work.

There are a number of ways that counselors can help explore the meaning of commitment. Once again, leaving aside all preconceived notions or assumptions about relationships will enable the counselor to keep an open mind. A slow and careful exploration of attitudes about commitment may open the door for greater understanding between the clients. Keeping the focus on the potential meaning that can permeate rituals and gently exploring resistance can lead to deeper understanding for the clients as individuals and as a couple.

Relationship Formation

The myth about the instability of gay and lesbian relationships is fostered by the rapid merging that so often takes place by these couples (McKenzie, 1992). Men meet at a bar and within days or weeks may have moved in together. In our practices it is not rare to see individuals who live hundreds of miles apart move in together within weeks of meeting. Neither is it unusual to hear individuals say something like, "She came home with me the night we met and has never left."

Dating is a complicated process regardless of sexual orientation. For both gay and nongay adults, dating more than one person simultaneously brings up issues (sexual exclusivity, time, attendance at events where other "dates" may be present, and so on) that may become so stressful that a decision is made to date only one person at a time. Helping clients recognize the "red flags" that indicate possible relationship insecurity, learn to communicate more directly and clearly, and ask the questions that lead to greater intimacy may take place well after the relationship is in place rather than in the early stages of getting to know each other. Sometimes, relationships are formed with ambivalence. A client recently said, "I know that Roy and I will move in together very soon even though I only met him last month. He lives at home with his parents, and about the only way we can have private time is at my place. I gave him a key after we had been out only three times. It was just a lot easier that way. He gets off from work earlier than I do, and he will go home and get dinner started so it is about ready when I get there. Last week when I walked in, he had rearranged the furniture. At first I was shocked, but then I realized that he has a better eye for decorating than I do so I let it go. He is quickly making my place into his home. One night last week we were getting friendly on the sofa, and the phone rang. I froze since the answering machine was on the end table. It was Jimmy, the other guy I have been dating, asking me to go out with him the next weekend. I had to talk fast to keep Roy from bolting. I have more fun with Roy so I guess I will have to quit dating others." There is little data that gives insight into the course of relationships formed so quickly (Kurdek, 1995). Anecdotal evidence suggests that some of these relationships falter and some last for years.

Breaking Up

There is also much diversity in the ways gay and lesbian couples end their relationships. Although the issues that lead to termination (for example, money, infidelity, lack of sexual interest, changing personal interests) are similar, in our practices there are two patterns that occur with some frequency. Some relationships tend to end only when the terminating partner has found a new relationship, and often the relationship may not end but simply be redefined (Kirkpatrick, 1991). The latter case is a rather familiar one. Perhaps Rosetta's comments will illuminate this more clearly. "Nita and I have been together for ten years, and really after the sixth year we no longer had much in common. We had stopped having sex and pretty much lived parallel lives. I tried to get her to talk about this, but she would just sit and say nothing. I moved into our second bedroom, and she didn't say a word. After a couple of years, I began to look around even though I was afraid to leave her. When I met Rosie, I knew it was time for me to go. One day I just told Nita that we were done, packed up my clothes, left, and have never looked back. All those things we had bought together I just left with her. There was no negotiation, no conversation at all. Rosie is not much of a talker either, but I am trying to get a better agreement about facing our differences from the beginning."

Scott and Kerry had been together for about two years when they came for counseling. Scott had decided that the relationship was over and wanted help in telling Kerry so they could figure out what to do. "I care about Kerry a lot. I just don't want to be his lover any longer. I think of him more as a friend now, a friend I do not want to lose. I want him to move into the guest room and for us to be roommates, but he says he would have a hard time sleeping in the room next to me if I brought someone home one night. Actually, for the last six months I have been sleeping in the guest room, and I've had a few dates. Kerry doesn't like it, and I don't like hurting him. He is like my best friend though, and I want him to know that he will always have a place in my house. But we can't be lovers any longer." In fact, Kerry and Scott finally did come to an understanding about being roommates, and four years later they still live together, travel together, and even have some of their finances blended. Kerry's comments illuminate their new relationship. "As friends, our relationship works better than before. I manage money better than Scott does, so when we travel I take care of all expenses. He always pays me back once we get home. At first it was weird to sleep next to him as his friend. But that's just the way things have grown, and I think both of us are happy with the agreement we have. The people I date don't understand. I guess most people don't. He is like a brother to me, and I can't imagine not living with him or at least very near him."

Naturally, both of these illustrations reveal something about the way some gay and lesbian couples negotiate the boundaries around their relationships. Codependency can be an issue in these relationships, but there is also a lot of room for these couples to create unique and effective relationships. A more recent trend in the gay male community is for a couple to seek a third person who becomes an equal part of their household. In order for such complex relationships to work successfully, good communication and trust are essential.

Tips For Practitioners

The techniques of counseling gay and lesbian couples do not differ markedly from those used with all couples. Like Susan at the beginning of the chapter, understanding the unique challenges and opportunities that these couples face will lead you to explore specific areas that might not otherwise surface when working with nongay couples. Recognizing the long-term potential that exists for all persons who form relationships, letting the couple serve in the role of instructor when unfamiliar topics come up, and constantly affirming the strengths of the relationships will provide the kind of atmosphere where effective counseling can take place.

Expect Language Difficulties   One problem that plagues the gay and lesbian community relates to language. The terms that are used to describe relationships vary. Susan talked about this. "Is she my *partner,* or is that too businesslike? Maybe the term *girlfriend* suggests a more casual relationship than what we really have, but *lover* seems to say that the relationship is based on sex, and we certainly have more than that between us. I sometimes call her my spouse, or, jokingly, my wife or husband. There's just not a word that really describes what we have." You might want to ask the couple what terms they use to describe their relationship. Such exploration will often lead to important underlying information.

Expect Diversity: Revise Traditional Notions of Relationship Counseling   Probably by now you have learned that there are few patterns that define gay and lesbian relationships. Understanding that the absence of community-accepted models is both a burden and an opportunity for these couples to create what works for them will enable you to interact from a more neutral and open base. Be aware that gay and lesbian couples of color may face particular challenges (Greene, 1996).

Make Assumptions Explicit   Approaching gay and lesbian couples without assumptions about the nature and functioning of the relationship will make the counseling more effective. Similarly, be aware that gay men and lesbians often do not discuss the assumptions they bring to their relationships. Listening for the ways assumptions can undermine both the relationship and the counseling is critical. Stereotyping can go on between the couple and between the couple and the counselor and interfere with the effectiveness of both relationships.

Expect HIV Issues to Surface   For gay men, HIV is almost a daily issue even if neither partner is HIV-positive. Inquire about their understanding and practices relative to safe sex. If the couple is serodiscordant (one is HIV-positive, and the other is HIV-negative), you must ask about their efforts to maintain safe sex. Researchers (Rabkin, Remian, & Wilson, 1994) have shown that sometimes even long-term serodiscordant couples occasionally relapse into unsafe sex. You will read more about HIV disease in Chapter 10.

Celebrate Relationships   Given society's ambivalence about gay and lesbian relationships, it is important for the counselor to find ways to help the couples celebrate what they have created. Likewise, the counselor is in a unique position to make positive comments about milestones in gay relationships (Igartua, 1998). Congratulating a couple who has recently moved in together or making positive comments about their work in counseling can support the couple and give them confidence, especially when they are facing disapproval from family and friends. For some, making the decision to spend holidays together, apart from families who refuse to welcome the couple, can make a statement about increased commitment to the relationship. When you acknowledge this step, the couple will have more confidence in the relationship they are creating.

BIBLIOGRAPHY

Atkinson, D. R. (1998). *Counseling diverse populations.* Boston: McGraw-Hill.

Blumstein, P. & Schwartz, P. (1983). *American couples: Money, work, sex.* New York: William Morrow.

Boswell, J. (1994). *Same-sex unions in post-modern Europe.* New York: Random House.

Cabaj, R. & Klinger, R. (1996). Psychotherapeutic interventions with lesbian and gay couples. In R. Cabaj & R. Klinger (Eds.), *Textbook of homosexuality and mental health.* Washington, DC: American Psychiatric Association.

Clifford, D., Curry, H., & Leonard, K. (1996). *A legal guide for lesbian and gay couples.* 10th ed. Berkeley, CA: Nolo Press.

Cole, S. (1999). Single in a couple's world: The elusive lesbian date. *In the Family,* January, 7–9.

Greene, B. (1996). African-American lesbian couples: Ethnocultural considerations in psychotherapy. *Women and Therapy, 19*(3), 49–61.

Hart, J. (1996). Same-sex couples and counseling: The development of multicultural perspective. In G. Sullivan & L. Leong (Eds.), *Gays and lesbians in Asia and the Pacific: Social and human services.* New York: Harrington Park Press.

Hawkins, R. L. (1992). Therapy with male couples. In S. Dworkin & F. Guiterriez (Eds.), *Counseling gay men and lesbians: Journey to the end of the rainbow.* Alexandria, VA: American Counseling Association.

Igartua, K. (1998). Therapy with lesbian couples: The issues and the interventions. *Canadian Journal of Psychiatry, 43*(4), 391–407.

Kirkpatrick, M. (1991). Lesbian couples in therapy. *Psychiatric Annals, 21*(8), 491–496.

Klinger, R. (1996). Lesbian couples. In R. Cabaj & T. Stein (Eds.), *Textbook of homosexuality and mental health.* Washington, DC: American Psychiatric Association.

Kurdek, L. (1988). Relationship quality of gay and lesbian cohabiting couples. *Journal of Homosexuality, 15*(3–4), 93–118.

———. (1994). The nature and correlates of relationship quality in gay, lesbian, and heterosexual cohabiting couples: A test of the individual difference, interdependence and discrepancy models. In B. Greene & G. Herek (Eds.), *Lesbian and gay psychology: Theory, research and clinical applications.* Thousand Oaks, CA: Sage.

———. (1995). Developmental changes in relationship quality in gay and lesbian cohabiting couples. *Developmental Psychology, 31*(1), 86–94.

Marcus, E. (1998). *Together forever: Gay and lesbian couples share their secrets for lasting happiness.* New York: Anchor Books.

McKenzie, S. (1992). Merger in lesbian relationships. *Women and Therapy, 12*(1–2), 151–160.

McWhirter, D. & Mattison, A. (1984). *The male couple: How relationships develop.* Englewood Cliffs, NJ: Prentice-Hall.

Peplau, L. (1991). Lesbian and gay relationships. In J. Gonsiorek & J. Weinrich (Eds.), *Homosexuality: Research implications for public policy.* Newbury Park, CA: Sage.

———. (1996). Gay and lesbian relationships. In R. Savin-Williams & K. Cohen (Eds.), *The lives of lesbians, gays, and bisexuals: Children to adults.* Ft. Worth, TX: Harcourt Brace.

Peplau, L. & Cochran, S. (1990). A relationship perspective on homosexuality. In D. McWhirter, S. Sanders, & J. Reinisch (Eds.), *Heterosexuality/homosexuality: Concepts of sexual orientation.* New York: Oxford University Press.

Peplau, L., Veniegas, R., & Campbell, S. (1996). Gay and lesbian relationships. In

R. Savin-Williams & K. Cohen (Eds.), *The lives of lesbians, gays and bisexuals.* Fort Worth, TX: Harcourt Brace.

Rabkin, J., Remian, R., & Wilson, C. (1994). *Good doctors good patients: Partners in HIV treatment.* New York: NCM Publishers.

Reilly, M. & Lynch, J. (1990). Power-sharing in lesbian relationships. *Journal of Homosexuality, 19*(3), 1–30.

Renzetti, C. M. (1992). *Violent betrayal: Partner abuse in lesbian relationships.* Thousand Oaks, CA: Sage.

Sanders, G. (2000). Men together: Working with gay couples in contemporary times. In P. Papp (Ed.), *Couples on the fault line: New directions for therapists.* New York: Guilford Press.

Schreurs, K. & Buunks, B. (1996). Closeness, autonomy, equity and relationship satisfaction in lesbian couples. *Psychology of Women Quarterly, 28*(4), 577–593.

Slater, S. (1995). *The lesbian family life cycle.* New York: Free Press.

RESOURCES

Internet Resources:
www.buddybuddy.com/toc.html is an Internet resource offering information in support of gay and lesbian relationships.

Newsgroups:
The Marriage Mailing list (*majordomo@abacus.oxy.edu* with a one-line message: subscribe marriage).

The Domestic Partner Mailing list (*majordomo-domestic@cs.cmu.edu* with a one-line message: subscribe domestic).

COUNSELING BISEXUAL AND TRANSGENDERED CLIENTS

The Case of Melissa

Melissa has been working in private practice for about three years. Prior to opening her practice, she worked in a number of different nonprofit companies, including several social service agencies where she worked with individuals, couples, and families. In each of these settings, she worked with a small number of clients who were struggling with sexual orientation issues.

Most of Melissa's clients were trying to determine if they were gay or straight, and Melissa felt that she did a good job helping her clients process feelings and work through the various stages of coming to terms with their sexual orientation and coming out to others. All of these clients ended up self-identifying as gay or lesbian. Melissa was proud of her ability to work with gay clients as she had received no such training in her graduate program. She had gained knowledge and skills by attending conferences and workshops and reading various books. She also made it a point to attend events that were sponsored by the gay and lesbian community as a way to keep up-to-date with current events and issues. Generally, Melissa felt very confident about her ability and skills to work with gays and lesbians.

"You're not going to believe this," said Marcy. "You're really not going to believe this. . . ." Marcy had been a client of Melissa's for the past six months, and they both felt they had a good working relationship. "I know that since I've been seeing you in therapy, I've proudly identified as a lesbian. I've marched right up front every year at Pride Day; I even went to the big March on Washington in 1993 and was planning to go to the upcoming Millennium March in Washington. I've had a girlfriend practically since I was 16. I know I dated guys in college and even thought I was in love a time or two; however, I've always known deep down inside that I was a lesbian. Being with a woman fits for me in every aspect—

sexually, spiritually, and emotionally. I mean, all the evidence is there, isn't it? I'm lesbian, right? Wrong. For the past month or two we've been talking about the breakup between Anna and me. You know the story. We'd been together 5 years, although it seemed like 50, but unfortu-nately, we just stopped getting along. We couldn't agree about anything, and we hadn't had sex in months. As you know, I've been dating women here and there and having a good time, but lately I started hanging out with this guy at work and we get along great. He's funny and intellectual, and he has an amazing personality. I'm so afraid to admit this to you, but here goes: I am so sexually attracted to him. I mean, when I see him, the bells and whistles go off and my heart starts pounding—it's un-believable. I've been so afraid to tell you; in fact, I'm afraid to tell any-one. My lesbian friends would absolutely disown me, probably never speak to me again, and call me a traitor, or worse. Well, I've told you this much; I might as well be honest about the whole thing. Last week he and I started a sexual relationship, and I am really enjoying myself. In fact, what I've begun to realize is that I am attracted to both men and women and even more important, I'm beginning to rethink this whole notion of who I am and am coming to terms with the fact that I'm bi-sexual, that a lesbian identity really doesn't fit me. Yes, I'm still attracted to women, but I'm also attracted to men. Amazing, huh? So, what do you think?"

Melissa paused before she answered. Her internal dialogue was racing: "Bisexual? What in the world was Marcy saying? What do you mean you're bisexual? I thought you told me you were lesbian. You've been in relationships with women most of your life. What do you mean you're now bisexual? Is it okay just to switch sexual orientations halfway through your life? Surely Marcy must be going through a phase or maybe a midlife crisis that has manifested in rebellion and rejection of her sex-ual orientation. This doesn't make any sense to me; however, I want to be empathic and nonjudgmental. I really want to help Marcy work through this process and be the best person she can be."

Later that night, Melissa attended her local counseling association meeting. Before the program she had a chance to talk to some of her colleagues about different sexual identities. Most of them dismissed the idea of switching in midlife to a "new" orientation, saying that either you're gay or you're not, and claiming to be bisexual was just another way of succumbing to internalized homoprejudice. They discounted bi-sexuality, calling it a "cop-out." Bisexuality, they said, was a wonderful excuse for people who were afraid to come out of the closet. One col-league, however, said that bisexuality was indeed a valid sexual orienta-tion. She explained to Melissa and the others that the relationship be-tween sexual orientation, sexual identity, and sexual behavior is not as clear-cut as we'd like to think. Self-identifying as bisexual is valid regardless of whether the client had previously identified as heterosexual or homosexual. The important thing is to help clients process their feelings and concerns as they begin the often turbulent journey through the coming out process. Her colleague also shared some information about a number of self-identified bisexual clients he was working with, including a self-identified gay man who not only had a male partner but also a female sexual partner with whom he had sexual encounters on a regular basis. Both he and his male partner accepted and communicated regularly about this secondary relationship, and for his client, having intimate relationships with both a woman and a man made him feel whole sexually and emotionally. Melissa's colleague also counseled a female client who had been married to a man but throughout the marriage had maintained female lovers. Her husband was aware of these relationships and felt very secure in their marriage. The key, it seemed, to making this type of arrangement work was open communication.

As she listened closely to her colleague, Melissa realized how little she really knew about homosexuals and heterosexuals. Clearly, some people didn't fit in either of those categories, and that was acceptable. In addition, even though sexual orientation may be immutable, it appeared that one's sexual identity could change over time, and even more confusing, someone's sexual behavior could contradict how he or she self-identified. "The possibilities seem to be endless," thought Melissa. "I'd better start educating myself and my clients."

The program that evening proved even more interesting to Melissa as she began to realize that even gender is not clear-cut. The topics that evening were transgenderism and transsexualism. The presenter shared clinical information about a heterogendered couple she was working with in which the "husband" identified himself as transgendered. Paul and his wife had been married for about four years, and for the past two years he had begun to adopt what are stereotypically viewed as feminine characteristics and mannerisms. For example, he started wearing feminine clothing, wearing his hair longer, shaving his legs, and so forth. In fact, he began referring to himself as Paula. Wearing female clothes and acting female made Paula happy—made her feel whole. Paula truly believed that she was a woman trapped in a man's body, and honoring her true female self made her feel healthy and authentic. At first, Jane, his wife, laughed off his behavior and attributed it to eccentricity: "That's my crazy husband for you; he's just a little bit weird." The night Paul told Jane about his inner turmoil will be etched in her mind forever. From that day forward, her life has never been the same. Realizing that this wasn't just eccentricity or play behavior, but that this was real, had been very difficult for Jane. She missed her husband, the man she had married, and she didn't want to be with a woman even though she loved Paul, or Paula as he preferred to be called, very deeply. But the thought of her life alone, without Paul (or Paula) was more than she could bear.

Ever since he was a kid, Paul knew he was different. He knew he didn't fit in, and he knew something didn't match, but he just didn't know what. About five years ago, he started to realize what didn't match; he realized he was a woman trapped in a man's body. Since then, Paul and his wife had been trying to cope with his transformation. Clearly, the issues for both of them were enormous: The more Paula dressed and acted feminine, the more comfortable and authentic he felt. Conversely, the more female he became, the more uncomfortable and horrified Jane felt. At this point, Paul was not considering sex-reassignment surgery; in fact, he seemed content using hormones and electrolysis as long as he could dress and act as a female. For his wife, Paul's transformation to his true female self was torturous. She felt betrayed and resentful of Paul, but at the same time she knew it was healthy and appropriate for him to pursue becoming female. Most of the time, she felt a huge sense of loss, overwhelming grief, and bitterness about the "unfairness" of it. She hated going out in public with him because people would refer to Paul as "ma'am." What was even worse were the times they were perceived as a lesbian couple; she really resented this assumption—not because she wasn't okay with gays and lesbians, but because she was heterosexual. She had married a man and didn't want to be in a relationship with a woman but neither did she want to lose Paul (or Paula). He was her soul mate, the one she wanted to spend the rest of her life with and whom she loved.

The presenter discussed the myriad issues associated with this case, including how she validated Paula and her experience as a transgendered person while at the same time supported and validated Jane as she tried to process and work through her emotions and grief.

Melissa left the meeting overwhelmed by how much she didn't know about sexual orientation and transgenderism. Clearly, knowledge and experience with gays and lesbians were not enough to work effectively with the broad and complex experiences of bisexual and transgendered clients.

Counseling Bisexual and Transgendered Clients

Bisexuals and transgendered clients pose similar challenges to counseling practitioners in that both threaten traditionally held beliefs and socially sanctioned dichotomous thinking. Bisexuality blatantly challenges the notion that there are only two valid sexual orientations—heterosexual and homosexual—and transgenderism violates the belief that there are only two valid genders—male and female. Not surprisingly, mental-health practitioners who feel somewhat comfortable working with gays and lesbians often feel confused and inadequate working with bisexual or transgendered persons because these clients don't fit the molds of orientation or gender. This chapter seeks to dispel the misconceptions and stereotypes associated with bisexuality and transgenderism as well as to illuminate the unique issues faced by these often ignored and marginalized groups. Treatment issues and intervention considerations will also be explored. We will first explore bisexuality, bisexual behavior, and the challenges associated with a bisexual sexual orientation.

Bisexuality

Bisexuality challenges dichotomous perceptions of homosexual and heterosexual orientations. Bisexuality violates culturally maintained binary categories that are based on the premise that each orientation category has a mutually exclusive opposite (Ochs, 1996). Bisexuality implies overlap and ambiguity, making both heterosexuals and homosexuals uncomfortable. Some heterosexuals are uncomfortable with bisexuals because anything that isn't heterosexual is perceived as abnormal. Likewise, some gays and lesbians are uncomfortable with bisexuals because they are seen as "undecided" or just unwilling to admit that they're really queer. Therefore, all too often, bisexuals are ignored and dismissed, forced to remain invisible, and isolated as they struggle to work through the complex issues associated with developing and adopting a positive sexual identity.

To understand bisexuality, certain questions must be answered, such as What is bisexuality? What makes someone bisexual? Why can't bisexuals just identify one way or another, as either straight or gay? and If bisexuals are gay anyway, why do I have to treat them differently?

Definitions

The term *bisexuality* refers to the experience of erotic, emotional, and sexual attractions to persons of the same and other-gender (*other-gender* is used here purposely in recognition of the fact that the term *opposite-gender* is noninclusive and implies that there are only two genders). To make matters even more confusing, the term is often used to describe one's sexual behavior when, in fact, sexual behavior does not necessarily reflect sexual identity. Individuals who engage in bisexual behavior may identify as homosexual, bisexual, lesbian, gay, heterosexual, or transgendered, or choose not to identify at all (Firestein, 1996).

Bisexual identity refers to those individuals who have decided to accept the term *bisexual* as an identity label. Persons who identify as bisexual feel attracted to men and women and believe they could potentially become involved with either men or women (Dworkin, 2000). Seeking to further clarify these often confusing terms, Guidry (1999) specifically delineates between the notion of bisexuality and a bisexual. Bisexuality refers to sexual behavior with both men and women, while being a bisexual refers not only to the capacity for sexual arousal and behavior with both men and women but also to someone who consciously self-identifies as bisexual, rather than as heterosexual or homosexual. The reader may recall in the case at the beginning of the chapter that one of the presenter's clients was a self-identified gay male who also had sexual relationships with a woman. He continued to self-identify as gay, yet he was sexually involved with both a man and a woman. However, Marcy, after years of identifying as lesbian, was beginning to realize that describing herself as bisexual more accurately characterized her feelings and attractions.

Understanding and defining bisexuality and bisexual behavior and recognizing the existence of a bisexual sexual orientation are beginning steps toward being able to work effectively with bisexual clients. It is also important to understand and dispel the culturally pervasive myths and stereotypes associated with bisexuality. The following is a list of commonly held myths regarding bisexuality.

Common Myths Associated With Bisexuality and Bisexuals

Myth   Bisexuality is immature, pathological, or just a phase on the journey to identifying as gay or lesbian.

Fact   For some, bisexuality is a phase between heterosexuality and the adoption of a positive lesbian or gay identity, or, alternatively, bisexuality might be a phase along the journey of adopting a positive heterosexual identity. For others, bisexual behavior may be experimental or situational. For many individuals, however, bisexuality is a valid and authentic sexual orientation and should be accepted as such. Research (Firestein, 1996) indicates there is no evidence to support that bisexuality is associated with pathology or maladjustment.

Myth   Bisexuals can never be satisfied with just one gender; therefore, they are destined to live a life of promiscuity, or at best, a lifetime of serial monogamy marked by interchanging genders and never able to commit to long-term monogamous relationships.

Fact   Just like their heterosexual and homosexual counterparts, some bisexuals practice monogamy while others practice polyamory, that is, concurrent sexual or romantic relationships with more than one partner (Rust, 1996). To say that someone who is bisexual is inherently unable to commit to one gender or another because of a basic flaw in his or her orientation is as absurd as saying that someone who is attracted to both blue-eyed and brown-eyed individuals would require two lovers rather than be able to commit to someone with either color of eyes (Rust, 1996).

Myth   The existence of bisexual orientation is automatically erased by the current relationship, that is, a self-identified bisexual in a heterosexual relationship is "returning to heterosexuality," and vice versa, a bisexual involved in a homosexual relationship is really gay or lesbian. In other words, the gender of the relationship defines the orientation for bisexuals.

Fact   Most people who consider themselves bisexuals do so because they are attracted to both genders; believe they have the potential to become involved with both genders; or in the past have had relationships with both genders and choose not to adopt a lesbian, gay, or heterosexual identity because this would, in fact, deny these very real feelings and meaningful past relationships (Rust, 1996). It is unfair and inappropriate to question someone's bisexuality because he/she is single or involved in a relationship with a person of only one gender (Rust, 1996).

Myth   Heterosexuals, homosexuals, and bisexuals are distinct, nonoverlapping categories of sexual orientation.

Fact   Numerous studies indicate that a substantial number of people, most of whom identify as heterosexual and certainly more than identify as gay or lesbian, have had sexual attractions and encounters with both genders. Heterosexual, homosexual, and bisexual are all valid sexual orientations.

The Emergence of Bisexuality

For over a century, researchers and theorists alike have been struggling to fully understand and characterize the notion of bisexuality. For example, in an attempt to provide a framework for psychosexual development, psychoanalytic theorists identified bisexuality as an evolutionary stage that one passes through as he or she develops a heterosexual sexual identity. In fact, Freud (1963) and many of his contemporaries believed that all human beings have some homosexual feelings and found the notion of inherent bisexuality helpful in understanding why some individuals deviated from heterosexuality and developed a homosexual identity. Still others disavowed the notion of innate bisexuality and viewed bisexuality as a defense or a way to mask and hide an undesirable homosexual identity (Fox, 1996). Both of these psychoanalytic views clearly fostered the notion that homosexuality was an illness, and the associated notion of bisexuality was merely a phase on the journey to developing a "healthy" hetero-sexual orientation.

As the reader may recall from Chapter 1, the landmark Kinsey (Kinsey, Pomeroy, & Martin, 1948, 1953) studies suggested that both homosexuality and bisexuality were simply variations of human sexuality. Instead of pathologizing bisexuality, Kinsey and his team suggested that sexuality can be viewed across a continuum, ranging from homosexuality to heterosexuality, with bisexuality lying somewhere in the middle.

Bisexuality Versus Homosexuality

The landmark decision to remove homosexuality from the *Diagnostic and Statistical Manual (DSM)* in 1973 paved the way for the emergence of gay and lesbian identity development models. Recall from Chapter 2 that these models are traditionally characterized by the following sequential stages: self-awareness of being different from the heterosexual norm, romantic and sexual experiences with the same gender, self-identification as gay or lesbian, disclosure to others, and the end stage, which typically culminates in the adoption of a positive gay or lesbian self-identity (Cass, 1979; Coleman, 1982; Troiden, 1988). In general, these models are based on the assumption that sexual orientation is dichotomous, that is, one is either heterosexual or homosexual. Similar to psychoanalytic theorists, gay and lesbian identity theorists found themselves trapped in a binary paradigm of sexual orientation, and the concept of bisexuality was often seen as either a phase or a sign of arrested development. Only a few models recognized that bisexuality was a valid sexual orientation (Coleman, 1982; Troiden, 1988). In recent years, however, theorists have begun to recognize the shared path of bisexual and homosexual identity development (Cass, 1990). Moreover, theorists have realized that although sexual identity may be long-lasting, it may not be immutable across time since individuals have different experiences throughout life that may bring into question an established homosexual, heterosexual, or bisexual identity (Fox, 1996).

The Fluidity of Sexual Behavior

As well as expanding traditionally held ideas of sexual orientation, the Kinsey, Pomeroy, & Martin (1948, 1953) research revealed that a large number of those surveyed had had both homosexual and heterosexual sexual experiences at some point in their lives. Approximately 42% of the men and 25 to 27% of the women reported that they had experienced a sexual encounter with the same gender. Subsequent studies confirmed these data, clearly suggesting that significantly many more people have same-gender sexual experience than self-identify as homosexual and bisexual. In fact, most of the participants probably self-identify as heterosexual. It stands to reason, however, that at least some of these individuals could be considered as bisexual based on past and current sexual attractions and sexual behavior even though they may not choose to self-identify as bisexual because of the stigma attached to bisexuality (Fox, 1996).

As noted in Chapter 1, the Kinsey data clearly suggest that sexuality and sexual behavior are much more fluid than previously assumed. A strictly dichotomous view of sexual orientation is inappropriate and inaccurate, yet continued classification of people as either "straight" or "gay" is the norm. Klein, Sepekoff, & Wolf (1985) recognized that there were multiple factors related to sexual orientation, including sexual attraction, behavior, and fantasies, as well as emotional and social preference, heterosexual or homosexual lifestyle, and the way one self-identifies. In an attempt to illuminate the multifaceted nature of sexuality as well as to understand how sexuality may change over time, he developed the Sexual Orientation GRID on which individuals rate themselves on a seven-point heterosexual, homosexual, bisexual scale for each factor across time (Klein, Sepekoff, & Wolf, 1985).

Types of Bisexuality

In an effort to characterize bisexuality and bisexual behavior, Ross (1991) proposed eight types of bisexuality, which describe the different circumstances under which same-gender sexual encounters can occur.

1. **Defense bisexuality** occurs as a type of defense mechanism when an individual is transitioning, exploring, or trying to deny a homosexual orientation. Clients may identify as bisexual as they move through the coming out process. Identifying as bisexual may feel somewhat safer than accepting a homosexual orientation because at least it has a base in heterosexuality.
2. **Married bisexuality** occurs when an individual engages in homosexual behavior outside the marriage, and his/her spouse may or may not be aware of this behavior. Engaging in homosexual behavior outside the marriage without the partner's knowledge is likely to create feelings of guilt and shame. Issues to address with this client might include discovering his/her sexual orientation, practicing safe sex, and deciding how and when to share this information with the spouse.
3. **Ritual bisexuality** occurs when homosexual behavior is socially sanctioned for some or all members of a given society or cultural group. Throughout history and across different cultures, bisexual behavior has not only existed but has also been viewed as acceptable and appropriate behavior or a normative rite of passage.
4. **Equal bisexuality** occurs when gender is not a criterion or is transcended as a primary factor in the choice of a potential sexual partner.

5. **Latin bisexuality** refers in some cultures, particularly Latin cultures, to heterosexual males who take only the inserter role, or "top," in anal intercourse with another male. As long as the male is the "top," this behavior is somewhat acceptable and not perceived as homosexual.
6. **Experimental bisexuality** is homosexual behavior that is infrequent or happens only a few times. This person is likely to continue to self-identify as heterosexual.
7. **Secondary bisexuality** occurs only when no heterosexual outlets are available, for example, in a prison setting. Therefore, as a sexual being the individual decides to be sexual with whoever is available, regardless of gender.
8. **Technical bisexuality** is homosexual behavior that occurs as a result of male or female prostitution activities. In this case, economics is the key factor, that is, a trick is a trick, regardless of gender.

Klein (1993) offered the following categories of bisexuality based on the premise that sexuality and sexual behavior are fluid, adding that sexual orientation may change over time. Specifically, one's sexual identity may not be consistent across one's life span and it may even contradict current behavior or self-identification.

1. **Transitional bisexuality** refers to individuals who are moving throughout the phase of coming out as either homosexual or heterosexual. This is often a stage clients move through as they address the tasks of coming out to self or others.
2. **Historical bisexuality** refers to those individuals who currently identify as heterosexual or homosexual and have had past experiences with the same or opposite gender, respectively. To define oneself by one's sexual partner, for example, I am lesbian when I am in a lesbian relationship and heterosexual when I am with a man, seems disingenuous to bisexual individuals. Individuals who are bisexual remain bisexual regardless of their partner's gender.
3. **Sequential bisexuality** refers to individuals who have had relationships with both genders but not during the same time period. Again, the gender of the partner does not define sexual orientation.
4. **Concurrent bisexuality** refers to those individuals who have had relationships with both men and women at the same time. This type of bisexuality is often the most difficult to accept as it implies that the individual has the "best of both worlds." Having an intimate relationship with two people of different genders simultaneously is likely to be challenging and require open and honest communication.

Bisexuality Identity Development

Given that sexual behavior and identity are fluid, how does an individual proceed to identify as bisexual and accept a positive bisexual orientation? Weinberg, Williams, & Pryor (1994) conducted a comprehensive longitudinal study of both men and women who identified as bisexual, and as a result of their research, proposed the following model of bisexual identity development.

Stage 1: Initial Confusion   The individual experiences attractions to both sexes and initially feels unsettled, disoriented, and often frightened. He/she is not sure how to categorize these new feelings and yet is uncomfortable trying to fit into either heterosexual or homosexual categories.

Stage 2: Finding and Applying the Label of Bisexuality   The individual names his/her behavior as bisexual and begins to make sense of long-standing feelings for both sexes.

Stage 3: Settling Into the Identity   The individual begins to self-identify as bisexual, becoming more self-accepting and less concerned with how others perceive him/her.

In terms of bisexual identity development, Weinberg, Williams, & Pryor (1994) viewed bisexuality identity as an add-on to an already-established heterosexual identity. Fox (1996) cautions against this assumption because it is important to note that although some people develop a bisexual identity after first identifying as heterosexual, others adopt it after maintaining a long-term lesbian or gay identity.

Just as there are different developmental stages and tasks for bisexuals, there are also age and gender differences. Box 6.1 lists a few of those developmental milestones.

THE NOTION OF BIPHOBIA, OR PREJUDICE AGAINST BISEXUALS

Biphobia, or, more accurately, biprejudice against bisexual persons, is manifested in many of the same ways as homoprejudice—for example, institutional and cultural discrimination, hatred, stereotyping, and verbal and physical harassment.

To be specific, biprejudice is similar to homoprejudice in that it is manifested in culturally pervasive negative and stereotypical messages about homosexuality and bisexuality. This constant barrage of oppression may lead to feelings of self-hatred, low self-esteem, and self-doubt. Like their gay and lesbian counterparts, bisexuals face the dilemma of choosing whether to be visible or invisible. Staying hidden can lead to alienation and isolation, fueling feelings of

BOX

6.1   *Milestones in Bisexual Development Process*

- Bisexual men and women have their first heterosexual experiences in their early teens.
- Bisexual men have their first homosexual attractions in their early to middle teens, and bisexual women have their first homosexual attractions in their middle to late teens, similar to gay men and lesbians. Bisexual men and women have their first same-gender sexual experiences in their early twenties, somewhat later than their gay and lesbian counterparts. Bisexual men and women have their first homosexual relationships in their early twenties.
- Bisexual men and women first self-identify as bisexual in their early to middle twenties, somewhat later than gays and lesbians self-identify.
- Bisexual men and women typically first disclose their sexual orientation to another person during their twenties, most likely to disclose to friends, relationship partners, or a therapist and not as likely to disclose to family, co-workers, or school friends.

—*Fox, 1996*

shame and self-loathing, while increased visibility can lead to blatant discrimination and oppression.

Biprejudice is different from homoprejudice because bisexuality itself is often dismissed as fictitious. Society might grudgingly acknowledge gays and lesbians, but bisexuals are more often ignored and denied (Ochs, 1996). In addition, bisexuality presents a threat to both the heterosexual and homosexual communities, the media is rife with negative stereotypes of bisexuals, and there is a general lack of visible positive bisexual role models (Guidry, 1999). Biprejudice from the heterosexual communities is expressed in the following ways (Ochs, 1996):

- Bisexuality threatens the hierarchy where heterosexuality holds a dominant, preferred space. The idea of bisexuality makes people uncomfortable with themselves by making visible what many have felt or acted on and chosen to keep secret and unnamed.
- The tendency is to view bisexuality as synonymous with nonmonogamy. Media tend to inflate this concept by portraying bisexuals only as having more than one partner at the same time.
- Bisexuality is identified with the spreading of HIV/AIDS via images of straight men sneaking out and having sex with men.

Biprejudice from the gay and lesbian community is expressed in the following ways (Ochs, 1996):

- Bisexuals are perceived as not committed to the gay and lesbian community because "allegedly" they have the option of choosing heterosexuality. They are therefore seen as less oppressed, because it seems that at any moment they could make the decision to switch over to the privileged side. In addition, bisexuality implies choice and threatens the platform on which gay and lesbian rights fight for civil rights, that is, sexual orientation is not a choice and therefore gays and lesbians should be afforded the same rights as heterosexuals.
- There is historical tension between lesbians and bisexual women, some of which originates in the feminist community. Bisexual women are perceived as "sleeping with the enemy" or succumbing to male power— previously, identified lesbians who reidentify as bisexual are seen as traitors and vilified.

Bisexuals are often caught between the two communities, legitimized by neither, and often misunderstood and much maligned. Mental-health practitioners have the opportunity to serve as allies to bisexual persons, providing affirmative therapy and recognizing bisexuality as a valid sexual orientation with its own set of issues and challenges.

TREATMENT ISSUES

Accepting a stigmatized identity or nonheterosexual identity is difficult under any circumstances. Bisexuals are further challenged because they are marginalized and often vilified by both the heterosexual and the gay and lesbian communities. It is essential, therefore, that mental-health practitioners recognize and validate bisexuality as an authentic sexual orientation. Bisexuals who previously identified as heterosexuals are often caught off guard by their new attractions to both men and women and can be overwhelmed with feelings of confusion, guilt, and shame. Mental-health practitioners can help bisexual clients move through the coming out process, the grieving and letting go of heterosexuality and its associated privileges, and facilitate the process of adopting an alternative sexual identity.

Clients who have previously identified as lesbian or gay face the fear of being rejected and ostracized by the gay and lesbian community. As discussed in the case at the beginning of the chapter, Marcy was afraid to tell her therapist and her friends of her new relationship with a man. Clients who formerly identified as gay and lesbian often find themselves reeling from a completely new sexual identity crisis. After years of feeling different from the heterosexual norm and finally finding and accepting a safe and valid identity in the gay and lesbian community, it can be extremely frightening to think about risking not belonging, and even more painful to realize that the gay community may not be supportive of the new bisexual identity (Matteson, 1996). Clinicians are in a position to help facilitate this often painful process by validating bisexuality as an authentic sexual orientation, guiding the client toward affirmative resources and support groups.

Counseling Couples With Mixed Orientations

As noted in the myths associated with bisexuality, it is erroneous to think that a bisexual orientation is automatically erased by the current relationship—that is, a self-identified bisexual in a heterosexual relationship is "returning to heterosexuality" and vice versa or a bisexual involved in a homosexual relationship is really gay or lesbian.

Mental-health professionals are encouraged to use inclusive language that does not deny either partner's orientation. Avoid defining a relationship with two women as *lesbian*. This may in fact deny that one is bisexual and the other is lesbian; a preferred descriptor is *homogendered*. To define a couple as *heterosexual*, denying sexual orientations, may also be inaccurate; the term *heterogendered* might be preferred. As with any discussion related to identity, listen to how your clients define the relationship and use their language as your cue.

Issues to Consider

When counseling mixed-orientation couples it is important to consider the following dynamics:

1. Recognize and address the effects of externalized and internalized homoprejudice or heteroprejudice and biprejudice.
2. Be prepared to address the concerns of the nonbisexual partner who is either heterosexual or homosexual. Be sure to provide accurate nonbiased information about bisexuality and bisexual behavior. Address empathically the myriad feelings associated with coming to terms with a bisexual partner, such as confusion, betrayal, jealousy, and insecurity.
3. Help facilitate the process of coming out as a bisexual person.
4. Be prepared to assist with issues related to monogamy and polyamory. Couples may need help negotiating an open relationship in which the bisexual partner may be permitted to have relationships outside the original relationship. To effectively manage open relationships, partners must establish communication, trust, a certain level of acceptance and discussion of the homosexual/heterosexual feelings of the partner, and a commitment to making the relationship work (Fox, 1996).

Counseling Transgendered Clients

Just as bisexuality challenges the notion of dichotomous sexual orientations, transgenderism threatens traditionally held binary and polarized concepts of biological sex and gender. A comprehensive discussion of transsexuality and transgenderism is beyond the scope of this chapter, and the reader is encouraged to visit the websites and other resources listed at the end of the book. The remainder of this chapter is designed to introduce the reader to the relevant concepts and issues associated with transgenderism and transsexuality. One must first understand the relationship between biological sex and gender and the role of anatomy in determining sex, gender, and sexual orientation. Then it is necessary to address and dispel the culturally held myths and stereotypes regarding gender roles and behavior. Finally, some general treatment considerations will be explored.

Myths

The concept of transgenderism can be quite confusing because we are all culturally bound to strict constructs of male and female. These constructs are held tightly in place by the following myths (Denny & Green, 1996).

- There are only two genders, male and female.
- Your gender is immutable: If you are female, you will always be female; and vice versa, that is, if you are male, you will always be male.
- Any exception to two genders must not be taken seriously because it's sick, gross, immoral, or just plain perverse.
- Everyone must be classified as one gender or another; anything else is just not natural.

Important Terms

In order to dispel these myths and stereotypes, it is necessary to define a few terms.

Biological sex refers to one's chromosomal sex, including internal and external genitalia.

Gender identity refers to one's sense of being male or female as defined by social construct. In our culture one's gender identity is supposed to match one's biological sex. Females in our society have a great deal of latitude to be androgynous or adopt stereotypical male behaviors or dress. Males, however, are more limited by strict behavioral definitions of what it means to be male and are definitely taught how not to be female. For example, boys are admonished not to "act like a girl," "throw like a girl," or "cry like a girl." The clear implication is that any female behaviors and mannerisms are strictly forbidden.

Intersexuality refers to an individual who is born with physical evidence of sexual ambiguity, and a gender is often assigned or reassigned at birth. This involuntary surgery is rather controversial since it may contradict or violate the person's internal sense of self and well-being, leaving the individual with a life-long sense of having been robbed of an essential part of self. Activists assert that these surgeries should no longer be performed. It should be possible to live without being assigned an identity as male or female until the person him/herself is old enough to make that decision.

Transgenderist refers to someone who identifies with both male and female roles or as a member of an alternative gender. Many transgenderists live full-time as members of the sex opposite from their biological sex but have no desire for genital modification surgery. Many may modify appearance with hormones, electrolysis, or plastic surgery.

Cross-dresser is preferred to *transvestite* and refers to a woman who prefers to wear men's clothing or a man who prefers to wear women's clothing. Persons do so for a variety of reasons, including eroticism and recreation. *Drag kings* or *drag queens* are cross-dressers for the purpose of entertainment, displaying exaggeration of gender stereotypes.

Transsexual refers to persons who have a long-standing desire to live as the sex opposite from their biological sex. They are also categorized as *MtFs* (male to females) and *FtMs* (female to males). The angst associated with this state of incongruity is tremendous, and many of these individuals experience severe depression, substance abuse, suicidal ideation, and low self-esteem. This, coupled with verbal and often physical abuse from family and peers, makes for a painful and tormented existence.

Sex reassignment is a complex process that includes mental-health therapy, electrolysis, hormonal therapy, and living in the new gender role for at least a year or other prescribed period of time. These requirements are based on the Harry Benjamin Standards, the physician who popularized the term *transsexual* and who developed standards of care for mental-health and medical practitioners who treat transsexuals. Transsexual clients can be either postoperative or preoperative depending on whether they have had surgery to modify their genitalia. This process can be physically challenging. The effects of the hormonal therapy can be too extreme, too little, or even adverse, and reassignment surgery may not meet expectations.

Not surprisingly, these clients may be resentful of having to undergo therapy at all since, unfortunately, many know much more about transsexualism than the therapist does. Nevertheless, the surgery is expensive and usually will not be covered by insurance unless the client seeks therapy and is diagnosed with Gender Identity Disorder, pathologizing as a mental disorder what is really a physical disorder.

Transgendered and transsexual people face significant oppression. As one "lives out," challenges arise with families, friends, and the workplace. People often react strongly and violently when they learn that someone is transgendered. Many transgendered and transsexual people live in overwhelming fear of exposure, which can lead to unemployment, ridicule, rejection, and, even worse verbal, physical, and sexual assault. Unfortunately, because of societal prejudice, much of the violence goes unreported since transgendered individuals have little legal recourse or support.

Advocacy

The removal of the category Homosexuality from the *DSM* was revolutionary for gays and lesbians; therefore, transgendered activists are also seeking the removal of the diagnostic categories Gender Identity Disorder and Transvestite Fetishism. These categories perpetuate myths and stereotypes regarding gender and damage a person's right to live his or her life in whatever gender is comfortable or fits (Lombardi, 1999).

Activists even challenge the diagnostic category Gender Dysphoria, a classification that is used to describe individuals who are extremely distressed with feelings of mismatched gender and biological sex. Although transgendered individuals do indeed experience overwhelming stress and angst, Gender Dysphoria is an unfortunate descriptor (Denny & Green, 1996) as it needlessly pathologizes a set of behaviors that have been present in many cultures throughout history and is clearly a very real phenomenon for some individuals.

Therapeutic Issues

Most important, accept and understand that transgenderism exists as a healthy alternative to strictly polarized male and female gender roles. Be aware of and sensitive to the overwhelming stress associated with transgenderism and transsexualism. The pressure on clients to keep this a secret can be enormous. These clients are at high risk for substance abuse, suicidal ideation, and depression.

In working with transgendered and transsexual clients, therapists are encouraged to be empathic and supportive. The process of adopting a transgendered or transsexual identity is similar to the grief process, characterized by stages of denial, anger, grief, and acceptance. Emerson & Rosenfield (1996) propose the following stage theory and suggestions for intervention.

Denial   Many clients and their significant others assume that this is just a phase or eccentricity. Mental-health practitioners can educate clients and normalize the existence of transgenderism. Therapists can suggest readings and help clients and others recognize that the person is not sick, crazy, or perverted.

Anger   Transgenderism evokes intense feelings of confusion and stress for both the client and his/her significant others. Significant others may react in shock, horror, disbelief, or anger and rage. Persons who are transgendered also experience a multitude of feelings, including, self-blame, self-hatred, loss of self-esteem, depression, fear, and suicidal ideation. Therapists can assist by validating feelings and helping both the client and his/her significant others express feelings and effectively communicate with each other.

Bargaining   Continued cross-dressing or pursuit of sex-reassignment surgery can be perceived as selfish. Significant others may make threats or promises to try and dissuade the client, believing that the transgendered person's transformation process is abnormal and inappropriate. Therapists can help normalize the process and subsequent transformation of the client.

Depression   This stage is characterized by feelings of loss and sadness. Clinicians can facilitate the grieving process and at the same time celebrate the client's steps toward wholeness and congruency.

Acceptance   There is no longer a desire to change the person who is transgendered, and significant others begin to accept him/her for who he/she is. Clearly, throughout the process, access to accurate, nonbiased information is absolutely necessary for both the transgendered client and his/her significant others. Support groups are also helpful for both client and significant others.

Tips for Practitioners

Examine Your Biases and Stereotypes   Both bisexuality and transgenderism challenge culturally sanctioned dichotomous thinking. Society tends to treat people in these "gray areas" as deviant and abnormal. Recognize that bisexuality is a valid sexual orientation. Explore your own biases and stereotypes regarding gender and male and female roles. How much do you adhere to restrictive gender expectations in your own life? How might this affect your work with transgendered clients?

Educate Yourself   Be aware that knowledge about the issues associated with counseling gays and lesbians is not enough to understand and address the issues related to bisexual and transgendered clients. In the case at the beginning of this chapter, Melissa was amazed at how little she knew about sexual orientation and issues related to being transgendered. Actively seek information about bisexuality and transgenderism. Visit the Internet sources listed at the end of this book, and become familiar with local resources and support groups.

Be Flexible   Accept and understand the fluid nature of sexuality and sexual behavior. Take time to explore what the client really means when he/she identifies as bisexual, because sexual behavior and sexual identity may not always match. Understand that heterosexuality and homosexuality are not mutually exclusive nor is sexual identity immutable across time. Examine your own beliefs and values about monogamy and polyamory. For example, if you value monogamy in your relationships, how comfortable would you be helping clients negotiate open and flexible sexual arrangements? Be prepared to address issues of simultaneous, multiple relationships, understanding that relationships can be modified and adapted to meet the needs of the partners.

Avoid Focusing Solely on the Client's Sexual Orientation or Gender Identity   Understand that not all issues will be related to the client's identification as bisexual or transgendered. Bisexual clients have reported going to a counselor to talk about issues related to parenting and having the counselor focus only on issues related to the experience of dating both men and women.

Be Willing to Serve as a Social Change Agent   Be willing to serve as an advocate for your bisexual and transgendered clients. Bisexuality is a valid sexual orientation and should be treated as such. Challenge your local and national professional counseling organizations to include discussions and presentations regarding the issues related to bisexuality and transgenderism. Advocate for your clients by working to depathologize transgenderism and transsexualism.

BIBLIOGRAPHY

Cass, V. E. (1979). Homosexual identity formation: A theoretical model. *Journal of Homosexuality, 4*(3), 219–235.

———. (1990). The implications of homosexual identity formation for the Kinsey model and scale of sexual preference. In D. P. McWhirter, S. A. Sanders, & J. M. Reinisch (Eds.), *Homosexuality/heterosexuality: Concepts of sexual orientation*. New York: Oxford University Press.

Coleman, E. (1982). Developmental stages of the coming out process. *Journal of Homosexuality, 7*(2/3), 31–44.

Denny, D. & Green, J. (1996). Gender identity and bisexuality. In B. A. Firestein (Ed.), *Bisexuality: The psychology and politics of an invisible minority*. Thousand Oaks, CA: Sage.

Dworkin, S. H. (2000). Individual therapy with lesbians, gays and bisexuals. In R. M. Perez, K. A. DeBord & K. J. Bieschke (Eds.), *Handbook of counseling and therapy with lesbians, gays and bisexuals*. Washington, DC: American Psychological Association.

Emerson, E. & Rosenfield, C. (1996). Stages of adjustment in family members of transgender individuals. *Journal of Family Psychotherapy, 7*(3), 1–12.

Firestein, B. A. (Ed.). (1996). *Bisexuality: The psychology and politics of an invisible minority*. Thousand Oaks, CA: Sage.

Fox, R. C. (1996). Bisexuality in perspective. In B. A. Firestein (Ed.), *Bisexuality: The psychology and politics of an invisible minority*. Thousand Oaks, CA: Sage.

Freud, S. (1963). *An autobiographical study.* Translated by J. Strachey. 1925. Reprint, New York: Norton.

Guidry, L. L. (1999). Clinical interventions with bisexuals: A contextualized understanding. *Professional Psychology: Research and Practice, 30*(1), 22–26.

Kinsey, A. C., Pomeroy, W. B, & Martin, C. E. (1948). *Sexual behavior in the human male.* Philadelphia: W. B. Saunders.

———. (1953). *Sexual behavior in the human female.* Philadelphia: W. B. Saunders.

Klein, F. (1993). *The bisexual option.* New York: Harrington Park.

Klein, F., Sepekoff, B., & Wolf, T. J. (1985). Sexual orientation: A multi-variable dynamic process. *Journal of Homosexuality, 11*(1–2), 35–39.

Lombardi, E. L. (1999). Integration within a transgender social network and its effect upon members' social and political activity. *Journal of Homosexuality, 37*(1), 109–126.

Matteson, D. R. (1996). Counseling and psychotherapy with bisexual and exploring clients. In B. A. Firestein (Ed.), *Bisexuality: The psychology and politics of an invisible minority*. Thousand Oaks, CA: Sage.

Ochs, R. (1996). Biphobia: It goes more than two ways. In B. A. Firestein (Ed.), *Bisexuality: The psychology and politics of an invisible minority*. Thousand Oaks, CA: Sage.

Ross, M. W. (1991). A taxonomy of global behavior. In R.A.P. Tielman, M. Carballo, & A. C. Hendricks (Eds.), *Bisexuality and AIDS: A global perspective*. Buffalo, NY: Prometheus Books.

Rust, P. C. (1996). Monogamy and polyamory: Relationship issues for bisexuals. In B. A. Firestein (Ed.), *Bisexuality: The psychology and politics of an invisible minority*. Thousand Oaks, CA: Sage.

Troiden, R. R. (1988). *Gay and lesbian identity: A sociological analysis.* Dix Hills, NY: General Hall.

Weinberg, M. S., Williams, C. J., & Pryor, D. W. (1994). *Dual attractions: Understanding bisexuality*. New York: Oxford University Press.

SEXUAL MINORITY YOUTH

The Case of April

April was a relatively new high school counselor. Prior to becoming a counselor, she had worked for years as an eighth-grade English teacher. She loved teaching, but after ten years she was ready for a change. About five years ago she decided to switch careers and become a school counselor. It took her three years to complete her master's degree in counseling because she could attend classes only in the evening or during the summer. She was hired as a counselor and so far was doing well. She enjoyed her work and had good rapport with all her students. One of her strengths, at least in her opinion, was that she always welcomed an opportunity to talk with a student, which was more rewarding than shuffling papers, making schedule changes, or writing recommendations for college, even if it meant staying later or working on the weekends. The feedback from students and teachers indicated that she was well respected and liked for her personable style and willingness to talk anytime.

Meagan dropped in to talk to her about a really important issue. "Hey, you got a minute?" asked Meagan, as she threw her books on the floor and slumped down on the couch. "Sure," said April, with a smile. April was glad to make time to talk to Meagan as they hadn't yet talked about any personal issues. "I've been needing to talk to someone for a while, and I don't even know how to begin. I've heard from my friends that you're cool and that you don't freak out or anything—like last year when my friend Kim talked to you about being pregnant and whether or not she should have an abortion. She said you were really supportive and didn't call her folks immediately, or even the principal."

"Why don't you tell me what's going on," April said gently. "I'm here and ready to listen." However, April's thoughts were racing. Kim's struggle with pregnancy had been a real challenge for her. Fortunately, she had a couple of good friends who were veteran school counselors and with whom she could talk and strategize. What in the world was Meagan about to share? Would she be able to handle it?

"Like I said, I don't even know where to begin. I guess I'll just say it. I think—I think I'm different. I mean very different, different from my friends and different from the other kids at school," Meagan began. "I've felt this way for a while, probably since I was 10 or 11. I didn't know what it was, but I just felt different. I remember playing with my girl-friends, especially when we "made house." It wasn't just make-believe for me; in fact, it felt right in a weird sort of way. I really believed that I could spend the rest of my life with my friends, make a home, go to work, and spend time together. It just felt right. My friends were always pretending that their husband was a big rock star or something like that, and they'd fantasize about living in a big house with him. Not me—I just wanted to be with my girlfriends forever. Who needed a boyfriend or husband? Of course, I didn't tell anyone; they would have thought I was crazy. I just sort of pushed it away and tried not to think about it.

"I've had this feeling I was different for a long time, and I've always known it was wrong. I mean, please, . . . turn on the TV and you can see how different it is. Every show has some girl and guy kissing and making out, living together, and having babies together. I mean, that's normal; that's the way it's supposed to be, right? And God forbid that anyone 'different' is on TV, like on *Ellen* or *Will and Grace.* My family goes berserk—they laugh, make jokes, and even pretend they're throwing up. I used to love watching Ellen; in fact, I want to be Ellen. When she came out, I cried and cheered at the same time. What a shame they canceled her show. And those religious shows—oh my gosh. All you hear about is how all homosexuals are going to burn in hell because they're big-time sinners and hated by God. One day I asked my dad what a homosexual was, and I swear he almost choked. He said, 'Honey, why do you want to know that? You'll never be one of them. Fruits and lezzies are horrible, sick people—not normal like us.' 'Okay, Dad. I definitely don't want to be like *them.*' But you know what? Inside I still felt different, but I sure wasn't going to tell anyone. There is no way I'd tell my parents what I'm thinking and feeling; they would be so mad, they would kill me or at the very least, kick me out of the house.

"You know, school is even worse. It's definitely not okay to be different here. Kids that are different are absolutely hated. For instance, there are some really sweet guys who are tortured by the other kids. Some of the guys are always calling them names like 'sissy' or 'fag,' spitting on them, kicking them, or shoving them against lockers. Sometimes they just beat them up for the fun of it. It's unbelievable, and no one says a word. The teachers, even the principals, know it's going on, and no one does a thing to stop it. There are a couple of teachers who are 'different,' if you know what I mean. All the kids know and make fun of them behind their backs. It would be so cool if they would just be themselves. Then I could look around and say, 'Aha! There's a teacher and she's different and that's okay.' But no way, they'd never do that.

"Last summer things just got worse. I got a huge crush on my brother's girlfriend, Valerie. I mean a real crush, mushy feelings. I felt warm and excited when I was around her; it was terrible. I didn't know what to do with my feelings, so I'd avoid her or be mean to her when she was around, and I totally trashed her to my brother. Of course, I couldn't tell anyone what was really going on. I decided that I'd better get it together, so I started dating boys. What a joke that was! They were sweet, but I just wasn't comfortable with them. When I'd go to parties with them, I'd start drinking or getting high as soon as we got there. By the time we left, I was toasted and that made it much easier when it came time to fool around. It was nice and fun, but it just didn't feel right. I really can't explain it. When I'd get home, I would go straight to bed and relive the night, except this time I'd picture going out with Valerie to the party, only having a beer or two, and at the end of the night making out with her and really enjoying it. This went on most of the summer. You never would have known what was going on with me. On the outside I seemed happy, but on the inside I felt horrible. I felt like something was really, really wrong with me, like I was sick or perverted or maybe just losing my mind.

"Actually my friends did start to think something was wrong with me or at least that I was acting a little crazier than usual. I was drinking every night and going out with different guys. Then one night it happened. There was this new girl at a party, and while we were outside catching a smoke, we started kissing. I couldn't believe it. It was amazing. It felt so good—just like you're supposed to feel when you kiss a guy. We didn't talk about it—it just happened and then we went on our way. I could hardly sleep that night. I kept replaying that kiss over and over again. The next morning, though, I felt horrible. I couldn't believe what I'd done. I had kissed a girl. Oh my gosh, something really is wrong with me. I felt like taking a bunch of pills and just ending it right there. I felt so alone and scared. There was no one I could talk to about what had happened, not even her. In fact, I didn't see her again until this past weekend. And there she was and all I wanted to do was kiss her and hold her in my arms. Oh my God, what do I do? There's something wrong with me. I need help. I feel so scared and alone. I even hated coming to talk to you. I don't know what you think of me or what you're going to do, but I just couldn't take it anymore and had to talk to someone or else I'll go crazy. Can you help me?" Meagan started to cry uncontrollably.

April let Meagan cry. "Wow!" thought April "I considered Kim's pregnancy a challenge, but what in the world do I say to Meagan? It seems as if she may be gay or lesbian, but I definitely don't want to label her something she's not. She's in so much pain. I'm glad she talked to me and felt safe enough to share what's going on, but what do I do with her? I don't remember learning anything about this in graduate school, and I haven't a clue how to begin. I'm scared to explore this issue with her. What if her parents or the administration find out? They'll think I made her gay or talked her into something she's not. Anyway, isn't she too young to be thinking about this? I thought people didn't become gay until they were adults, when they could decide whom they want to date and after they've had a lot of heterosexual experience. I really don't know what to do."

THE EXPERIENCE OF SEXUAL MINORITY YOUTH

The labyrinth of adolescence is difficult to navigate in the best of conditions. According to Adlerian psychology (Dreikurs, 1953; Mosak & Dreikurs, 1967) and Levinson (1978), as discussed in Chapter 1, there are a number of tasks that are faced across a person's life span. During adolescence the tasks of establishing work goals, creating a life structure, and shaping a dream of adult life are most intense. Adolescence is a critical developmental stage, a time to explore, try out new roles, test one's sense of individuality, and develop new ways of relating to parents. It is also a time of burgeoning sexuality and of experiencing deeper relationships with peers. Adolescence is characterized by relationships: learning how to relate to others, to parents, and perhaps most important, to an ever-changing self. Imagine how difficult and complicated these tasks must be for sexual minority youth, particularly since coming to terms with self means accepting a stigmatized identity (Ryan & Futterman, 1998). Amazingly, many gay and lesbian youth are living out and leading visible lives. They have stepped forward proudly, effecting revolutionary change as they refuse to lead lives hidden in shame and secrecy. Sexual minority youth struggle with the same issues as their heterosexual counterparts; however, their developmental process can be thwarted by oppression and shame. Home, school, and religious organizations can be hostile environments where gay youth are forced to suppress their self-identity. As a result, some sexual minority youth struggle through adolescence without support and validation, moving into adulthood with a negative self-image and lacking the skills to relate authentically to others. Others courageously blast out of the closet at an early age, demanding equal treatment and opportunities.

The premier challenge for many sexual minority youth is to develop a positive self-identity in a society that generally sees gays as immoral, deviant, and perverted. Hostility and oppression breed feelings of isolation, low self-esteem, fear, and anger in these youth, leaving them at high risk for depression, anxiety, substance abuse, and even suicide. Given the potential severity of these problems, it is unfortunate that the needs of sexual minority youth are often ignored. Some counselors prefer to ignore or overlook the existence of gay and lesbian youth. Being gay is often thought of as only an adult phenomenon, and sexual minority youth are forgotten, relegated to invisibility. This cloak of invisibility is further exacerbated by the youth's being a sexual minority within a minority group, such as a female adolescent or an adolescent of color.

The purpose of this chapter is to explore the various experiences and challenges faced by sexual minority youth. Included in this discussion is an exploration of cultural homoprejudice and its devastating impact. Various strategies and interventions for assisting with positive identity development will also be discussed.

FEELING DIFFERENT

It is estimated that gay and lesbian adults represent between 4 and 17% of the population (Gonsiorek & Weinreich, 1991). Accordingly, there are approximately 3 million sexual minority youth (Deisher, 1989; Herdt, 1989). This estimate suggests that approximately 1 in 20 youths is gay; therefore, each time a middle or high school teacher meets with a class, at least one or more students is probably a sexual minority (Ginsberg, 1998).

According to the literature, some personal awareness of same-sex erotic feelings predates puberty, and awareness of same-sex attraction becomes increasingly crystallized during puberty (Hershberger & D'Augelli, 2000). Specifically, same-sex attraction begins at about age 10, the same age when heterosexual youth begin to feel sexual attractions (McClintock & Herdt, 1996). The age of self-labeling of same-sex sexual orientation varies between 13 and 16 (D'Augelli & Hershberger, 1993; Hershberger & D'Augelli, 2000).

Feeling different in a hostile world is enormously stressful. The formative tasks of adolescence, such as developing relationships and intimacy, are precluded by the arduous task of hiding one's feelings of differentness. Meagan, in the case at the beginning of this chapter, had felt from a young age that she was different from her friends. Instinctively, she knew she couldn't share her feelings with anyone. Much of her time and energy was spent trying to hide and squelch her feelings rather than attending to the normative tasks of early adolescence. As a result, for Meagan and other sexual minority youth, the tasks of adolescent exploration are circumscribed by stress, hypervigilance, self-monitoring, and an overwhelming sense of fear—fear that one's differentness will be exposed.

THE SETTINGS

The traditional settings that adolescents navigate and use as springboards for development can be pitfalls for sexual minority youth. Instead of providing opportunities for socialization and facilitating growth and identity, they become sources of pain and confusion. The following discussion presents the different environments in which adolescents develop, including society at large, home, school, and religious organizations, to help the counselor understand the various challenges gay and lesbian youth must face.

Society

Society, in general, is plagued by homoprejudice (Logan, 1996), heterosexism, and rigid gender roles. Culturally, homosexuality is viewed as immoral, inferior, and just plain wrong. From birth we are imprinted with heterosexual aspirations and propelled toward heterosexual markers, such as school dances, dating, the prom, and eventually marriage. It's a given that these milestone events assume heterosexuality; however, it's ironic that prior to marriage, it is also assumed that they are sexless. In other words, we give adolescents permission to play heterosexual house or have trial relationships, but we are absolutely incensed if they ever act on their sexual feelings and attractions. The implicit message suggests that you can be whoever you are as long as you're heterosexual and you can do whatever you want as long as you're sexless.

Sexual minority adults are often ostracized because they are perceived to represent eroticism. In other words, gays and lesbians, by virtue of being different from heterosexuals, are often seen only in sexual terms and hated for being different. Imagine society's dismay with gay youth. Heterosexual adolescents are monitored closely and expected to move through various tasks playing pretend adult roles yet remaining virtually sexless. Even though sexual minority youth may not be sexually active, by virtue of deviating from heterosexuality, they too are sexualized and therefore ostracized. Consequently, the concept of gay youth challenges not only the assumption of heterosexuality but also the idea that teens are innocent and sexless. Tragically, gay youth must shoulder the burden of the betrayal of adolescent sexuality; in addition, they are further vilified for being gay and different (Owens, 1998).

Home

Instead of comfort and asylum, home is likely to be another source of negativity and rejection for sexual minority youth. Parents assume heterosexuality and are therefore predisposed to reject sexual minority kids (Owens, 1998). Expectations and anticipation of future life events are all centered on the assumption of heterosexuality. For example, Meagan was very clear about what her family thought about gays and lesbians by their reactions to TV shows with gay and lesbian characters. She knew that they thought queers were horrible and sick and going straight to hell. No wonder Meagan was afraid to share her feelings; she thought her family would disown her, hate her, or even worse. In fact, when faced with sexual minority offspring, many families do react with shock, disappointment, and even anger, or worse. Studies indicate that approximately 33% of gay youth have been verbally abused by family members and up to 10% have been physically attacked by family members due to their different sexual orientation (Berrill, 1990; Pilkington & D'Augelli, 1995). In 1994, Bradford, Ryan, & Rothblum found that in a sample of 1925 lesbians, 24% had been harshly beaten or physically abused while growing up. Harry (1989) found that gay adolescents were significantly more likely to be physically abused than their heterosexual counterparts, especially if they exhibited stereotypical feminine characteristics. A general characteristic of sexual minorities is that they are usually not accepted, or even hated, by their families. Other minority groups experience prejudice and discrimination from the majority group and find safe haven and validation from their family members—safe in terms of being able to rely on their family for support. This, however, is not true for sexual minority youth regardless of ethnic background.

School

School is a wonderful environment for teens to socialize and develop peer relationships but usually not a great place to be gay. Identified by the U.S. Department of Justice as probably the most frequent targets of hate crimes (Gibson, 1989) on a typical day at school, sexual minority youth are faced with a constant barrage of verbal and sometimes physical abuse. Meagan, in the case at the beginning of this chapter, is painfully aware of how kids who are "different" are treated by their classmates. They are teased mercilessly, harassed, and physically abused, and for the most part, no one, not even the teachers, does anything to stop the violence.

The results of the first national survey of sexual minority youth, conducted by the Gay, Lesbian, Straight Educators Network (GLSEN) (1999), revealed that 69% reported having experienced some type of verbal, physical, and sexual harassment/assault while on school property. Ninety percent reported that they have been harassed verbally by negative remarks or derogatory name-calling, such as dyke, sissy, or queer. Most reported hearing these bigoted comments from other students; 30% reported hearing them from faculty or other staff members. Moreover, a third of the students reported that no one ever intervened when they were being harassed, and if someone did intervene, it was usually another student and rarely a faculty or staff member. To put this in context, GLSEN estimates that sexual minority youth hear antigay epithets at least 25 times per day or every 14 minutes. Over half of the respondents said they experienced some type of verbal abuse on a daily basis; however, less than two-thirds of them felt comfortable reporting the incidents to a staff member.

Previous studies have revealed that sexual minority youth are frequently the targets of physical threats and violence, such as having had objects thrown at them, been chased, or been spat on (Pilkington & D'Augelli, 1995). Annually, one in every six sexual minority youth will be beaten up so badly that he/she will have to see a doctor (Safe Schools Coalition of Washington, 1996; Bart, 1998). Other studies indicate that dual or triple sexual minorities are at an even greater risk for violence and abuse, both at home and in the community (Hunter, 1992; Savin-Williams, 1994).

As one student recalls:

> Everyday was a nightmare. I was called names like fag and sissy and pushed up against the lockers. People would stop in the hall to tease me, using the crowd to build momentum and encourage more and more kids to join in the abuse. I used to hate going to school and would try any excuse in the book to avoid it. I would pretend I was sick or had a doctor's appointment or just blow off school altogether. And it's not like I could go home and complain about what was happening at school. See, it's definitely not cool to be gay but to be African American and gay . . . that's something else altogether. My parents would have killed me.

School can be a dangerous and lonely place. There are few, if any, role models to provide guidance and support to harassed and abused sexual minority youth. Gay and lesbian historical figures are virtually invisible in textbooks and coursework.

In addition, if there are any gay and lesbian faculty or administration, they are generally deeply closeted, choosing to remain invisible because of their own fear of exposure, sending a resounding message that it's not okay to be gay. Sexual minority youth have no one to turn to and no way of refuting societal stereotypes and negative portrayals of gay adults.

Religious Organizations

Suffice it to say, many religious organizations and institutions are clearly not places of solace for sexual minority youth. Instead of providing spiritual comfort and support, they often are places that loudly proclaim that gays are immoral, perverted, and hated by God (Bass & Kaufman, 1996). Sexual minority youth are faced with being called sinners, feeling further alienated and despised.

ADDITIONAL STRESSORS

Multicultural Issues

Membership in multiple minority groups looms large as a significant stressor for sexual minority youth. Caught in the crossfire of dual or even triple identities, they further suppress their different sexual identity for fear of insurmountable discrimination and ostracism. As noted in the previous anecdote, coming home to complain about derogatory taunts or name-calling because of ethnic background is quite different from coming home to seek support because you were called a dyke or sissy (Owens, 1998). To be gay is to lose face, embarrassing the family in front of a majority culture that may already denigrate and belittle you. In the African American culture, homosexuality is looked at with disdain because it's perceived as an affliction of the white community (Sears, 1991). For the Asian community, homosexuality is viewed as unnatural and a serious threat to the expectations of traditional gender roles, marriage, and bearing many children (Chung & Katayama,1998). As for the Latino community and the heavy influence of Catholicism, homosexuality flies in the face of masculinity or machismo, threatening rigid gender roles and expectations.

The Media

The media significantly contributes to cultural prejudice toward sexual minorities. Traditionally, sexual minorities have been portrayed as either stereotypical, foppish characters or completely asexual. The media typically portrays gay and lesbian adolescents as angst-ridden and confused. Conversely, heterosexual teens are never seen struggling with their sexual orientation. The occasional positive gay character is usually sexless and rarely connected to the gay community. He/she exists as cheery, asexual, and uninvolved—a perfect heterosexual gay person (Kielwasser & Wolf, 1992). The shows *Ellen* and *Will and Grace* have been revolutionary in their attempts to honestly portray gay and lesbian people. In these shows, the characters actually date and spend time with both gay and nongay friends and family. Ellen's historical coming out on national television gave the viewing public insight into the challenges and opportunities associated with publicly acknowledging one's sexual identity. Unfortunately, the more typical inaccurate and pervasive portraits of gays fuel stereotypes and fears and prohibit sexual minority youth from identifying with positive role models. In fact, according to a recent study of sexual minority youth aged 14–17, a large number believed that gay men were always effeminate and lesbians were always masculine. In addition, over half of the respondents thought that all homosexuals were unhappy (Ryan & Futterman, 1998).

THE DEVASTATING IMPACT

Faced with an ongoing onslaught of cultural prejudice, verbal and physical abuse, religious condemnation, and familial rejection, these youth may begin to implode. Having nowhere to turn and overwhelmed by feelings of shame, guilt, and self-loathing, sexual minority youth flail around trying to find avenues of escape. Alcohol and other drugs are seen as refuges from the pain and torment. In an effort to conform to heterosexual standards, Meagan tried to date boys. Plagued by feelings of dissonance and incongruity, she would have to get drunk or high so she could "play straight." It is quite common for sexual minority youth to combine drug abuse with sexual promiscuity or hypersexuality in an effort to prove heterosexuality or hide homosexuality. Mixing the two can be extremely deleterious for sexual minority youth.

Inquisitive gay youth may seek out gay bars to socialize and meet other young people like themselves. Unfortunately, they find themselves caught up in the adult gay world, a highly sexualized atmosphere fueled by alcohol, without the developmental tools that they need to draw boundaries and make effective decisions. Caught up in the impulsivity of adolescence, feelings of invincibility, and the ongoing turbulence of an identity struggle, sexual minority youth are more likely to have unprotected sex, putting themselves at risk for HIV and other sexually transmitted diseases. According to Remafedi (1987), almost 50% of gay youth studied had a history of sexually transmitted diseases and 45% reported that they never used a condom. These findings were confirmed by a 1996 study conducted by the Los Angeles County Department of Health (1996), which found that 55% of the young men surveyed reported having unprotected anal sex within the last 6 months. Young women are also having risky, unprotected sex, according to a study by Einhorn & Polgar (1994).

Gay youth are at a greater risk for substance abuse and more likely to use drugs and alcohol than their heterosexual peers, using drugs and alcohol to ameliorate emotional pain and to reduce sexual inhibitions and internalized prohibitions against same-sex sexual behavior (Savin-Williams, 1994).

According to one client:

> Yeah, I just drank all the time. I remember I went to my senior prom, and, of course, I went with a guy even though I really didn't want to. Anyway, we went to the prom and I proceeded to get really drunk. I was so unhappy. I just didn't want to be there with him; I really wanted to be with my best friend. I mean, she was more than a friend— we used to kiss and hang out together. Of course, she was at the prom, too, with some guy. All I wanted to do was be with her, so I got drunk, had sex with my date to keep him happy, and, thankfully, I passed out because at least then that horrible night was over.

Faced with a multitude of stressors, some sexual minority youth run away from home; others are kicked out of their house because of their sexual orientation. According to a study conducted by the Hetrick-Martin Institute (Hunter, 1992), up to 40% of gay/lesbian youth had been violently assaulted and almost half of those assaults were gay-related. A significant number of those assaults occurred at home; as a result, many gay youth choose to escape the abuse and live on the streets. Although exact numbers are unknown, it's estimated that one in four homeless youth may be lesbian or gay (Ryan & Futterman, 1998). Out on the street, sexual minority youth are left to fend for themselves, hustling for food and shelter. It's not surprising that over half turn to prostitution to support themselves (Savin-Williams, 1994). Homeless sexual minority youth are at an even higher risk for significant mental and physical problems, such as depression, HIV and other sexually transmitted diseases, pregnancy, and suicide (Ryan & Futterman, 1998).

Suicide

Faced with family and peer rejection and fear of being exposed, gay and lesbian youth may consider suicide the only option to end the pain and remain permanently hidden. Although frequently challenged and dismissed as a political tactic, the estimation is that 30% of adolescent suicides are related to sexual orientation. According to a study conducted by the U.S. Department of Health and Human Resources and quickly suppressed by the Bush administration in 1989, gay youth were reported to have attempted suicide 2 to 3 times more often than their heterosexual counterparts (Gibson, 1989). The controversy swirled because the author targeted homoprejudice as the primary contributing factor, as well as put the responsibility on a society that continues to deny that sexual minority youth even exist. Subsequent studies have confirmed these findings (D'Augelli & Hershberger, 1993), suggesting that suicide is indeed higher for gay youth. Just as sexual minority youth of color are more frequent targets of violence, they are also at greater risk of suicide than their white counterparts (Bell & Weinberg, 1978).

MEETING THE CHALLENGE

In spite of these harrowing statistics, it is important to recognize that many gay and lesbian youth are choosing visibility, living out proudly at school and home. In fact, according to GLSEN (1999), there are over 700 gay/straight alliances and other support groups across the nation. These organizations are designed to ensure that schools are environments where all students are nourished and supported, regardless of sexual orientation or gender identity. Gay and lesbian youth are coming out in the classroom and in their neighborhoods. They're taking their girlfriends or boyfriends to the prom or other school-sponsored activities. These out youth are courageously living their lives, no longer will-

ing to succumb to homoprejudice and oppression. Mental-health practitioners are challenged to support these youth by helping to create an affirmative
environment.

The Counselor's Response

Professional counselors are ethically obligated to work with sexual minority
youth by creating a positive and affirming environment where gay and lesbian
youth can safely explore their feelings and issues, and, as a result, successfully
navigate the journey of adolescence. Counselors who refuse to treat, or ignore,
sexual minority youth and continue to hold biased and judgmental attitudes interfere with these youths' development, and are therefore engaging in unpro-
fessional practice (Hershberger & D'Augelli, 2000). Unfortunately, many
counselors face a serious dilemma: They are ethically required to work with
sexual minority youth but lack any kind of formal training. It has been clearly
documented that counselors receive little, if any, exposure to the myriad issues
facing sexual minorities (Buhrke, 1989; Buhrke & Douce, 1991).

Moreover, in recent years, mental-health organizations such as the American Psychological Association (APA), the American School Counselor's Association (ASCA), the American Counseling Association (ACA), and the National
Education Association (NEA) have upped the ante, so to speak, challenging
counselors to take a more active role by actively affirming sexual minorities,
providing support and accurate information, and advocating for a reduction in
discrimination and oppression.

Tips for Practitioners

The primary goal of counseling sexual minority youth is to decrease the effects of homoprejudice and increase the chances for these youth to develop a
positive self-identity. To do so requires the facilitation of positive social relationships, self-understanding, and self-acceptance (Owens, 1998). The following suggestions are offered to community agencies, private practitioners, and
school counselors who are working with sexual minority youth.

Explore Internalized Homoprejudice   According to Logan (1996), we are
all raised in a homoprejudiced society that teaches us that homosexuality is
wrong and inferior to heterosexuality. Explore the impact of those negative
messages and the ensuing myths and stereotypes you have about sexual minority youth. Explore your own feelings about sexuality, sexual identity, and
behavior. Assess your comfort level with your own sexuality. Sexual minority

youth are hypervigilant, looking for the familiar signs of prejudice and disdain, looking for any sign or inappropriate comment as proof that you are "just like the rest of society." In the case at the beginning of the chapter, Meagan was looking for someone she could talk to, someone who wouldn't judge her or immediately contact her parents or the school administration. Meagan trusted April because she had dealt effectively with Meagan's friend Kim when she had a controversial problem and Meagan had heard that April could be trusted. Remember, as a counselor, you have the responsibility to prove yourself worthy of the client's trust and self-disclosure.

Educate Yourself   Many graduate counseling programs are failing to prepare counselors to work with sexual minority youth. It is your responsibility to educate yourself by reading related literature and books, or by attending workshops and other types of continuing education programs. In recent years there has been an increase in the number of programs related to the issues facing sexual minorities offered at both local and national conferences. If you are currently a student in a graduate program, challenge your professors to include sexual minority issues in all courses rather than as a section of a multicultural/diversity course.

Allow Adolescents to Explore Their Sexuality   Don't assume that a youth's confusion automatically signifies underlying heterosexuality or homosexuality—this is a time for exploration. Many sexual minority youth don't crystallize their sexual identity until late adolescence, and same-sex sexual behavior does not necessarily cement sexual orientation. For example, boys may engage in group masturbation, competing to see who can have an orgasm first, and girls may be very affectionate with each other, holding hands, walking with their arms around each other, and even kissing. This does not necessarily mean they are gay or lesbian.

Use Inclusive Language   Avoid premature labeling and categorizing. Allow gay and lesbian youth the chance to experiment and have new experiences in a safe and affirming environment. Encourage kids to seek out social and recreational opportunities where they can meet, interact, and explore who they are.

Challenge Negative and Derogatory Comments   Interrupt name-calling and use of phrases that demean gays and lesbians. Talk honestly about stereotypes and myths and about how hurtful slurs can be to people. Share what being gay really means and what it doesn't mean.

Provide Accurate and Positive Information Regarding Sexual Minorities   Be prepared to address the devastating effects of homoprejudice, the full spectrum of sexuality, sexual identity, and behavior, including safe-sex practices. Have books and other materials readily available, and maintain a list of gay-positive websites.

Ensure and Respect Confidentiality   Maintaining the highest level of confidentiality is paramount to an effective counseling relationship and even more critical when working with sexual minority youth. In a hostile, homo-prejudiced environment, breaching confidentiality can have devastating effects. Unfortunately, many school counselors are afraid to discuss issues related to sexual orientation because of threat of parental retribution or sanctions by management or school administration. The client's right to privacy and confidentiality is clearly protected when counseling sexual minority youth. Lambda Legal Defense and Education Fund (LLDEF) firmly supports this protection and states that in order for parents to take legal action against a counselor for affirming sexual minority youth, there would have to be proof of harm or brainwashing. To date, there have been no successful cases (GLSEN, 1999).

Do Not Assume Heterosexuality   Be inclusive in your language and attitudes—there are gay students, faculty, staff, and parents. Use language that sends a message of recognition and acceptance. Homoprejudice and heterosexism are insidious and pervasive within the home, school, and community agency environments. Agencies that invite husbands and wives but not gay couples, encourage kids to date the opposite sex, or offer health care exclusively to heterosexual married couples are engaging in acts of discrimination.

Advocate   Make your office a safe zone where students, faculty, and agency staff know they have a safe space to be open about all issues, particularly those related to sexual orientation. To delineate a safe space, use pink triangle "safe zone" magnets or stickers available from GLSEN, or other gay symbols such as the rainbow flag. Encourage gay and lesbian faculty and agency staff to be visible and serve as role models and consider bringing in outside speakers and representatives of the gay community. Ask yourself the following questions. Are you sexual minority–friendly? Do you have gay-friendly symbols in your office, such as a "safe space" pink triangle or a rainbow flag? Do you have age-appropriate gay-related books and other materials visible? Do you have culturally diverse posters on the wall? Do you have gay-friendly videos or other media available? Do you have a reading list that includes materials related to sexual minorities? Do you have a working relationship with the local gay community, including counseling centers, religious institutions, and community centers?

Provide Training   Educate the faculty and agency staff. Include in your training programs the effects of internalized and externalized homoprejudice, the experiences of sexual minority youth, and the coming out process. Teach faculty and agency staff how to understand and develop the skills to meet the needs of sexual minority youth.

Have Resources Available   Make sure that the school library or agency resource center has appropriate and accurate resources dealing with sexual minority issues. Encourage the school library or agency resource center to celebrate gay history month.

Mentor   Be willing to mentor a gay/straight adolescent support group. Encourage other faculty and agency staff to be part of the group and its activities.

Work With School Administration   School counselors are often stymied by fearful and prejudiced administrators. School administrators can no longer afford to ignore sexual minority youth and their abusers. All students have the right to a safe school environment and the right to feel accepted and valued. In 1997, the Office of Civil Rights released a new Title IX federal statute that prohibits sex discrimination, and for the first time, stated that gay students are protected from sexual harassment. Unfortunately, it doesn't forbid discrimination based on sexual orientation; however, it does prohibit actions that create a sexually hostile atmosphere.

Be Aware of the Cost of Ignorance   In the 1996 case of *Nabozny v. Podlensy,* one student fought back against harassment, costing a school district nearly $1 million. Because of his sexual orientation, the student suffered brutal verbal and physical abuse by classmates. Over a four-year period, he was kicked, urinated on, and at least once was beaten so badly that he required surgery. He complained to teachers, school counselors, and administration to no avail. More recent gay-related discrimination cases have been settled out of court, sending a clear message that schools can no longer ignore sexual discrimination against sexual minority youth.

Work to Effect Change Within the School Environment   School counselors are uniquely challenged by the potential barriers associated with school systems. Parents, teachers, and administrators are more often formidable opponents rather than allies in the battle to make schools an affirming environment for all students. One counselor explained the enormity of her task by sharing a story about her school. In her office she had hung a poster that celebrated diversity; over the summer an administration official had torn it down and left the pieces on her desk. Refusing to bend to homoprejudice, she now has a "safe zone" sticker on her filing cabinet, and each year she is taking small steps to educate and effect change in her hostile school setting. The essential point is to continue trying by putting up "safe zone" stickers, keeping gay and lesbian materials in view, and trying to find allies and other support. When preparing to effect change in your school, consider the following suggestions.

Create a Mission Statement   Write a mission statement for your school that is inclusive of sexual orientation, setting the tone for acceptance and affirmation of all students. For legal assistance and ideas, contact the Lambda Legal Defense and Education Fund. Promote equality and protection for all students and staff.

Adopt Policies   Write and adopt policies against sexual harassment, and include sexual orientation. Take a clear stand of zero tolerance against antigay harassment; Be clear that it will not be tolerated and that swift action will be taken against the perpetrators.

Counsel Gay Youth and Their Families   At some point, sexual minority youth may consider coming out to their families. Be willing and able to process with your client the possible repercussions. Role-play the situation and potential outcomes, and make sure she or he has support. Proceed with caution since families may react in a hostile manner, placing the adolescent in jeopardy or in physical peril. Be sure to validate the adolescent's need for family support and acceptance; at the same time recognize and validate that families need time to adjust and accept sexual minority children. Reactions may include shock, denial, anger, sadness, and rejection. Prepare adolescents and their families for the wide range of feelings. Allow for a mourning process, time to mourn the loss of the dream of heterosexuality and time to deal with feelings of guilt, shame, and anger. Educate families about gay identity development. Provide accurate and positive information, dispelling myths and stereotypes. Encourage communication and conflict resolution. Teach active-listening skills, and challenge negative self-talk and negative communication patterns. Be willing to assert yourself as a professional counselor: Intervene and challenge verbal and physical abuse. Encourage parents to find support through PFLAG, an organization where they can meet other parents who have experience with sexual minority children and friends.

BIBLIOGRAPHY

Bart, M. (1998, September). Creating a safer school for gay students. *Counseling Today,* 26–39.

Bass, E. & Kaufman, K. (1996). *Free your mind: The book for gay, lesbian, bisexual youth—and their allies.* New York: HarperCollins.

Bell, A. P. & Weinberg, M. S. (1978). *Homosexualities: A study of human diversity.* New York: Simon & Schuster.

Berrill, K. (1990). Anti-gay violence and victimization in the United States: An overview. *Journal of Interpersonal Violence, 5,* 274–294.

Bradford, J., Ryan, C., & Rothblum, E. D. (1994). National lesbian health care survey: Implications for mental health care. *Journal of Consulting and Clinical Psychology, 62*, 22–242.

Buhrke, R. A. (1989). Incorporation of lesbian and gay issues into counseling training: A resource guide. *Journal of Counseling and Development, 68*, 77–80.

Buhrke, R. A. & Douce, L. A. (1991). Training issues for counseling psychologists in working with lesbian women and gay men. *The Counseling Psychologist, 19*, 216–234.

Chung, Y. B. & Katayama, M. (1998). Ethnic and sexual identity development of Asian-American lesbian and gay adolescents. *Professional School Counseling, 1*(3), 21–25.

D'Augelli, A. R. & Hershberger, S. L. (1993). Lesbian, gay, and bisexual youth in community settings: Personal challenges and mental health problems. *American Journal of Community Psychology, 21*, 1–28.

Deisher, R. W. (1989). Adolescent homosexuality: Preface. *Journal of Homosexuality, 17*, xiii–xv.

Dreikurs, R. (1953). *Fundamentals of Adlerian psychology*. Chicago: Alfred Adler Institute.

Einhorn, L. & Polgar, M. (1994). HIV risk behavior among lesbians and bisexual women. *AIDS Education and Prevention, 6*, 514–523.

Gay, Lesbian, Straight Educators Network. (1999). First-of-its-kind school climate surveys lesbian, gay, bisexual, transgender students, showing pervasive harassment at school. [on-line] Available: glsen.org/pages/sections/library/news/9909-241.article.

Gibson, P. (1989). Gay male and youth suicide. *Report of the secretary's task force on youth suicide*. Washington, DC: U.S. Public Health Services.

Ginsberg, R. W. (1998). Silenced voices inside our schools. *Initiatives, 58*, 1–15.

Gonsiorek, J. & Weinreich, J. (1991). The definition and scope of sexual orientation. In J. Gonsiorek & J. Weinreich (Eds.), *Homosexuality: Research implications for public policy*. Newbury Park, CA: Sage.

Harry, J. (1989). Parental physical abuse and sexual orientation. *Archives of Sexual Behavior, 24*, 350–361.

Herdt, G. (1989). Gay and lesbian youth: Emergent identities and cultural scenes at home and abroad. *Journal of Homosexuality, 17*, 1–42.

Hershberger, S. L. & D'Augelli, A. R. (2000). Issues in counseling lesbian, gay, and bisexual adolescents. In R. N. Perez, K. A. DeBord, & K. J. Bieschke (Eds.), *Handbook of counseling and psychotherapy with lesbian, gay and bisexual clients*. Washington, DC: American Psychological Association.

Hunter, J. (1992). Violence against lesbian and gay male youths. In G. M. Herek & K. T. Berrill (Eds.), *Hate crimes: Confronting violence against lesbians and gay men*. Newbury Park, CA: Sage.

Kielwasser, A. P. & Wolf, M. A. (1992). Mainstream television, adolescent homosexuality and significant silence. In R. E. Owens (Ed.), *Queer kids: The challenges and promise for lesbian, gay and bisexual youth*. Binghamton, NY: Hayworth Press.

Levinson, D. (1978). *The seasons of a man's life*. New York: Ballantine Books.

Logan, C. R. (1996). Homophobia? No, homoprejudice. *Journal of Homosexuality, 31*(3), 31–53.

Los Angeles County Department of Health, HIV Epidemiology Program. (1996, February). *Young men's survey: Los Angeles—August 1994–January 1996*. Paper presented to Los Angeles County Adolescent HIV Consortium, Los Angeles, CA.

McClintock, M. K. & Herdt, G. (1996). Rethinking puberty: The development of sexual attraction. *Current Directions in Psychological Science, 5*, 178–183.

Mosak, H. H. & Dreikurs, R. (1967). The life tasks III, the fifth life task. *Journal of Individual Psychology, 5*(1), 16–22.

Nabozny v. Podlensy. (1996). 92 F.3d 446 (W.D. Wisc).

Owens, R. E. (Ed.). (1998). *Queer kids: The challenges and promise for lesbian, gay and bisexual youth*. Binghamton, NY: Hayworth Press.

Pilkington, N. & D'Augelli, A. R. (1995). Victimization of lesbian, gay and bisexual youth in community settings. *Journal of Community Psychology, 23*, 33–56.

Remafedi, G. (1987). Adolescent homosexuality: Psychosocial and medical implications. *Pediatrics, 79*, 331–337.

Ryan, C. & Futterman, D. (1998). *Lesbian and gay youth: Care and counseling*. New York: Columbia University Press.

Safe Schools Coalition of Washington. (1996). *Safe schools anti-violence documentation: Third annual report*. Seattle, WA: Safe Schools Coalition of Washington.

Savin-Williams, R. C. (1994). Verbal and physical abuse as stressors in the lives of lesbian, gay male and bisexual youths: Associations with school problems, running away, substance abuse, prostitution and suicide. *Journal of Consulting and Clinical Psychology, 62*, 261–269.

Sears, J. T. (1991). *Growing up gay in the South: Race, gender, and journeys of the spirit*. New York: Harrington Park Press.

Spiritual Issues for Gay Men and Lesbians

The Case of Pat

Pat had seen Anthony for three sessions when the issue of coming out to his parents was first discussed. Anthony was a 31-year-old youth minister in a conservative rural church. He had struggled with his sexual orientation for years and had been most conflicted by the tension between living up to the high expectations that others had for him and living his own life. He had spoken about being gay with an older minister who advised him to move slowly, pray, and not tell others. But he had come to the point where his life felt like a total lie, and he knew he was not being true to his belief in God as long as he denied who he was. He had come for counseling for help in finding a new career.

As Pat listened, she felt uneasy. She had read reports of youth ministers who seduced boys who had been placed in their care. She worried that Anthony was going to tell her he was involved in that kind of activity, or that he was involved and would not tell her. She found herself feeling uncomfortable because the church she attended had taken strong stands against homosexuality. She had counseled other gay and lesbian clients, but Anthony was her first gay client who worked with church youth. She found herself distracted by her own thoughts and refocused on what Anthony was saying. He spoke about his plan to come out to his parents the following weekend. He loved his parents and was simply not willing to lie to them any longer. Pat thought his plan seemed reasonable and respectful.

Pat redirected the conversation to the issue of his work. As Anthony spoke about how much he enjoyed working with young people, Pat found herself internally rejecting the notion that Anthony might be a sexual predator. He clearly loved what he was doing and saw every activity as an opportunity to witness to his faith. He was creative and inspiring as he talked about his commitment to stay in the job for several more months so he could complete several projects "his kids" had planned. When she asked what kind of work might come next, she felt herself feeling sad when Anthony spoke about his fears of a job that would involve working with children or youth. He was simply too uncomfortable to place himself in a situation where others might accuse him of sexual abuse. Pat was moved by his commitment to his own integrity and realized that Anthony was trying to make this difficult change in his life with enormous respect for those who cared about him. Anthony ended the session talking about his excitement from a date he had been on the previous weekend.

During the week Pat found herself caught between her own religious beliefs and her feelings for Anthony. Over dinner one night she asked her husband, Jim, what he would think if the youth minister in their church turned out to be gay. She was troubled by his quick insistence that the man should be fired immediately. She listened quietly as Jim repeated the church's stance about the sinfulness of homosexuality. Later she realized that her relationship with Anthony was causing her to look at homosexuality in a different way, and she was not sure what that might mean about her own faith.

Anthony came into her office the following week and immediately broke into deep sobs. As he stammered out what had happened, Pat found her own anger rising. When Anthony told his parents, his mother blew up at him and threw him out of the house. As he was leaving, she said, "I would rather have you lying here in a coffin than to have heard what you just told me." On Monday when he went to work, the minister called him in and said that his mother had called and told him that Anthony was homosexual and should not be working at the church. Anthony responded truthfully when asked if he was gay. The minister then told him that he was not welcome at the church any longer and that he should get his things out of the office immediately. Pat was astonished by these events, angry that his parents had been so judgmental, and stunned that his mother had been so vindictive. She pushed aside her own feelings to help Anthony sort through his distress. As she watched him struggle, her respect for him grew enormously.

Over the next few weeks, Anthony began to move on. He found a job that at least gave him some income. He tried several times to speak with his parents, but they would not respond to him. He had continued dating the man he mentioned earlier, and it was clear that the relationship was becoming important. He could see that both good and bad had come from his decision to come out to his parents. What troubled him the most was his personal loss of his spiritual connection. He could not bring himself to go to another church, and he felt adrift without the steady religious practice that had been so meaningful to him. Pat could feel this sense of loss and found herself thinking that the church had failed both Anthony and his parents. If their church had tried to develop an understanding of homosexuality, Anthony's parents might have been able to respond differently, and he might still feel strengthened by his faith.

Months later Anthony had created a new life. He had been promoted at work and was beginning to attend graduate school. He and his boyfriend had moved in together and had a happy social life. His parents still did not welcome him back into the family, but he was not letting that get him down too much. He continued to struggle with his religious beliefs. Pat understood his struggle because counseling Anthony had led her to struggle with her own faith.

She spoke up in her Sunday school class when the issue of homosexuality came up. She encouraged the group to try to learn more about what it means to be gay or lesbian and offered to bring some people in to talk with the class about this topic. Once again, she was stunned by the hostile response. Her church friends were absolutely unwilling to consider her suggestion, and later her husband told her that he thought she was crazy to express herself that way. Although Pat knew she had done the right thing, she found herself wondering how to reconcile her own new understanding about homosexuality with the teachings of her church. She worried about the gay youth in her congregation and wondered if their parents were getting the kind of information that would help them when their children finally came out. She knew there were no easy answers and, for the first time, began to understand how gay men and lesbians who stayed in the closet might feel. Still, she kept silent about these questions even as she knew they were leading her to examine other aspects of a faith she had taken for granted.

HOMOSEXUALITY AND RELIGION

The religious domain presents one of the most complex challenges to gay men and lesbians. Most of us grow up with some kind of orientation to religious organizations. We are taught that they are the source of much meaning in life or, perhaps, that they serve no useful function. Whatever our personal beliefs may be, religion impacts many aspects of our daily life. Whether it is the debate about prayer in the schools or even scheduling events on Yom Kippur or other days that have religious significance, our lives revolve around religious issues. Gay men and lesbians are like others in their search for spiritual and religious understanding and their need for a community of people who share and celebrate their faith. But, virtually all the mainline religious organizations condemn homosexuals and brand them as sinners simply because of their sexual orientation. How can one make peace with a religious organization that casts you out simply because of who you are?

The clash between many religious organizations and homosexuality brings to the surface one of the most fundamental questions about sexual minorities: Is homosexuality a deviant choice (and therefore sinful) or is it one more aspect of the divine diversity that exists in nature? The way one responds to this question determines whether or not homosexuality is seen as a moral issue or a civil rights issue. The hard line that most denominations take about homosexuality leads many gay men and lesbians to stay in the closet or to go back in the closet when they go to worship (Abraham, 1993). The internal conflict between self-affirmation and potential rejection can become particularly intense in the religious domain. Many sexual minorities reject religious life entirely because of judgmental and rejecting statements they routinely encounter. Others may drift toward New Age or even pagan practices that are more accepting (Cherry & Sherwood, 1995). Obviously, the debate about this issue is intense, and it is a conflict that is unlikely to be resolved anytime soon.

Sexual minorities are not the first group to experience rejection or limited status within religious organizations. In the early Christian church there was intense debate among the Jewish membership before gentiles were allowed to belong. Scriptural proscriptions exist that severely limit the role of women to fully participate in religious life. For centuries, people who were left-handed were seen as possessed by Satan. In modern times, the Bible has been used to justify the oppression of black people, divorced people, and others who are different. Fortunately, many of these teachings have been abandoned. African Americans and whites worship together. People who are divorced may now remarry in the church. Still, most mainline churches continue to be uneasy about gay men and lesbians who seek membership. On the surface it would appear that the one safe place where gay men and lesbians would find acceptance would be in the Christian church. Because of its emphasis on the nature of sin (all people are sinners) and the universal nature of God's love, one would expect that homosexuals would be welcome even if they are seen as sinners. However, most Christian churches, and particularly, conservative Christian groups, view homosexuality as a special kind of sin. Staunch in their belief that gay men and lesbians seek special rights through the promotion of a "homosexual agenda," they condemn all homosexuals. This tension and subsequent debate within large Christian and Jewish groups is observed carefully by gay men and lesbians, and it is easy to understand why many would be reluctant to expose themselves in religious organizations that are so afraid of them.

The Metropolitan Community Church (MCC) was created with the express intention of ministering to gay men and lesbians. Visible in most major cities, the MCC has congregations that are predominantly, but not exclusively, gay or lesbian. As successful as it has been, this one organization cannot meet the needs of all sexual minorities who seek participation in religious life. Many people prefer to worship in the faith communities that were part of their family lives. However, a local congregation of the MCC will be a valuable resource for clients who are seeking religious support and are afraid to approach more well-known religious organizations because of fear of rejection and condemnation.

Most organized religious bodies have taken public stands against homosexuality. Some are vociferous in their objection to the gay rights movement and actually go on the offensive in encouraging their congregations to condemn those who are gay and lesbian as well as their allies. Rev. Fred Phelps of Westboro Baptist Church in Topeka, Kansas, has created a web page (www.godhatesfags .org) that demonstrates what many would call the offensive nature of this attack. Conservative religious leaders stridently denounce the "homosexual demons" among us. They present gay men and lesbians as evil people who have an agenda that is anti-Christian and antifamily. And, as we discussed in Chapter 1, they exhibit strategies of direct attacks in their television ministries or place advertisements like the ones on conversion therapy in national media. Most mainline Protestant and Jewish groups participate in this discussion about homosexuality and religion within their organizational structures.

In spite of the offensive nature of many religious groups' statements about homosexuality, in most large cities there is a growing and visible gay and lesbian presence in mainline religious organizations. Typically, these congregations are located in the central city, and many continue to exist or even thrive because of the influx of sexual minorities. This rapidly expanding body of believers is actively at work within the larger religious organizations, educating and advocating for full participation in religious life. Perhaps this new interest in religion is merely a reflection of the growing visibility of gay men and lesbians in all aspects of contemporary life; or maybe it is a natural result of the level of suffering within gay communities as thousands died from HIV/AIDS. Perhaps it is the recognition by many within religious organizations that gay men and lesbians are human beings who have been unjustly branded as outcasts by generations of the faithful who simply did not have the opportunity to experience and know them as fellow believers. It is evident that change is coming.

It has become routine to read in the media each summer about the debates and votes taken on acknowledging and welcoming homosexuals as legitimate participants in the full array of religious practices and sacraments. In 1999, the Reform branch of Judaism voted to open marriage to persons of the same sex. And in 2000, although Methodists, Presbyterians, and Episcopalians stepped back from inviting homosexuals into full church membership, the votes are becoming increasingly close. Some ministers openly defy church policy by blessing "holy unions" even though such ceremonies have no legal recognition.

While there are encouraging signs that large religious bodies are beginning to understand sexual minorities, gay men and lesbians, as well as their families, often have a difficult time finding religious organizations that welcome and understand them. Frank's parents had requested a joint counseling session after he had come out to them and wanted them to meet his partner, Wes. With Frank present, they explored the following dilemma:

> We have wondered for a long time whether or not Frank might be gay, so his news was not exactly a surprise. And we have met Wes and he seems like a fine person. What troubles us is that they want to come to church with us as a couple. We went to talk to our minister, and he told us in no uncertain terms that homosexuality is sinful and that Frank and Wes will not be welcome. That's what has us in a bind. We love Frank and just want him to leave Wes at home when it comes to religious services. We can't understand why he gets so upset at this. After all, we are willing to have them in our home. It looks like they could respect the fact that we do not want our minister and friends to be offended by their presence in our family.

Situations like these and that of Anthony in the case at the beginning of this chapter bring a new awareness to many religious people that there is a community out there that needs help. This awareness has led to an intense debate within religious organizations and within the gay and lesbian community. It is not within the scope of this book to review the theological discussion about the rightness or wrongness of the church's admonitions against homosexuality. What is important is to take a look at the consequences of this debate as it influences the spiritual lives of gay people.

The Perspective of Organized Religion

This is not a book about theology; rather, we hope to present information that will help counselors and other mental-health professionals understand the dilemma facing sexual minorities as they seek to build spiritual lives. At the same time, understanding how organized religion views homosexuality can provide the necessary context for developing a sensitivity to these important issues. Box 8.1 presents information about the current positions taken by major Christian denominations about homosexuality.

Judeo-Christian Heritage

In the United States the dissent about homosexuality is most prominent in the Christian church. The questions that many major denominations puzzle over are complex. Shall we ordain gay men and lesbians? What access do they have to the sacraments? How do we value and support their relationships when they cannot be legally married? If we become more accepting of the "gay lifestyle," aren't we endorsing promiscuity or, even worse, sin? How do we reconcile the church's historic stand against homosexuality with our own personal understanding of this part of God's creation? Even an organization as conservative as the Roman Catholic Church has issued a public teaching that encourages the parents of gay and lesbian children to love rather than reject them. Individuals like Pat in this chapter's case, as well as many congregations, are beginning to

---

BOX 8.1

Where Christian Churches Stand

- **Catholic:** Forbids same-sex unions. Expects priests to be celibate.
- **Episcopal:** Same-sex unions not forbidden but bishops recently defeated a resolution to create liturgy for same-sex commitment blessings. Ordained gays must remain celibate.
- **Lutheran:** Evangelical Lutheran Church discourages same-sex unions. Clergy rosters open to celibate gays.
- **Presbyterian:** In June 2000, Presbyterian Church (USA) convention voted narrowly to forbid clergy from performing same-sex unions. Noncelibate homosexuals not allowed to hold church office.
- **Southern Baptist:** Opposes gay unions and ordination of gay ministers.
- **Unitarian:** Permits same-sex unions and ordination of gay clergy.
- **United Church of Christ:** Policy determined by individual congregations but the denomination has a history of blessing same-sex unions and places no expectation regarding celibacy for gay clergy.
- **United Methodist:** In May 2000, delegates at Convention overwhelmingly approved motions against same-sex unions and for disciplining clergy who perform them.

---

understand that sexual orientation is only an issue when sexuality is expressed in harmful and destructive ways.

The debate about homosexuality in the Christian church revolves around understanding specific Bible verses that appear to condemn homosexual acts. The more conservative church organizations promote a literal interpretation of the scripture and often take the offensive against gay men and lesbians. These literalists can be seen most clearly in the stands taken by the Southern Baptist Convention, which not only publicly states that women must be subservient to men, but also promotes a boycott against the Disney Corporation because it has employment policies that give domestic partner benefits to its gay and lesbian employees, as well as hosts periodic Gay Days at Disney theme parks.

Within more mainline denominations, congregations and individuals speak up and reach out to the gay community. Jack Spong (1988), former Episcopal Bishop of the Diocese of New Jersey, has written about and practices a Christian faith that does not discriminate on the basis of sexual orientation. Controversial within and his denomination, Spong represents the new and more loving understanding of homosexuality within the Christian tradition. Spong has openly ordained gay men and lesbians and promotes their full inclusion in church life. Glaser (1994) provides a more modern look at the Bible and homosexuality, giving gay men and lesbians information that will help them counter the more strict interpreters of Scripture. Helminiak (1994) draws from the research of biblical scholars who see Scripture in a particular context that cannot be interpreted strictly today. Goss (1993) goes so far as to suggest an active role of social protest for gay men and lesbians within religious organizations.

Christian groups are not the only religious organizations encountering this struggle. In the Jewish faith, a similar tension can be seen between the more conservative and liberal congregations. Kahn (1989) reports that both Orthodox and Conservative Jewish thinkers point to specific verses in the Old Testament to justify their belief that the prohibitions against homosexuality are a commandment (mitzvah). The Reform movement within Judaism does not see traditional Jewish law as binding. Much like the more accepting Christian denominations, they see the teachings of the Torah as reflective of historical, social, and scientific understandings of a specific era that is vastly different from contemporary life. Today's world demands a different interpretation and understanding of these ancient "truths." The Reconstructionist movement within Judaism endorses and supports gay men and lesbians and sanctions their relationships. Still, many Jewish gay men and lesbians experience religious organizations that are every bit as conflicted as those that Christians find. Much of the tension rises from a literal versus interpretative reading of Scripture. While admitting that the Torah does contain statements that appear to condemn homosexuality, some Jewish scholars point out that the proscriptions against homosexual contact do not take into consideration homosexual loving relationships. From this perspective, the scriptural admonitions can be seen as warning about exploitative sexual contact. It is this belief that has led the Reform movement in Judaism to formally bless same-sex commitments. When these blessings take place, the most frequent protest is not about condoning homosexuality but against a kind of discrimination that occurs when rabbis refuse to bless unions involving couples where one member is Jewish and the other is not.

Gay Buddhism

One of the attractions of the Buddhist faith is that the practice of meditation reinforces the legitimacy of individual experience. Rather than having an identified leader who describes the nature of spiritual experience, Buddhism is primarily the practice of exploring and discovering individual spiritual reality through meditation and offers an ethical system with an emphasis on suffering. Because Buddhism does not denounce homosexuality (Dynes, 1990), some gay men and lesbians often find in the freedom of meditation an affirmation and expression of their spirituality that grounds them solidly. Behavior is not seen as either good or bad (attributes of a moral system) but more as activity that either relieves or causes suffering. Much like Reform Judaism's interpretation of the Torah's comments about same-sex contact, all sexual behavior is to be seen in terms of its role in creating or lessening suffering (Kolvig, 1995).

In San Francisco, when a Zen center was being consecrated, the gay and lesbian membership was uncertain whether or not to tell the well-known Master that he would be addressing a membership that was predominantly gay and lesbian and finally decided to remain silent. They expected a typical dedication address that would not be challenging; instead, the Master focused on his belief that gay men and lesbians who were not out of the closet were not practicing Zen (Barret & Barzan, 1996).

Of course, Buddhism is not so well established that one would expect to find groups identified with the Gay Buddhist Fellowship in most cities. Followers may have to find retreats and other gatherings of gay men and lesbians who practice Buddhist meditation in order to feel a part of this community. Fortunately, the Internet provides an abundance of information on various opportunities within the Buddhist tradition.

Native American Spiritual Life

Within the Native American culture there is a growing visibility of what has come to be known as the two-spirited people. Like other indigenous cultures, Native Americans have traditionally understood gay men and lesbians as magical people who possess male and female spirits. Two-spirited people are believed to possess special spiritual powers and tend to be honored rather than reviled in their communities. Their gatherings (see Resources at the back of this book) involve traditional Native American spiritual rituals and have become a source of support for Native American gay men and lesbians (Brown, 1997). Their minority sexual status is seen as a gift that enables them to have a special relationship with the spiritual world. A statement on the two-spirit web page shows this opportunity:

> Some of us see things that no one else sees. Some of us hear things that no one else hears. Spirit is at your doorstep! What are the messages? Initiate the dialog with Spirit. Learn the benefits of heartfelt prayer. Notice how energy moves through you, what works and what doesn't. You don't have all the answers, but Spirit can guide you, is guiding you, if you pay attention.

Native American spiritual life as a whole is deeply grounded in nature. Rituals and celebrations bring together people to honor the Great Mother and to renew spiritual connectedness. The role of the two-spirited person in the tribe is often one of leadership in these activities.

Paganism

Some gay and lesbian people turn to pagan gatherings to celebrate their spirituality. Much like Native American practices, paganism is grounded in nature and structured around the cycles of nature. Living in harmony with the natural environment, and opening oneself to the energy fields found in nature, one can find this experience to be very intense and freeing. There is probably more misinformation among the general public than there is understanding about this religious group. Like within other spiritual traditions, there is much diversity within paganism. Wicca is one spiritual group that believes all people should live harmoniously with nature. Witches are part of this tradition but are not always seen as magical creatures. Popular among some lesbians, the goddess culture also traces its roots to pagan practices. Women attracted to the goddess culture honor the power of the feminine and often isolate themselves from the corruptive influences of masculine energy. Similarly, in the gay male culture a group called the Radical Fairies holds celebrations in rural areas, where men can connect with each other without the interference of feminine energy. While certainly less well known, these groups can provide a strong spiritual community, especially to gay men and lesbians who feel rejection and hostility in more traditional religious organizations. Be careful not to view them as worshipers of Satan or as cults. Although less visible than other religious practices, pagan practices have existed in cultures throughout the world, and pagans see themselves as more connected to the natural energy that allows our environment to exist.

SPIRITUALITY AND RELIGION

The general public has a tendency to see religion and spirituality as one and the same. Defining spiritual experiences has become the domain of organized religion despite that many people have daily spiritual awarenesses that are not connected to religious teachings.

A fundamental struggle for gay men and lesbians is to find ways to overcome the clash between homoprejudiced religious institutions that assert their authority and personal spiritual experiences that connect them with a Supreme Being who offers love and acceptance. For many sexual minority clients this struggle begins in adolescence. In most religious groups, adolescents are carefully taught ways to integrate their emerging sexuality into their religious lives. Such nurturing is not available for most gay and lesbian youth. Rather than being encouraged to embrace their sexuality, most gay youth learn to hate and fear rather than celebrate their sexuality. Deprived of assistance from families, schools, and churches in learning how to affirm both themselves and their sexual orientation, and feeling pressure to live up to the family expectations to learn a particular religious orthodoxy, leads many gay youth to compartmentalize their sexual orientation. Outwardly they participate in their religious organizations, yet inwardly they are involved in a sometimes powerful struggle to reconcile their religious beliefs with their emerging sexual identity. Safe in the compartment, some remain unconscious about their gayness; others hope that through prayer or "being good," God will take way this demon. Others completely reject religious institutions and participation in a personal spiritual experience, and some resort to an active search for another, more accepting, religious organization.

Gay and lesbian clients may struggle with renouncing the authority of the church as well as with finding ways to affirm the lessons of inclusive and spiritual connectedness that come from their authentic spiritual experience. Assisting gay men and lesbians to step away from external religious authority may challenge the counselor's own acceptance of religious teachings.

Fortunately, gay men and lesbians frequently have experience in claiming the primacy of their own authority. D'Augelli (1992) pointed out that because they often feel different from other family members, they learn to separate early from the family. As they acknowledge a sexual orientation that may lead to rejection by their families, they have learned to trust their own experiences rather than the dictates of the family. D'Augelli's work suggested that this early emancipation enables gay men and lesbians to become independent as they create their life goals. Others may push themselves to achieve as a way to compensate for what has been labeled a deficit. For counselors, this means that in exploring the spiritual beliefs of gay men and lesbians, an analogy can be made between the clients' need to rely on an internal understanding that leads them to live contrary to their families' wishes and the similar task that can be undertaken with an authoritarian religious organization. Understanding the need for creative resolutions to this dynamic is important. Encouraging gay clients to look beyond the confines of the religious worldviews they may have learned as children is equally important. Celebrating the spiritual aspects of everyday life and pointing out that personal authenticity and adherence to truth are significant spiritual values can be a point of emancipation (Barzan, 1995). Assisting with understanding that an ability to love a person of the same sex is indeed a great spiritual blessing may help gay clients affirm their sexual identity.

Most counselors will benefit from a model that helps them understand the difference between spiritual and religious authority. In separating these two experiences, clients are better able to see that their own life events can be a source of authority. A model that will help clients work through the shame, guilt, and condemnation espoused by many religious groups is essential. The model identified in Figure 8.1 will help clients actively explore a gay-positive spiritual world with a greater internal sense of authenticity and integrity. Understanding that metaphysical experience takes many forms and that what we call spirituality and religiosity may be quite different experiences allows the client to add flexibility to previously rigid positions. Like all people, gay men and lesbians have the same capacity to affirm their own spiritual experiences as more direct and possibly even more valid spiritual experiences that lead them toward Truth.

Religion is one of an almost infinite number of expressions of one's personal and communal spirituality, and Christianity is but one among many world

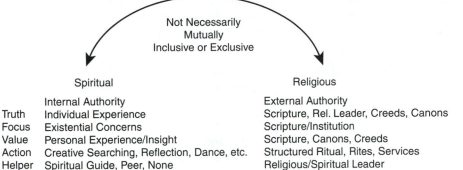

FIGURE **8.1**

Spiritual and religious dichotomy.

religions. Learning about other religious traditions can be helpful. Realizing the meaning that can be found in non-Western traditions like Buddhism, Islam, or primitive traditions, or even dismissing the religious canon entirely, is essential.

PERSPECTIVES WITHIN THE GAY AND LESBIAN CULTURE

It used to be rare to hear gay men and lesbians talk about participating in religious organizations. Today, however, there is a growing awareness of the opportunity to explore both religious and spiritual questions in established religious organizations (O'Neill & Ritter, 1992). Also, social conversations are much more apt to include references to religious activities. Lee & Busto (1991) collated the results of a survey printed in a national magazine read largely by gay men and lesbians. From the 648 responses, 83% reported being raised in the Christian tradition, 11% identified as Jewish, and the remaining 6% had no particular religious instruction during their childhood. By 1990, most respondents reported not participating in their family's religious organizations. Forty-six of these subjects continued to maintain an affiliation (Protestant, 22%; Jewish, 6%; gay Christian, 12%; Eastern faiths, 4%), with the largest group (28%) naming their religious affiliation as a 12-step recovery program. Over 33% of the participants in this survey reported that they did not belong to any religious or spiritual community; over 84% stated that spirituality was very or somewhat important. Only 52% saw religion as similarly important. These results parallel those reported by a 1988 Gallup poll and a similar survey conducted by the *San Francisco Chronicle* (Ritter & Terndrup, 2002). While these data may be out-of-date now, they do reflect a level of disaffiliation with religious life within the gay community.

The reasons that some gay men and lesbians give for abandoning all spiritual activity are varied. Many report that during their adolescence and young adulthood they were very active in religious life. They talk about how devout they tried to be, and the alienation and sense of aloneness that evolved as they realized that a higher power was not going to take away their homosexuality. Because of the intensity of their suffering and the acute judgment they continue to witness in most mainline religious organizations, they conclude that trusting any spiritual or religious teaching will just lead to more suffering.

Challenges in Claiming Spiritual Life

The primary challenge that gay men and lesbians face in embracing their spirituality is to give up the worry of condemnation that comes so loudly from the religious organizations that do not accept them. Given the positive potential of living out (Chapter 2), counselors may find themselves in the role of consciousness-raising around some of the issues that emerge from participation in traditional religious organizations. For example, as gay men and lesbians seek accommodation with traditional religious organizations, they are likely to find a mixed welcome. Some organizations embrace and warmly welcome them. Others will tolerate them but encourage them to be quiet about their sexuality. There are few that seem to genuinely understand how oppressive the experience is for people to participate in religious activities that continue to marginalize them. During religious services the frequency of baptisms, bar/bat mitzvahs, and even weddings reminds gay and lesbian members of their differences. There are few moments that honor, much less acknowledge, their relationships. Some religious groups even bless their members' pets and homes but still refuse to provide community support for gay and lesbian relationships. Many hide behind the fact that they cannot bless these relationships because they are illegal. Although coming out of a loving tradition, most of these organizations fail to recognize an opportunity to creatively bless nontraditional relationships. When this issue is not addressed, gay men and lesbians once again must find ways to a kind of faith that recognizes the failure of the organization to properly reflect the teachings on which it is based (McNeill, 1995).

Some gay and lesbian clients will undoubtedly project onto their religious organizations their own internal shame. Helping them begin to see that the real problem lies within is a step for them toward opening more fully to the idea of religious or spiritual practice. Some totally reject religious life and hold on to a bitterness and cynicism that will come up in counseling sessions. Others choose nontraditional beliefs and practices, such as Wicca and other nature-based connections to the spiritual world. An increasing number continue to participate in organizations that outwardly reject them but appear to be tolerant and "welcoming."

The Emergence of Literature on Gay and Lesbian Spirituality

There is a growing body of literature that reflects the level of discussion about gay and lesbian spirituality. This literature unfortunately does not come from well-designed research studies. As is true with research on homosexuality in general, research into the spiritual lives of gay men and lesbians is scarce. However, various authors are beginning to provide books that allow the reader to understand the complex issues that surround this topic. While not at all exhaustive, mentioning a few of them will provide a sense of the topics being discussed.

As early as 1984, Catholic theologian Matthew Fox outlined a four-step process of spiritual development for gay men and lesbians: (1) creation, in which the gay self is truly embraced; (2) letting go, in which the pain of rejection is acknowledged and released; (3) creativity, which leads to the rebirth of the soul; and (4) transformation, in which the individual extends compassion and a sense of celebration to others. These steps mirror the coming out process but employ a different language. Gay men and lesbians who participate in religious communities display similar needs as their nongay peers: a sense of something greater than self, a sense of community, answers to universal questions, and moral guidance (Perlstein, 1996). In the early 1990s, Thompson (1994), a gay man living with AIDS, interviewed 16 gay men, writers or thinkers like James Broughton, Clyde Hall, Ram Dass, Malcolm Boyd, and Robert Hopcke, who have contributed to the understanding of gay spirituality. This book, *Gay Soul*, recounts these interviews and provides insight into their thoughts on one specific question: What is gay soul and how might it be expressed? Later, Thompson (1997) describes the development of gay identity through spiritual reflection. Peter Gomes (1996), former minister at Harvard Memorial Church in Boston, outlines a way to read the Bible that shows the way understanding scripture has changed over the years, with particular emphasis on the issue of homosexuality. White (1995), a former colleague of Jerry Falwell and Pat Robertson, tells his coming out story against the backdrop of the fundamentalist Christian movement. Glaser (1998) encourages gay men and lesbians to affirm the deeply spiritual experience of gaining integrity and wholeness through coming out. Along those same lines, McNeill (1995) urges gay men and lesbians to celebrate their sexuality as a gift from God. Wann (1999) details various ways that congregations can affirm their gay and lesbian members. Ferry (1994) describes his experience as a gay minister and offers insights from within the church. Scanzoni & Mollenkott (1994) raise the issue of the appropriate Christian response to gay and lesbian neighbors. Books like these serve as beacons to gay and lesbian people who are seeking a greater spiritual life. They also help inform the debate for religious organizations and homosexuality.

Tips for Practitioners

When you work with gay and lesbian clients in the area of spirituality, you need to be aware of the possibility that your own faith may be challenged. Just as Pat in the case at the beginning of this chapter became troubled, sometimes the inhumanity of religious organizations will generate discomfort in you as well as in the client. Learning about nontraditional religious experiences, such as Wicca and Buddhism, will help you be a stronger resource for clients who choose that path to spiritual life. Just as in working with clients who are coming out, you may know more about spiritual and religious resources than your clients and may need to step into a role that resembles that of a case manager. The following suggestions are offered as guidelines as you begin to access this important part of all clients' lives.

Keep an Open Mind or Open a Closed One Most counselors probably have little information about paganism, Buddhism, or New Age religions. Some may have been taught that such spiritual expressions are inappropriate or even sinful. Few, however, have had an opportunity to examine the origins of these practices or to understand their place in the larger scheme of metaphysical experience. The Internet offers virtually unlimited resources for those who want to learn. Suspending (at least for a while) your judgmental attitude about some of these practices is an important first step. To be effective, you must develop a tolerance for ambiguity and not press too quickly for resolution. Attempts to "save" or even encourage clients to become active in religious or spiritual life are clearly inappropriate, but could happen subconsciously. You must be very alert to subtle signals that promote your own values. Clients may be quick to identify counselors who struggle to honor an individual who talks about participating in a pagan solstice event. When such internal conflict is present, effective counseling is probably not going to take place. Letting the client know that this material is new to you and seeking further clarification may lead to increased understanding. If, after reflection, you realize that there is simply too much clash in values for you to be of help, refer the client to a counselor who is more able and experienced to explore this area of the client's life.

Understand the Wounds Left From Religious Rejection A central issue in the lives of gay men and lesbians is to resolve the conflict between mostly negative religious instruction about homosexuality and their own experience

(Ritter & O'Neill, 1989). Encouraging clients to tell you about their suffering in organized religion may enable you to provide a healing environment. Be particularly cautious in referring gay and lesbian clients to religious leaders who may simply draw more blood from the wound as they negatively judge homosexuality. Imagine how you might feel if your religious tradition condemned you for an aspect of your being you were not able to change (i.e., your gender or handedness). Develop empathy for the hurt such rejection may cause and for the sense of fear at the idea of exploring spiritual life.

Be Aware of the Connection Between Spirituality and Eroticism

Some gay and lesbian clients may speak about the intense spiritual energy they experience in sex (Connor, 1993). The discussion about the links between spirituality and eroticism is not limited to gays and lesbians and can be seen throughout the professional and popular literature. There are structured experiences, such as the one offered by The Body Electric, an organization in Oakland, California, that provide training for gay men who want to explore this connection. Learn about other resources that may be available in your area, and be aware of the possibility that accessing the spiritual world through eroticism may be a valuable path for gay men and lesbians who have rejected the traditional church.

Offer to Meet With Family Members

There are times when a joint meeting with family members who are also struggling with these issues can be helpful. One client asked for a joint meeting after her parents refused to have her partner join the family for Christmas celebrations. Because the extended family had the tradition of attending religious services, they had told Dolly not to bring her partner, Wendy. Dolly's mother had said, "We can't possibly go to church and have Wendy with us. How would we explain her presence to our friends? No, she is not invited." Even after a joint session, Dolly's parents were adamant, but she felt supported by the counselor when she told her parents that she would not be present at this family event and that in the future she would attend only those family functions that included Wendy. Joint sessions will not always resolve the issue but can provide important opportunities for you to observe the client in the family context, as well as for the client to feel additional support.

Be Attentive for Potential Client Projections

Often clients will talk about their family's or church's rejection in the context of religious issues although the problem may be that at deeper levels, they are struggling with their own self-condemnation and rejection. A tip to this situation can be seen when clients repeatedly focus on the family's or church's rejection and seem unable to move on. Encouraging your client to explore his or her "stuckness" on an internal level can bring up deeply held but unconscious self-condemnation. Questions that explore the client's beliefs about God (or a higher power) can cause the internal struggle to surface. "You believe that you were created by God. Do you also believe that he made you gay? Would he have done this to punish you? How do you reconcile your own belief in a loving God with the rejection from your church? Do you think this is the way God wants you to be treated?" Perhaps when these attitudes are examined in a supportive atmosphere, the client can move on.

Find Supportive Resources in Your Community   Getting to know the local religious leaders who understand the pain created from condemnation and rejection by religious organizations can be very valuable. Asking gay and lesbian clients to give you names of supportive ministers, priests, and rabbis is just the first step. Make an appointment with these persons, and ask them how they would respond to a gay or lesbian client. In one instance a counselor thought she had found a valuable resource until she asked how the priest would welcome gay men and lesbians to services. "I'm just not able to make references to gays in sermons. A friend in another parish started doing that and pretty soon the gays had taken over the 11 A.M. mass. I would not want that to happen here. But, if they want to come I will not turn them away." This man might not be helpful to someone who is seeking acceptance in a safe spiritual community. Another counselor reported that he knew the Methodist Church would condemn him. When that counselor referred him to a minister who had gay men and lesbians in leadership in her congregation and publicly introduced gay couples who joined the congregation, the client was astounded. Knowing where to refer clients for spiritual and religious activities and being able to recommend books to clients who are not ready to come out in religious organizations are often extremely helpful.

Be Aware That Some Clients Who Are Religious/Spiritual Leaders May Be Wondering About Their Sexual Orientation   What if Anthony in the case at the beginning of the chapter had come in just to talk about changing careers? If he had not brought up the fact that he was gay, what might be clues that he really wanted to explore that aspect of his life but was afraid to trust that the counselor would be understanding? Often clients who are afraid to bring up their sexual orientation mask that anxiety in statements like "I just don't fit in" or "I am so different" or "I am tired of people asking me why I don't date." Review the suggestions made in Chapters 1 and 2 about ways you can sensitively explore sexual orientation, and see how they will apply to the area of spiritual/religious concerns.

Become an Activist   In the area of advocacy there is no better place for you to become an ally for gay and lesbian clients than in the religious/spiritual domain. Volunteer to speak to religious groups, or write op-ed pieces for your local newspaper. Articulate how your own understanding of gay men and lesbians has changed as you have got to know them. Become an advocate for including homosexuality in religious instruction. Write about your clinical experiences in professional journals. The opportunities are unlimited, and the chances of making a significant difference are great.

BIBLIOGRAPHY

Abraham, K. (1993). *Stand up and fight back: A young person's guide to spiritual warfare.* Ann Arbor, MI: Servant Publications.

Barret, B. & Barzan, B. (1996, October). Spiritual experiences of gay men and lesbians. *Counseling and Values, 41,* 4–14.

Barzan, R. (1995). *Sex and spirit: Exploring gay men's spirituality.* San Francisco: White Crane Press.

Brown, L. B. (1997). *Two-spirit people: American Indian lesbian women and gay men.* Binghamton, NY: Herrington Park Press.

Cherry, K. & Sherwood, Z. (Eds.). (1995). *Equal rites: Lesbian and gay worship, ceremonies, and celebrations.* Louisville, KY: Westminster/John Knox Press.

Connor, R. P. (1993). *Blossom of bone: Reclaiming the connection between homoeroticism and the sacred.* San Francisco: Harper.

D'Augelli, A. R. (1992). Teaching lesbian and gay development: From oppression to exceptionality. *Journal of Homosexuality, 22*(3/4), 213–227.

Dynes, W. (1990). *Encyclopedia of homosexuality.* New York: Garland.

Ferry, J. (1994). *In the courts of the Lord: A gay minister's story.* New York: Crossroads.

Fox, M. (1984). The spiritual journey of the homosexual . . . and just about everyone else. In R. Nugent (Ed.), *A challenge to love: Gay and lesbian Catholics in the church.* New York: Crossroads.

Glaser, C. (1994). *The word is out: The Bible reclaimed for lesbians and gay men.* San Francisco: Harper.

———.(1998). *Coming out as a sacrament.* New York: Geneva Press.

Gomes, P. (1996). *The good book: Reading the Bible with mind and heart.* New York: Avon Books.

Goss, R. (1993). *Jesus acted up: A gay and lesbian manifesto.* New York: HarperCollins.

Helminiak, D. (1994). *What the Bible really says about homosexuality: Recent findings by top scholars offer a radical view.* San Francisco: Alamo Square Press.

Kahn, Y. (1989). Judaism and homosexuality: The traditionalist/progressive debate. *Journal of Homosexuality, 18*(3–4), 47–82.

Kolvig, E. (1995, October). A talk on gay spirituality and the dharma. *San Francisco Gay Buddhist Fellowship Newsletter,* 4–7.

Lee, K. & Busto, G. (1991, Fall). When the spirit moves us. *OUT/LOOK, 14,* 83–85.

McNeill, J. J. (1995). *Freedom, glorious freedom: The spiritual journey to the fullness of life for gays, lesbians, and everybody else.* Boston: Beacon Press.

O'Neill, C. & Ritter, K. (1992). *Coming out within: Stages of spiritual awakening for lesbians and gay men.* San Francisco: Harper.

Perlstein, M. (1996). Integrating a gay, lesbian, or bisexual person's religious and spiritual needs and choices into psychotherapy. In C. Alexander (Ed.), *Gay and lesbian mental health: A sourcebook for practitioners.* New York: Harrington Park Press/Haworth Press.

Ritter, K. & O'Neill, C. (1989). Moving through loss: The spiritual journey of gay men and lesbian women. *Journal of Counseling and Development, 68*(1), 9–15.

Ritter, K. & Terndrup, A. (2002). *Foundations for affirmative psychotherapy with lesbians and gay men: A mirroring perspective.* New York: Guilford Press.

Scanzoni, M. & Mollenkott, V. (1994). *Is the homosexual my neighbor? A positive Christian response.* San Francisco: Harper.

Spong, J. (1988). *Living in sin?* New York: Harper & Row.

Thompson, M. (1994). *Gay soul: Finding the heart of gay spirit and nature.* San Francisco: Harper.

———.(1997). *Gay body: A journey through shadow to self.* New York: St. Martin's Press.

Wann, M. C. (1999). *More than welcome: Learning to embrace gay, lesbian, bisexual, and transgendered persons in the church.* St. Louis, MO: Chalice Press.

White, M. (1995). *Stranger at the gate: To be gay and Christian in America.* New York: Simon & Schuster.

GAY AND LESBIAN PARENTING

The Case of Ken

Ken has been in private practice as an LPC for the past ten years in a medium-sized Midwestern city. During this time he has seen his clientele develop from exclusively adolescents to a majority of adults with an emphasis on relationship counseling. In the past two or three years he has had a number of men and women come in for counseling on issues relating to their sexual orientation and relationships. Generally, he is comfortable working with gay men and lesbians, but occasionally an issue comes up that creates confusion for him. When Jessie and Elise, former clients, came in to discuss becoming parents, he struggled with his own beliefs about marriage and parenting. He obtained the following history from them in the initial sessions.

Jessie and her partner, Elise, both 33, had talked about having children for several years. They had postponed the decision because there seemed to be so many issues to consider. How would their child deal with the many challenges that come with having lesbian parents? Who would get pregnant, and how would this happen? Were their careers stable enough to allow them to parent successfully? What kind of support might they get from their extended family? How would they manage the emergencies that would surely arise? How would having a child impact their relationship? Did they want to co-parent with a gay couple? If so, how might their parenting experience be enriched or complicated? They began to realize that they would never be able to anticipate all of the questions, and that in many ways staying so focused on these questions was just delaying the decision. After all, most straight couples don't seem to be concerned with finding the "right" answers to questions like these. Jessie and Elise had been together for eight years and considered themselves committed and ready. They wanted their child to have

163

a father as well as two mothers and decided to explore co-parenting with a gay couple they knew well.

Henry and Marcus, in their mid-thirties, had talked about having children since they had gotten together six years ago. They had considered ways of becoming parents and had decided they wanted to co-parent with a lesbian couple. They met Jessie and Elise at their church, and the two couples had become great friends, going on vacations together and even getting to know each other's extended families. They were enthusiastic when Jessie and Elise approached them with the idea of sharing a child.

The two couples spent a lot of time together discussing the possibility of co-parenting. They knew a lot about each other's values and goals and felt comfortable that they would be able to provide a consistent environment for their baby. After consultation with a physician, they decided that Jessie and Marcus would be the natural parents of the baby to be conceived through artificial insemination. They spoke with the minister at their church about their plan, met with an attorney to understand the legal issues, and wanted Ken's help in making the final decision.

As Ken listened to them, he became unsure that he was going to be able to help. He had no trouble with gay persons who had had children in heterosexual marriages but found himself struggling to accept supporting these two couples. Listening to them was difficult because he was not sure if it was "right" for gay people to have children. He worried about the child and what responsibility he would have if the two relationships fell apart. The questions seemed complicated, and the possibility that the child might grow up bewildered by such an alternative family troubled him. He found himself wondering what would happen to the child if both the relationships deteriorated or if the two couples found themselves fighting over parenting decisions. However, he respected both of the couples and believed they would be effective parents. He wondered if he needed to refer them to someone who would be more comfortable working with them, and he told them this was the first time he had been consulted by gay persons who wanted to co-parent. He asked them to consider what they might do if the issues that worried him did come up. He saw that they were uneasy with his hesitation and said that he would do some research before their next meeting.

Ken consulted with a colleague who worked with many gay and lesbian couples and even attended a gay parenting meeting before he felt he could separate his own issues from the ones that the two couples were presenting. He went to a library to see what he might find about gay parenting, but there was not much there. When he searched the Internet, he was amazed at the number of sites that carried information for gay and lesbian parents. He began to see that these two couples were not as "extreme" as he had imagined, and he made note of some of the resources that all of them might use. As he challenged his own biases, he began to understand that gay men and lesbians have as good a chance to be effective parents as other people, and he was reassured that both his profession and the court system were beginning to address such parenting rights.

When they came for the next session, Ken felt prepared. As he listened to them discuss the issues they had identified, he encouraged them to move slowly, to explore their thoughts and feelings in depth, and to find even more trust between them. Since the four prospective parents knew each other well, they had a strong base of effective communication in place. What the counseling did was help them hear each other at deeper levels. At Ken's suggestion, they worked hard to get the support of their extended families. All of them became discouraged when three of the four sets of parents voiced disapproval. Marcus's parents were the only ones who seemed excited at the prospect of a grandchild, and they indicated that they would consider moving so they could provide support and watch their grandchild grow up. It was not possible to have complete answers to all of the questions that arose, but over time, it became clear that these young people had created a strong relationship and that they were ready to become parents. Having a relationship with a counselor they trusted also reassured them that when there were future difficulties, they had someone available who understood what they were trying to do and who could help them out.

Within two months, Jessie became pregnant through artificial insemination. The two couples shared the pregnancy and also met other gay and lesbian couples with children. They attended childbirth classes together and began to structure their lives to include the responsibilities of parenting. They told their co-workers and friends what was about to happen and developed closer relationships with other gay and lesbian couples that had children. When Cathy was born, there were grandparents, aunts, uncles, and a crowd of friends who celebrated with them. Those early days were challenging, of course, as each person began to understand his and her role in the "family" they had created. One parent was always available in an emergency, and the couples were able to be with Cathy, together as well as individually. They adored their daughter and were doing the best they could to be effective parents.

Myths About Gay and Lesbian Parenting

Most counselors have not worked with gay and lesbian couples that want to become parents. Many would find themselves, like Ken, struggling to understand and accept this kind of family. The most frequently cited unsettling issues pertain to the two myths that surround parenting by sexual minorities: Children who grow up with gay or lesbian parents are likely to become gay or lesbian, and children in gay or lesbian households are more likely to be sexually abused than those in nongay families. These myths are generally promoted by conservative religious groups who see the gay parenting movement as an attempt to "recruit" children into the "homosexual lifestyle." Unfortunately, the general public lacks access to the data that would enable them to refute these kinds of claims. We will look at each of these myths and the data related to them.

Sexual Orientation and Child Abuse

The research on the sexual orientation of the children of gay and lesbian parents suggests that their sexual orientation is not influenced by that of their parents. Bailey et al. (1995) analyzed the data from questionnaires received from 82 sons of 55 gay fathers. Of the 75 sons whose sexual orientation could be reliably determined, 68 stated they were heterosexual, and 7 identified as either gay or bisexual. The sexual identity of these sons did not appear to have been related to the number of years spent living in the gay father's home, the frequency of contact with the gay father, or the quality of the father–son relationship. There has been no reliable research suggesting that living with gay or lesbian parents has any influence on sexual orientation. The percentage of children from gay families who turn out to be gay is similar to that of the children who grow up in nongay families. This fact seems logical when one considers that most gay and lesbian adults report growing up in heterosexual families.

Similarly, there is no evidence that children who have gay or lesbian parents are any more likely to be sexually abused than children with heterosexual parents (Geiser, 1979; Richardson, 1981). The data on child sexual abuse and incest is clear: Over 99% of the adults who sexually abuse children identify as heterosexual. Children face no special risk of sexual abuse from having gay and lesbian parents.

This is not to suggest that there are not unique challenges facing children from these families. Any child who grows up in an oppressive environment is going to have to develop effective coping strategies. Learning whom to tell and how to manage the potential harassment that might follow is one of the tasks that gay and lesbian parents report to be most challenging.

Attitudes toward gay and lesbian parents are changing. In virtually all major cities in the United States, gay and lesbian parent groups meet regularly. They create play groups for their children and even plan vacations with other gay parents so their children will not be too isolated. As gay couples form relationships, it is no longer rare to hear them discuss the issue of parenting. The legal system has begun to understand the needs of gay parents, and social institutions that provide services to children are recognizing that gay parents are more visible than in the past. The emerging family within gay and lesbian communities is supported by research studies that indicate these families are successful (Patterson, 1992). Even though gay parenting has been a research topic for over 20 years, the sample sizes continue to be small and most of the findings are based on self-reports (Bell & Weinberg, 1978; Flowers, Barret, & Robinson, 2000).

PATHWAYS TO PARENTING

No one knows how many gay and lesbian parents there are. Estimates of the gay population vary between 4 and 10% of the general population, with the more contemporary figure placed at about 5% (Gagnon et al., 1994). The idea of two men or two women becoming parents used to be revolutionary. Today, the estimates of the number of children living with gay and lesbian parents range from 6 to 14 million (Editors of the Harvard Law Review, 1990; Patterson & Chan, 1996). As this number grows, it is evident that schools and other social institutions will need to consider ways to support gay and lesbian families.

The reasons that gay men and lesbians give for becoming parents are diverse (Patterson, 1994; Patterson & Chan, 1996; Barret & Robinson, 2000). Many gay men and lesbians recognize the rich experience that parenthood offers. Some see the opportunity of sharing their homes and lives with children who might otherwise remain in the foster-parent system. Others simply want to enrich their lives and relationships by involvement with parenting.

Most gay men and lesbians who are parents had their children while living in heterosexual marriages. Some who are gay or lesbian remain married and make an agreement with their spouses to keep their same-sex behavior closeted (Gochros, 1989). Others become parents through adoption or even serve as foster parents and then later adopt once they and the social agencies involved see that the children are well adjusted. Lesbians may become pregnant by donor insemination. Businesses exist that provide sperm for a fee, and there are men like Marcus and Henry who are willing to donate sperm. Some gay men may co-parent with a lesbian couple or locate an egg donor and surrogate mother who carries the baby to term. The latest approach being used by lesbians is called co-maternity. One partner donates an egg that is inseminated and then implanted in the uterus of the other, making one partner the genetic mother and the other the biological mother. Each of these paths involves significant legal hurdles that often create extreme stress for gay parents. Following is a discussion of some of these issues.

Legal Issues

When Jessie and Elise decided to co-parent with Henry and Marcus, they located an attorney who drew up legal documents that protected their joint rights to parenting. However, they live in a state where second-parent adoption by unmarried persons is not allowed. Therefore, Marcus and Jessie were the legal parents whose rights would be protected by law. A recent case in Florida highlights one of the potential problems (Grace, 1999).

Pam Query and Penny Kazmierazak became parents after Pam was artificially inseminated. Together they raised their daughter, Zoey. Four years later their relationship had deteriorated, and they agreed to go their separate ways. They went to court when Pam decided that Penny could no longer have contact with Zoey. Because they live in Florida, a state that does not allow second-parent adoptions, it is possible that Penny may have to give up the daughter she has come to love. The lower court in Florida ruled that Pam is Zoey's sole legal parent, and the case has gone before the appeals court. Cases like this one are no longer rare, just as it is not unusual for judges in child custody cases to have to make rulings about custody and visitation rights between former spouses.

A case in North Carolina illustrates the difficulty gay parents face in the court system. Kirk Smith and his partner, Tim Tipton, parented Kirk's two sons after his wife moved to Oklahoma with her boyfriend. The boys did well in school and seemed well adjusted to their unique family. Four years later, Kirk's wife sued for primary custody on the basis that the boys were being negatively impacted from living with two gay men. Now married to her former boyfriend, Kirk's wife determined that she could provide a more proper home environment for her sons. The case moved slowly through the legal system with rulings favoring both sides before it was heard by the North Carolina Supreme Court. The final ruling gave custody to the boys' mother. The primary justification was that the boys were living with a couple who were not legally married and that they sometimes witnessed the two men kissing as they greeted each other and sharing other intimacies. The lone dissenting judge, Justice John Webb, stated in his opposing opinion, "There is virtually no evidence showing these acts by the defendants have adversely affected the children. The test should be how the action affects the children and not whether or not we approve of it. . . . I do not believe that we should allow a change of custody on evidence that shows only that the defendant is a practicing homosexual" (LLDEF, 1998).

A particular issue that once-married gay parents have to resolve is how open to be about their sexual orientation. If their former spouses use homosexuality as a basis to sue for sole custody, contact with their children may be limited or forbidden. Any action that might cause the question of custody to come before the courts can evoke extreme anxiety. Informing their lawyers about their sexual orientation is a necessary first step. Seeing a counselor to work through their feelings about the possible loss of custody may also be useful. Janice came for counseling because she wanted her children to spend an extended time with her and her partner, Maureen. She had told her former husband when Maureen moved in with her, and the relationship between the parents seemed supportive and solid. Still, Janice worried that simply raising the question might bring up her ex-husband's unresolved anger and that the courts probably would not be sympathetic to her desire to bring her three children into her home for the summer months. Many gay fathers choose not to rock the boat for fear of having custody rights curtailed. Mark told us:

> I get along very well with my ex-wife. We have joint custody of Jace, and she did not seem at all upset when Bill and I moved in together. We have not had any discussion with Jace about our relationship. He sees that Bill and I sleep together and act like a couple but so far has not asked any questions. Jace stays with us almost half the time, and his mother, who is a physician and recently married a physician, makes more money than I do. I am paying an enormous amount of child support and know this is not fair. Still, I am afraid to go to court to have the support reduced. If I do that, I could end up seeing my son less than I do now. The easiest thing to do is to not rock the boat. I understand that Bill resents the money I am paying out, and I hope he will come to understand why I am afraid to bring this issue before the courts.

Although the legal system has not been totally supportive of gay parenting, there are a growing number of cases where gay men and women have been awarded at least partial custody. Until very recently, most state courts used the "nexus test" to determine custody disputes. Under nexus approaches the spotlight is on making a decision that is in the child's best interest. Many communities have created agencies that investigate the parenting situation and make recommendations to the courts. These children's law centers often are well briefed on gay parenting and can be powerful allies in courts. Still, the risk that these parents encounter in the legal system is enormous and is likely to remain so until politicians, legislators, and judges develop a clearer understanding about the ability of sexual minorities to perform successfully as parents. Most state courts continue to base their decisions in cases involving gay parents on negative stereotypes (McIntyre, 1994). All too often, judges and others in the legal system are not willing to examine their own prejudices and continue to make decisions that do not include an examination of the potential contributions gay men and lesbians can have as parents. Change appears to be coming slowly, and it is difficult to predict whether we are close to the time when the court system will treat gay parents more fairly. For that to happen, we will need more knowledge gained from research on gay parenting.

IMPACT OF GAY AND LESBIAN PARENTING ON CHILD DEVELOPMENT

One of the stereotypes of gay and lesbian people is that they are not interested in forming families that include children (Sanders, 1999). Even people who do know that gay men and lesbians are often parents tend to characterize their children as victims. One gay father spoke of his mother's comments about his college friend who was an openly gay father: "It really bugs me the way my mom goes on and on about Bob and his children. She thinks he is a good guy, but she will tell me and others, 'Those poor children having to live with a gay father.' That's just her homoprejudiced attitude showing through." The research on gay parenting has consistently shown that children with gay and lesbian parents are just like other children. Some do very well in school, some are fine athletes, some have trouble, and some are just average kids.

Tasker & Golombok (1997) conducted a longitudinal study that investigated the impact of lesbian mothers on their children's development. Beginning in 1976, they interviewed 39 children of 27 lesbian mothers and compared them with 39 children of 27 heterosexually identified women. Fifteen years later, they contacted 51 of the 54 mothers and were able to interview 46 of the 78 children in their original study. In terms of gender identity, gender role, sexual orientation, emotional development and sexual development, the children raised by lesbian mothers did not differ from those who grew up in heterosexual households. These adult children were no more likely to have utilized mental-health services nor did they report higher levels of anxiety or depression. Perhaps most interesting, while both groups of children reported having been teased when they were children, they did not report significantly different levels of teasing. The results from this study parallel those reported in other research on the children of gay and lesbian parents (Herek, 1991; Patterson, 1992).

Since most of the children of gay and lesbian parents were born in heterosexual marriages, studies of their emotional development must take into consideration that they have also been through the trauma of divorce. Studies that investigate this dimension of gay parenting also report no significant difference (Huggins, 1989). To summarize, the research on the children of gay and lesbian parents consistently shows the following:

- Most of the problems that the children of gay and lesbian parents report is connected to the disruption caused by divorce rather than by their parents' sexual orientation.
- Having been exposed to a broader range of diverse people, children of gay and lesbian parents are more open-minded and accepting of diversity than children raised by heterosexuals.

- Daughters of lesbian mothers have higher self-esteem; sons of gay fathers are more comfortable expressing caring and are less aggressive than girls and boys in heterosexual families.
- The preponderance of evidence suggests that children who grow up with gay or lesbian parents have similar psychological and physical profiles as those of children who have nongay parents.
- Gay and lesbian children who have gay or lesbian parents mature with significantly higher levels of parental support than gay and lesbian children in nongay households (Barret & Robinson, 2000).

Just like heterosexual parents, gay parents do not all use one parenting style (Patterson, 1994). Raising children in social environments that make negative judgments about gay parents means that these parents must make special efforts to help their children understand the potential for negative and discriminatory attitudes they may face. At this time there is no evidence that this teasing creates a significant problem for these children.

Issues of Gay and Lesbian Parenting

While the children of gay and lesbian parents do not differ significantly from children who have heterosexual parents, gay parents face several unique issues. Some gay parents report a lack of support within their own community when it comes to parenting. Coming out to their children is a topic that sexual minority parents often discuss with friends as well as counselors. Helping their children learn how to face oppressive and discriminatory aspects of the outside world is fundamental for effective parenting. Discovering ways to expose their children to other children who have gay parents makes up another parenting task. The following examines the ways that counselors can be of assistance with each of these issues.

Rejection Within the Gay Community

An unexpected issue that many gay and lesbian parents report is the rejection that can come from within their own community. Many gay and lesbian people totally reject the idea of family as promoted by heterosexuals. Some of these people believe that having children is a means for some gays and lesbians to "normalize" their lives. Adherents of this belief encourage gay and lesbian men and women to explore more fully what is unique about being a sexual minority (i.e., developing a meaningful life that does not include parenting) rather than re-create a heterosexual institution in the gay community. Some gay men and lesbians are uncomfortable around children, perhaps reacting to a fear of being seen as child molesters, and avoid any contact with young people.

Forming parenting groups is one way to lessen this potential isolation. Creating play groups where all of the children have gay or lesbian parents is another useful idea. Educating the gay and lesbian community about the experience of parenting or finding allies in church and other organizations assists gay parents in reducing isolation.

Coming Out

One of the most frequently mentioned concerns of gay parents is when and how to come out to their children (Barret & Robinson, 2000). Helping children understand homosexuality when they live in social environments that are not supportive is difficult, even when parents are not gay. For gay men and lesbians this is an emotionally laden task that brings up anxieties, such as fear of rejection by children and fear of hurting their children's self-esteem, along with the awareness that the relationship will be different and in many ways more complicated. One mother talked about this in counseling:

> It was only after my husband died that I felt like I could act on my sexual feelings toward women. My kids were grown and married so I had the freedom to explore without worrying about being caught. It did not take long for me to realize that I was a lesbian and that I wanted a relationship with a woman. I worried a lot about how my children and grandchildren would react and decided not to tell them until I had to. When I fell in love with Susan, I had the hardest time not sharing this joy with them. They asked me several times what was going on for they could tell I was happier. When Susan and I decided to move in together, I went to a counselor to figure out how to resolve the conflict I was feeling. I was afraid I was going to hurt my children and that they would not let me see my grandchildren any longer. And I was afraid that I was not honoring Susan or our relationship if I created a situation where we pretended we were just roommates. I wanted to tell the truth, but I also did not want to hurt the people I loved the most. What a dilemma! The counselor helped me to see that I could tell the kids and just let them be wherever they might be with this issue. Together we figured out a respectful way to let them know and gave them sufficient time to adjust to this change in me. It was not easy, and for a while I was afraid I had lost my son. He was angry and upset, but I just kept on telling him I loved him and that I could understand his distress for I had also been upset in realizing I was a lesbian. Three years later Susan and I are living together and my whole family has embraced both of us. What a miracle!

There are no definite rules about coming out to children. Common sense tells us that modeling honesty is a fundamental task for all parents, and that is certainly true for gay and lesbian parents. Some gay men and lesbians delay coming out because they are afraid of legal entanglements that could lead to loss of their children (Bozett, 1980, 1981, 1989; Spada, 1979). As a result, some parents keep this information confidential and work to hide their relationships. Others, especially those who became parents after identifying as gay or lesbian, see their sexual orientation as an essential ingredient of their parenting and sort through their options before having children. They like being gay or lesbian and want to help their children use this understanding to become more aware of the valuable contributions that people who are different make to our communities. Box 9.1 has some useful suggestions that can be used with clients considering coming out.

Dealing With the Outside World

As identified in Box 9.1, helping their children face potential discrimination from the outside world is a basic task for gay and lesbian parents. One of the most frequently mentioned concerns expressed by gay parents of young children is how much information to give them. Eventually others will ask questions about their home environments, and children need to learn ways to face possible rejection or taunting. This leads many gay parents to hold off speaking about their sexual orientation until the children are old enough to understand their parents and the outside world. In Box 9.2, read how Callie, the daughter of a gay father, handles situations like these.

Tips for Practitioners

In the future it will not be uncommon for counselors to encounter gay and lesbian clients who are parents or want to explore ways to become parents. Counselors are in a unique position to validate the creative and responsible contributions gay men and lesbians can make in their parenting roles (Shordone, 1993). As mentioned in Chapter 1, the primary issue to confront is the counselor's own discomfort with the notion that gay persons can be effective parents. Examining deeply held but often unconscious prejudices is the first step in providing sound counseling services. Beyond that, there is an abundance of information available that can assist counselors and gay parents be more effective in this aspect of life. The skills that are used in helping gay parents make decisions about their children are basically similar to those that would be used with heterosexual parents. Counselors who know some of the unique challenges faced by gay and lesbian parents can be instrumental in providing stability and assistance to these families. The ideas that follow are offered to give direction and to stimulate thinking about actions counselors can take.

Get Up-to-Date Information   Finding up-to-date information on the legal issues affecting gay and lesbian parents can be challenging, especially since the law changes quickly. In most urban communities there will be attorneys who are able to give you sound advice. The LLDEF, a gay-supported organization that provides legal assistance where the question of sexual orientation is before the courts, is another resource that can provide information.

**BOX
9.1**

Coming Out to Children

There is no one way to come out to children. The following suggestions have been adapted from a similar list for gay fathers published by Bigner & Bozett (1990). Use this list to help clients who are considering coming out explore some of the important issues.

- Come to terms with your own gayness before disclosing to children. This is critical. The gay parent who feels negative about his/her homosexuality or is ashamed of it is much more likely to have children who also react negatively. The gay parent must create a setting of acceptance by accepting him/herself. It is more likely to be a positive experience for everyone if the gay parent is ready and comfortable before telling his/her children.
- Children are never too young to be told. They will absorb only as much as they are capable of understanding. Use words appropriate to the age of the child. Details may be added as they grow older.
- Discuss your sexual orientation with children before they suspect or guess. When children discover their parent's sexual orientation from someone other than the parent, they often are upset that they had not been trusted enough to be told. It is exceedingly difficult for children to bring up the subject, and they are not likely to bring it up even though they want to.
- Disclosure should be planned. Children should not find out about their parent's homosexuality by default or discover it accidentally or during an argument between their parents.
- Disclose in a quiet setting where interruptions are unlikely to occur.
- Inform, don't confess. The disclosure should not be heavy or maudlin but positive and sincere. Informing in a simple, natural, and honest manner when the parent is ready is more likely to foster acceptance. If possible, discuss or rehearse what will be said with someone who has already experienced a successful disclosure.
- Children may need to be reassured that the parent is the same person they have known before and that the parent will not become the stereotype of a gay man or lesbian that is promoted by some in the media and organized religion. Honesty is the key.
- Expect questions, and be prepared with answers. Typical situations may include the following:
    - **Why are you telling me this?** My personal life is important, and I want to share it with you. I am not ashamed of being gay (or lesbian), and I hope you will not be ashamed either.

Coming Out to Children (continued)

- **What does being gay mean?** Gay means loving someone of the same sex and wanting to have an emotional and physical relationship with him or her just like heterosexual people do.
- **What makes a person gay or lesbian?** No one knows why this happens. You will hear a lot of debate about this, but the truth is we do not know the answer. Most gay and lesbian people remember knowing they were different since they were very young. Today, many researchers believe that sexual orientation is determined before birth.
- **Will I be gay or lesbian?** You won't be gay just because I am gay. It's not contagious. My parents were not gay, yet I am. The same is true for you. Some children who have gay parents are gay, but most of them are not. You will have whatever sexual orientation you already have.
- **What should I tell my friends?** It is often hard to know who to trust. The problem is that not all people understand what it means to be gay or lesbian. They might not like it or may just be uncomfortable about it, and some think of it as bad. I hope you will be careful about whom you tell. Most children don't talk about their parents' sexuality, but some may ask you about me. Most kids who have lesbian parents worry about this. Some have had bad experiences when they told others; others have kept it a secret or just told one or two people they really trust. I'll be glad to help you figure out what to do when this comes up. I hope you will not be hurt when other people don't understand.

(Source: *Excerpted from* Gay Fathers, *Revised Edition, by R. Barret and B. Robinson, pp. 91–93. Copyright © 2000 Jossey-Bass. This material is excerpted by permission of Jossey-Bass, a subsidiary of John Wiley & Sons, Inc.*)

Provide Information About Coming Out to Children   There are no easy answers or proven ways to help children and their parents face this situation. You will do best if you listen to the concerns and help the parents find ways to maintain their integrity, honor their relationships, and still provide essential information to their children. Some parents meet with schoolteachers, principals, and counselors to let them know what is happening. Others shield their children from the reality of their home lives by giving ambiguous responses such as, "It's none of their business." You may have a difficult time with your personal opinion about the proper course of action. If you have other clients who have faced this issue, they may be willing to serve as resources for a client who is struggling with coming out to his or her children.

BOX 9.2

Callie and her brother Chip lived under a joint custody agreement where they spent time with their mom and their dad, a gay man who died from AIDS. Two years before his death, she reflected on living with a gay father.

When I was in sixth grade, my dad explained to me about being gay, and it never really bothered me. I really don't know why it would be different living with a straight father because this is all I've ever had. I don't know what my friends' fathers are like, but I know they are real nice, too. It's hard for me to hear people talking about gay people at school when they don't even know anything about them. I really don't pay too much attention to them. I just think, "If only they knew." I sort of feel that I'm lucky to have this opportunity that they'll never have to understand what being gay really is. . . . If I were somebody who was brought up in a prejudiced family saying things that aren't true about gay people, I wouldn't ever find out what it's really like. I feel it's special for me to be in this situation with a gay father.

I've never told anyone about my dad. They think he's a single father. When he had lovers, I always told my friends that he was renting a room out and that he's a real good friend of ours. And they understand that completely. If I could change my father and make him straight, I wouldn't do it because I like him the way he is.

The bad thing about it is that I can't tell anybody because I don't know if they would understand. I would like to be able to tell a close friend things that happen, but I can't really risk that. I have some very good friends, but I don't know how they feel about gays. Most of my friends are prejudiced, and they really don't care, but you just can't go out and start talking about it. The good thing is that things are so open in my family. You don't have to hide anything from one other. Some fathers don't even tell their family they are gay. We have such a good relationship. I think knowing Dad is gay brings us closer together. Some fathers are closed and are not very open to their family. . . . When I walk into Dad's house, this is life for me, and when I walk out, I know what I'm supposed to be handling out there. I deal with the gay world in here—with my dad and his friends—and when I'm with my friends, I deal with it their way. . . . I don't think that if your dad is gay, you're going to be gay. You can't choose if you're going to be gay. You can't make somebody gay. You are just what you are. . . . I get very angry at people who don't understand. Sometimes I feel like screaming at them, "Shut up! You don't know what you're talking about."

(Source: *Excerpted from* Gay Fathers, *by R. Barret and B. Robinson, pp. 77–79. Copyright © 2000 Jossey-Bass. This material is excerpted by permission of Jossey-Bass, a subsidiary of John Wiley & Sons, Inc.*)

Be Aware That Gay and Lesbian Family Members May Not Be Legally or Biologically Related   The laws that govern most family configurations generally do not apply to gay and lesbian parents. Gay and lesbian parents who are unable to marry, who may not be able to adopt children in states that do not allow second-parent adoption, or who co-parent children with one of the partners as the "legal" parent encounter complexities far beyond those faced by typical heterosexual "blended" families. One may resent the time his or her partner spends with biological children or may feel threatened by a child's apparent preference for one parent over the other. Helping couples find other gay and lesbian families or recognize the alternative family network as a healthy replacement for extended families will stabilize these families. Keeping communication clear and trust high in situations like these will help couples negotiate these complicated issues.

Understand the Complexity of These Issues   Lesbians and gay men who start the process of becoming parents face an often bewildering array of issues. Do they come out to the adoption agency? What happens if their physician refuses to inseminate one of them? How do they restructure their lives so the well-being of their children is enhanced? You can follow the example of Ken in the case at the beginning of this chapter. He searched the Internet and read about the many support organizations that exist for gay and lesbian parents. He also attended a gay parents' support group and was able to begin to understand gay families in a new way. He also cautioned the couples to move slowly and to involve their extended families. These same resources are available to you.

Become an Advocate   You can assist your clients by using your position in the community to educate those who are unfamiliar with gay and lesbian parents. As you become more comfortable with your role as social activist, you will begin to get involved in helping your community become more accepting of all persons (Barret, 1998). Offer to put on a workshop for attorneys, perhaps hosted by your local chapter of the American Bar Association. Make a similar effort for teachers and other professionals who will routinely interact with gay and lesbian families. Learn ways to let judges and other legal officials know about the resources on gay and lesbian parenting. Approach the university in your hometown and offer to provide training for students in education administration. Just about any effort you make will be helpful.

Know Your Local Resources   In virtually all larger cities there will be attorneys who have handled custody cases involving gay and lesbian parents. There will be clergy who have assisted in blessing these new families, and physicians and teachers who have become comfortable providing support to gay parents. Learn the names of some of these people, and be willing to encourage your clients to talk with them as they make this important decision.

You will also find some professionals who have negative attitudes about gay parenting; gently advise your clients to avoid them. Naturally, one of the best resources will be people who have gone through the process themselves. Get to know some of the gay and lesbian parents in your community, and determine which ones will be valuable resources for your clients who want to know more about child-raising.

BIBLIOGRAPHY

Bailey, J., Bobrow, D., Wolfe, M., & Mikach, S. (1995). Sexual orientation of the adult sons of gay fathers. *Developmental Psychology, 31,* 124–139.

Barret, B. (1998). Gay and lesbian activism: A frontier of social activism. In C. Lee & G. Walz (Eds.), *Social action: A mandate for counselors.* Alexandria, VA: American Counseling Association.

Barret, B. & Robinson, B. (2000). *Gay fathers.* San Francisco: Jossey-Bass.

Bell, A. P. & Weinberg, M. S. (1978). *Homosexualities: A study of diversity among men and women.* New York: Simon & Schuster.

Bigner, J. & Bozett, F. (1990). Parenting by gay fathers. In F. W. Bozett & M. B. Sussman (Eds.), *Homosexuality and family relations.* New York: Harrington Park Press.

Bozett, F. W. (1980). Gay fathers: How and why they disclose their homosexuality to their children. *Family Relations, 29,* 173–179.

———. (1981). Gay fathers: Evolution of the gay father identity. *American Journal of Orthopsychiatry, 51,* 552–559.

———. (1989). Social control of identity by children of gay fathers. *Western Journal of Nursing Research, 10,* 550–565.

Editors of the Harvard Law Review. (1990). *Sexual orientation and the law.* Cambridge, MA: Harvard University Press.

Flowers, C., Barret, B., & Robinson, B. (2000). Research on gay parenting. In B. Barret & B. Robinson, *Gay fathers.* San Francisco: Jossey-Bass.

Gagnon, J., Laumann, E., Michael, R., & Michaels, S. (1994). *The social organization of sexuality.* Chicago: University of Chicago Press.

Geiser, R. L. (1979). *Hidden victims: The sexual abuse of children.* Boston: Beacon Press.

Gochros, J. S. (1989). *When husbands come out of the closet.* Binghamton, NY: Harrington Park Press.

Grace, J. (1999, June 21). Zoey had two moms. *Time, 153*(24), 57.

Herek, G. M. (1991). Myths about sexual orientation: A lawyer's guide to social science research. *Law and Sexuality, 133,* 157–161.

Huggins, S. (1989). A comparative study of self-esteem of adolescent children of divorced lesbian mothers and divorced non-lesbian mothers. In F. W. Bozett (Ed.), *Homosexuality and the family.* New York: Haworth Press.

Lambda Legal Defense and Education Fund. (1998, July 30). North Carolina Supreme Court takes custody from gay father. Press release obtained on-line from http://www.lambdalegal.org/cgi-bin/pages/issues/record?record=5.

McIntyre, D. (1994). Gay parents and child custody: A struggle under the legal system. *Mediation Quarterly, 12*(2), 135–149.

Patterson, C. (1992). Children of lesbian and gay parents. *Child Development, 63,* 1025–1042.

————. (1994). Lesbian and gay families. *Current Directions in Psychological Science, 3,* 54–62.

Patterson, C. & Chan, R. (1996). Gay fathers. In M. E. Lamb (Ed.), *The role of the father in child development.* New York: John Wiley.

Richardson, D. (1981). Lesbian mothers. In J. Hart and D. Richardson (Eds.), *The theory and practice of homosexuality.* London: Routledge & Keegan Paul.

Sanders, G. (1999, January). Normal families: Research on gay and lesbian parenting. *In the Family, 5,* 24–27.

Shordone, A. J. (1993). *Gay men choosing fatherhood.* Unpublished doctoral dissertation, City University of New York.

Spada, J. (1979). *The Spada Report.* New York: Signet Books.

Tasker, F. L. & Golombok, S. (1997). *Growing up in a lesbian family.* New York: Guilford Press.

Gay and Lesbian Health Issues

The Case of Ann ▼

*Ann has been working with gay and lesbian clients for the past 10 years.
She currently works at a local counseling center that was established
15 years ago specifically to meet the myriad needs of the gay and lesbian community. The center is staffed by mental-health therapists, health
educators, and chemical dependency counselors.*

Ann feels fortunate to work in such a rich setting as it allows her to
provide multidimensional services to her clients, many of whom were
afraid to seek services anywhere else.

Ann has always had a keen interest in approaching her clients holis-
tically, making sure she addresses the clients' physical health as well as
their emotional health. For example, she started her counseling career
during the second decade of the HIV epidemic. At that time, much of her
work was focused on issues related to testing HIV-positive or on making
sure her clients remained HIV-negative. Ann worked with the clients to
help them manage the physical toll of HIV as well as addressed the
psychosocial effects of the disease, and, inevitably, she helped clients
grieve and work through the dying process. Over the years, she had lost
so many clients, friends, and colleagues that she found herself emotionally drained, barely able to come to work in the morning. In fact, Ann
eventually had to take a leave of absence from the center to recover
from emotional and physical exhaustion.

In recent years, Ann noticed that the faces of HIV and AIDS had
changed. It was no longer a gay, white disease; the number of women
and persons of color infected by HIV dramatically increased each year.
Thanks to the Herculean education efforts regarding safer-sex practices, the number of gay men infected with HIV each year continued to
decline. New, powerful drug therapies seemed to have reduced HIV in
the United States to a chronic manageable disease.

There were new issues to contend with in the fight against HIV infection. For example, now that people with HIV were living longer, they needed help to reframe the experience as living with a chronic illness rather than preparing to die. In addition, the new drug "cocktails" were powerful, but like AZT and other early drugs, they had significant side effects. Clients had to be very careful taking their medication and follow a strict regimen to prevent building up resistance to the drugs. Drug therapies were changing so quickly that many times Ann found that she was much less knowledgeable than her clients. She was constantly having to go to the health educator's office to learn about the new drug treatments, the potential side effects, and dosage regimens.

Recently Ann noticed that some of her gay male clients would share that they had engaged in unsafe sexual practices. Many times this happened when they attended circuit parties or all-night dance parties. Drugs such as ecstasy, crystal methamphetamine, or "Special K" (ketamine) were an integral part of the dance scene, allowing the men to stay up all night dancing and having multiple sexual experiences. For some of her clients, drug binges would lead to sex binges, and because her clients were impaired by the drugs, sometimes they engaged in risky sexual behavior. Most would feel guilt and fear after this occurred, afraid that they had exposed themselves to HIV or some other sexually transmitted disease, like hepatitis B. Ann would empathically help her clients work through their feelings of guilt and shame, encourage them to get tested, and even role-play future situations where it could be challenging to negotiate safer sex. Other clients, however, did not feel guilty about taking risks, and, in fact, they seemed to feel self-righteous about their decisions to have unprotected sex. "Quite frankly," these clients would say, "they were sick and tired of worrying about 'catching' a disease, sick and tired of having fear of a disease control their lives and their penises; if they were destined to die anyway, at least they were going to have some fun along the way." Ann was unsure how to approach this devil-may-care, fatalistic attitude. Sometimes she felt angry and resentful toward clients who took unnecessary risks.

Drinking was also pretty common among her clients. Ann knew that many of her gay and lesbian clients frequented gay bars and dance clubs. It was nice to be in a public space where gays and lesbians were the majority rather than the despised minority. Some of her clients said they went to bars to have a few drinks just so they could work up the courage to talk to someone or ask him/her to dance. Unfortunately, some of her gay and lesbian clients couldn't have just one or two drinks; these clients found themselves drunk every night and sometimes unable to remember what had happened the previous night. Some of these clients would eventually come to terms with their drinking problem and ask Ann for help with sobriety. Usually Ann would refer these clients to the center's chemical dependency staff, but sometimes individual and group counseling wasn't enough. Often they would encounter prejudice either in treatment facilities or at traditional AA meetings. For example, one client whom she referred to a chemical dependency program left after a few days because the staff wanted to talk only about why he was gay. Other clients reported that they felt out of place and ostracized even at AA meetings. Ann wasn't sure where to turn or how to help her gay and lesbian clients stay sober.

Health concerns were certainly not limited to her gay male clients. She remembered working with a lesbian couple who were reeling from the impact of breast cancer. Julie and Donna had been together for about six years and agreed that they had a wonderful, loving relationship. Three years ago their world turned upside down when Donna was diagnosed with breast cancer. Since then she has undergone a radical double mastectomy, radiation, and a full course of chemotherapy. When Donna found the lump in her breast, she made an appointment with her doctor to have it checked. She wanted Julie to accompany her to the doctor but was afraid Julie's presence would force the issue of coming out. She wasn't ready to risk telling the doctor, as she was afraid he'd treat her differently or not as well after learning she was a lesbian. She went to the doctor alone, and when she found out she had breast cancer, the news was especially devastating to hear without Julie by her side. Having to hide her relationship with Julie made everything worse. Every time she had to fill out a new form that asked for her husband's name or when the nursing staff asked if she had a husband or a boyfriend, she wanted to scream.

During the surgery and ensuing treatment, Julie and Donna were constantly worried about being found out. For example, when Donna was in the hospital, Julie masqueraded as her sister so she could spend time with Donna in the recovery room. Dealing with the illness was difficult but so was dealing with the constant fear of being discovered. Both women were stressed and emotionally overloaded. The tension between the two partners grew, and they found themselves disagreeing constantly, bickering back and forth over any little thing. Things got worse when Donna returned home from the hospital to recover. Unfortunately, Julie's job required her to travel two to three times a month, and, reluctantly, she would have to leave Donna at home alone to fend for herself. Although Julie hated to do it, there was no way she could risk losing her job by staying home to care for Donna, even though that's what she wanted to do. If her boss found out she was a lesbian, she knew she would be fired, and the couple couldn't afford to lose Julie's income. Unfortunately, Donna's job wasn't very high-paying and did not offer good insurance benefits, so the couple had to rely on Julie's income to sustain them through this time of crisis. It was unfortunate that Julie couldn't add Donna to her insurance policy; she had very good health benefits that would really have helped ease the financial load. The tension at home continued to grow as Julie felt increased pressure from her job and tried to take care of the finances, daily stressors, and yet all she wanted to do was be at home taking care of Donna.

Most of the time, Donna felt lonely and isolated. Coping with a cancer diagnosis had been really difficult. She felt such a sense of sadness and loss; she also felt disfigured and unattractive. One night while Julie was out of town, Donna attended a support group meeting for cancer survivors. What a nightmare that had been! All the other women were heterosexual and wanted to talk only about how well or how poorly their husbands were dealing with their scars from breast surgery. Sitting in that group, Donna felt even worse and more alone. She had some of the same issues they did, but there was no way she was going to talk about her relationship with Julie. How could she share her financial problems or fears about being sexually attractive to her female partner with heterosexual women?

Ann worked with Julie and Donna for several months. Many of these sessions were spent helping the partners communicate more effectively with each other. Ann helped Donna and Julie learn how to listen and empathize with each other's fears and pain. Early on in the counseling relationship, Ann referred the couple to a local volunteer organization that provided support services to chronically ill lesbians and their significant others. The organization was set up like a buddy program, but instead of one buddy, a team of five or six women provided support services. Services included transportation to and from the doctor, housework, yard work, grocery shopping, and companionship. Having team support made a huge difference in Julie and Donna's lives. Julie felt less guilty and nervous going on business trips, and Donna didn't feel so alone and isolated. In addition to couples sessions with Ann, Julie and Donna both attended a support group for lesbian cancer survivors that was held weekly at the counseling center. Ann also provided the couple with a list of lesbian-friendly physicians and encouraged them to sign legal and medical power-of-attorney documents. All in all, Ann felt very positive about her work with Julie and Donna as they successfully negotiated learning how to live with cancer.

GAY AND LESBIAN HEALTH RISKS

There are no increased health risks associated with being gay or lesbian. In general, gays and lesbians face the same illnesses and diseases that heterosexuals do. The greatest challenge for this population is dealing with a medical community that has traditionally been uncomfortable and even unwilling to work with gay and lesbian patients. The purpose of this chapter is to address a number of health issues that are of particular concern to gays and lesbians, as well as to offer suggestions for promoting good physical health.

As recent as the late nineteenth century, same-sex erotic feelings and behavior were seen as a disease that must be cured. Homosexuality was thought to lead to all kinds of malaise, including nervous exhaustion, anxiety, chronic fatigue, uncontrollable masturbation, and even mental illness (Kauth, Hartwig, & Kalichman, 2000). The "illness" of homosexuality was treated in a variety of ways, such as forced opposite-gender behavior or marriage, surgical/chemical castration, electroconvulsive shock therapy, brain surgery, aversive therapy and institutionalization (Murphy, 1992). The landmark decision in 1973 to remove homosexuality from the *DSM* served as an important first step toward destigmatizing gays and lesbians. Unfortunately, the AIDS epidemic first emerged in the gay male community and refueled the fire linking homosexuality to illness. Two decades later, changing demographics, as well as the overwhelming and successful response from the gay community in response to the HIV pandemic, has served to weaken but has not completely eliminated the argument that homosexual behavior itself is unhealthy because it may lead to HIV/AIDS (Kauth, Hartwig, & Kalichman, 2000).

The relationship between health-care providers and their sexual minority patients has been tenuous at best. Most doctors assume that all patients are heterosexual, failing to ask about sexual identity or even to take the time to conduct a nonbiased sexual history. Many doctors are uncomfortable with same-sex erotic behavior, and their disapproval is implied in both verbal and nonverbal messages. Moreover, many are not sensitive or knowledgeable about particular issues or health risks that are pertinent to gay and lesbian patients. A review of the available literature (Stevens, 1992; Rankow, 1995) found a significant level of antigay bias in the medical community, ranging from thinking that homosexuality is immoral and disgusting to feeling extremely uncomfortable with the idea of treating a gay or lesbian patient. Based on these data, it's not hard to believe that some doctors have been observed providing reduced or minimal care to their gay and lesbian patients and even making rude and disparaging comments (Rankow, 1995). For example, a client shared that she had disclosed her sexual orientation to her doctor, and he had actually walked out the room, leaving his nurse to finish the exam. Needless to say, she felt horrified and ashamed. As a result, she refused to go to the doctor for years after that incident; she was never going to put herself in that vulnerable position again.

To its credit, the American Medical Association (AMA) has been making progress toward recognizing the needs of gay and lesbian physicians and their patients. In 1993, the organization voted to adopt a nondiscrimination policy toward gay and lesbian physicians. In October of that same year, the American Academy of Pediatricians publicly charged pediatricians to care for gay and lesbian adolescents. In 1996, the American Academy of Family Physicians adopted a policy supporting equal treatment of gay, lesbian, bisexual, and transgendered physicians, patients, and their families (Schneider & Levin, 1999). Also in 1996, the AMA authored a comprehensive report on the health-care needs of gay men and lesbians. Moreover, members of the Gay, Lesbian Medical Association (GLMA) are working hard to make AMA a leader in gay, lesbian health concerns.

HEALTH ISSUES RELATED TO LESBIAN AND BISEXUAL WOMEN

Lesbians are less likely to seek traditional health care for a variety of reasons. The reason most cited for avoiding the doctor is lack of financial resources. On average, women tend to earn less money than men and are, therefore, less able to afford health insurance and medical care. In addition, lesbians are usually not covered under their partner's health insurance policy, a privilege that is usually afforded to married heterosexual women. As a result, many women seek treatment from alternative health-care providers, such as a chiropractor, an acupuncturist, or a homeopathic doctor. In fact, some women would rather rely on self-care than seek help from a traditional health-care provider.

Lesbians avoid going to doctors because it potentially forces the issue of whether or not to come out. As in the case in the beginning of the chapter, Donna was afraid to take Julie with her to her doctor's appointment, in case the doctor "figured them out." Lesbians are afraid doctors will react negatively, misunderstand their needs, or, even worse, be rude or rough. Many office intake forms assume heterosexuality and routinely ask if a patient is married, and if so, ask for her husband's name. Typical medical interview questions include, "Are you sexually active?" If the answer is yes, "What kind of birth control do you use?" (White & Levinson, 1993).

Another reason that lesbians avoid the doctor is sometimes referred to as the myth of "immunity" (Rankow, 1995). Lesbians tend to believe they are immune to HIV and other sexually transmitted diseases (STDs) because they're not having sex with men. This myth is obviously perpetuated by the medical community, since some lesbians report that they have been specifically told by their doctors that they don't need regular pelvic examinations or PAP smears because they are definitely not at risk (Rankow, 1995).

Health Risks for Lesbians

STDs—Non-HIV-Related

Self-identified lesbians tend to have a lower risk of contracting STDs. As noted in Chapter 2, sexual identity may not be congruent with sexual behavior. For example, 75 to 90% of self-identified lesbians report having had sex with a man at least once during their lifetime (Rankow, 1995). In a recent survey of 1,086 lesbian and bisexual women, 53% reported having sex with at least one man since 1978 (Einhorn & Polgar, 1994). Clearly, lesbians who have sex with men or bisexual women who have sex with men place themselves at greater risk for STDs such as gonorrhea, herpes, and syphilis.

Women who are sexually active exclusively with other women are less likely to contract STDs such as syphilis, gonorrhea, and chlamydia (White & Levinson, 1993). Moreover, the chance of contracting herpes and infections from the human papillomavirus (HPV) are also rare but can occur. If a person is infected, however, STDs such as chlamydia, venereal warts, and vaginal infections can be transmitted between women; caution and safer-sex precautions should be used if one or both partners are infected.

Lesbian sexual activity may include kissing; breast stimulation; digital penetration of the vagina or anus; penetration with sex toys; use of sex toys; genital/genital, oral/genital, or oral/anal contact; and sadomasochism (Rankow, 1995). To decrease the risk of clients' contracting an STD, counselors should inform clients of guidelines for safer sex.

HIV/AIDS

The data also indicate that lesbians or women who sexually partner exclusively with other women are at low risk for contracting the HIV virus. It is still very important to educate all clients about HIV and AIDS. A comprehensive explanation of HIV and its progression is beyond the scope of this chapter; however, it is essential that mental-health practitioners understand HIV and be able to inform all clients about how to reduce the risk of HIV infection. HIV is a virus that is transmitted through sexual fluids or blood products. Transmission can occur if someone is exposed to these fluids. The HIV virus attacks and destroys important cells that make up the immune system. As these cells decrease over time, the person is susceptible to infection, in particular, opportunistic infections that healthy immune systems are able to combat easily. Acquired Immune Deficiency Syndrome (AIDS) is a late stage of HIV infection.

Transmission of the HIV virus between women who partner exclusively with other women is rare (AMA Council on Scientific Affairs, 1996). Lesbians are usually exposed to the HIV virus via unsafe sex with gay or bisexual men or

IV drug users or if the woman herself uses IV drugs (Kauth, Hartwig, & Kalichman, 2000). Occasionally there are single cases reported in which a lesbian claims to be infected by the HIV virus via sex with another lesbian. For example, a lesbian who denied having sex with men and denied any IV drug use appeared to have contracted HIV from her female lover, who had been an IV drug user and died from complications associated with AIDS (Kauth, Hartwig, & Kalichman, 2000). These cases, however, are rare.

Lesbians can also be exposed to HIV and other STDs via alternative insemination. Sperm banks regularly test potential donors for HIV, and the samples are tested at least once more six months later. Using fresh semen, however, can be risky, and potential donors should be HIV-negative and tested again at least six months later before the semen is used (White & Levinson, 1993).

Bisexual women are at a higher risk for contracting HIV and other STDs if they engage in unprotected sex with men who are IV drug users, if they use IV drugs themselves, or if they choose to have unprotected sex with men (Rila, 1996).

Lesbian and bisexual clients may need assistance in learning how to negotiate safer-sex practices with male partners. Moreover, ethnic minorities are at an even greater risk of contracting the HIV virus. For example, women accounted for 32% of the adult cases of HIV infection, and of those cases, 77% were African American or Hispanic (Centers for Disease Control and Prevention, 1999). Counselors must serve as educators by dispelling myths and stereotypes regarding lesbian sexual behavior, providing accurate information regarding the transmission of STDs and HIV, and instructing women how to practice safer sex using condoms and other latex barriers. Be aware that any safer-sex training must be culturally sensitive, as women from different minority backgrounds may be "punished" for trying to take an assertive role in sexual situations. In these cases, safer sex and related behavior should be placed in the context of good health practices and reproductive concerns in order to reduce the possibility of negative and angry reactions from male sexual partners (Kauth, Hartwig, & Kalichman, 2000). Safer-sex education and training should include how and when to bring up the issue of safer-sex timing issues and role-playing exercises to help the clients negotiate potentially difficult situations.

Breast Cancer and Other Cancers

Lesbians are at a lower risk for cervical cancer than women who have sex with men. Risk factors for cervical cancer include intercourse with a man at an early age and infection with HPV (White & Levinson, 1993). As noted earlier, however, a large majority of lesbians have had sex with men at some point in their lives, and regular PAP smears and pelvic examinations are recommended for all women regardless of sexual orientation.

According to the National Cancer Institute (2000), one in eight women will develop breast cancer during her lifetime with most cases occurring after age 50. There has been some speculation that lesbians are at a greater risk for breast cancer than heterosexual women, based on certain risk factors that are typically associated with lesbians. For example, lesbians are less likely to have children or wait to have children later in life, have higher rates of alcohol consumption, and are more likely to be overweight (Solarz, 1999); however, be aware of education tactics that specifically target lesbians as a high-risk population as this may cause undue stress and anxiety. Rather, explain that lesbians meet the profile of women who are more susceptible to breast cancer, but they are not necessarily at a higher risk simply because of their sexual orientation. In fact, lesbians may simply be at a greater risk because they are unlikely to go to the doctor for yearly examinations. The specific incidence of breast cancer in lesbian and bisexual women is unknown; however, regular breast self-examinations and mammograms after age 35 are recommended for every woman.

Mental-health practitioners are encouraged to help lesbian and bisexual clients access affirmative health care. Be aware of community health programs that are designed specifically to meet the needs of lesbian and bisexual women. Remember that women are more likely to seek support from peers. For example, Donna and Julie were able to access a buddy program, which helped provide support services to Donna when Julie was out of town. In addition, the women attended a support group specifically designed for lesbian cancer survivors. It would be useful to have a readily available list of providers who are competent and appropriate in their treatment of lesbian and bisexual women. Include on this list out lesbian doctors because a lesbian is more likely to seek health care from someone similar to herself. In addition, be prepared to facilitate the process of drawing up legal documentation such as legal and medical powers of attorney.

HEALTH ISSUES ASSOCIATED WITH GAY AND BISEXUAL MEN

In general, gay and bisexual men have no greater health problems than heterosexual men. One difference between the two groups is that men who have sex with men are likely to have a greater number of sexual contacts and are more likely to engage in anal intercourse and oral and digital anal contact than their heterosexual counterparts (Kauth, Hartwig, & Kalichman, 2000). Increased sexual behavior is in fact highly correlated with increased risk of contracting an STD. Encourage gay clients to practice safer sex, perform regular self-examinations, schedule yearly physicals, and find a gay-friendly doctor who fosters open and honest communication. Men who have sex with men are also more susceptible to a variety of oral and gastrointestinal infections and a number of viral infections, including HPV, herpes simplex, and hepatitis B. In fact, the AMA Council on Scientific Affairs (1996) recommends that men who are sexually active with other men receive the hepatitis B vaccine. According to a health report issued by GLMA (2000), men who have a history of receptive anal intercourse and anal STDs, particularly HPV, may be a greater risk for anal cancer. Early detection enhances survival rates, and gay men are strongly encouraged to schedule regular checkups.

HIV/AIDS

The advent of HIV forever changed how gay men relate to each other. It first appeared in the gay community almost 20 years ago and was often referred to in a pejorative sense as the "gay" disease or Gay Related Infectious Diseases (GRID) implying that by virtue of having sex with men, gay men somehow deserved this disease. Hundreds of thousands were infected by the HIV virus and died from AIDS-related complications before the U.S. government and the medical community appropriately responded to the epidemic. As a result, the gay community was forced to rally together and establish AIDS services organizations, raising money for research and basically inventing the concept of safer sex.

Thanks to the efforts of the gay community, however, HIV is no longer an automatic death sentence. Effective prevention tactics and promising new drug treatments have helped make HIV a chronic manageable disease. Clearly, prevention and safer-sex education programs geared toward gay or bisexual men have paid off; less than half of the current AIDS cases are men who were exposed to the HIV virus via unprotected sex with men, and only 40% of new infections are a result of men who have unprotected sex with men (Centers for Disease Control and Prevention, 1999). Rila (1996) suggests the following safer-sex guidelines for both men and women.

- Use latex condoms for vaginal and anal intercourse.
- Use latex condoms for oral sex on a man.
- Use household plastic wrap or latex barriers to prevent oral contact with vaginal fluids, menstrual blood, or blood resulting from vigorous sexual activity.
- Use condoms or latex gloves for putting fingers in the vagina or anus.
- Use latex gloves for putting a hand in the vagina or the anus.
- Do not use sex toys that have been in contact with sexual fluids; either wash with one part bleach to ten parts soapy water or use condoms.
- If sex toys are shared, clean them with one part bleach to ten parts soapy water.

- Use water-based lubricants. Do not use oil-based lubricants with latex products.
- Do not ingest semen, blood, urine, or feces; it is okay for them to contact unbroken skin.
- Direct rubbing of genitals together can be unsafe as partners can be exposed to blood or vaginal fluids.
- Use condoms and other latex items only once and then dispose of them.

Therapists working with clients infected with the HIV virus are likely to encounter the confusing world of anti-HIV drug treatment therapies. These new drug treatments are helping people stay healthy, but taking the new drug cocktails can be challenging and expensive, and any noncompliance with the medication regime can pose a risk of building up resistance to the new drugs.

Drug Cocktails

Early in the AIDS epidemic, doctors prescribed a single drug, usually AZT, until the individual showed signs of intolerance, and then a new drug would be prescribed. The current practice is to prescribe two or three drugs because no single virus can resist them all at the same time. The following is a brief list of current drugs used as drug cocktail therapy for HIV infection (Shalit, 1998).

Reverse Transcriptase Inhibitors: Nucleosides   This category includes drugs such as AZT, DDI, DDC—they work to prevent the HIV virus from replicating itself. AZT was the first drug used in the fight against HIV and had numerous negative effects, such as nausea, headaches, and insomnia.

Reverse Transcriptase Inhibitors: Nonnucleosides   This category includes drugs such as Rescriptor, Sustiva, and Viramune—they disrupt the virus from making new DNA by distorting the enzyme needed to replicate itself. These drugs are fairly promising when used in combination with other HIV-related drugs; however, it's easy to build resistance to them and a severe rash is a fairly common side effect.

The Protease Inhibitors   This category includes drugs such as Crixivan, Viracept, and Norvir—these drugs have proven to be highly effective in preventing the replication of the HIV virus, working to make the virus virtually undetectable. However, these powerful drugs can be hard to manage. For example, a daily dosage can include up to 15 or 20 pills. To further complicate matters, some must be taken with a meal, others on an empty stomach. In addition, these drugs are expensive; each drug is approximately $500 per month, making the cost of a typical drug cocktail $1000–$1500 per month. Unfortunately, these highly effective drug cocktails are virtually out of reach for clients without insurance or in a low-income bracket. These clients can access drug therapies through state-subsidized community health clinics.

The potential side effects of the drug cocktails can be formidable. For example, some of these drugs interfere with the liver, and others cause dry skin and hair loss; some even change the fat distribution in the body, moving it to the stomach and away from other places in the body, a phenomenon sometimes referred to as the "crix belly." Be aware that changes in one's physique resulting from the drug therapies can be emotionally challenging. For example, Wes was HIV-positive and doing very well. He had been taking a drug cocktail for some time now and, in his words, "had never felt better in his life." Recently, however, Wes had been disturbed by the weight gain he was experiencing in his waist. He was eating right and going to the gym regularly, yet he could not shed his big stomach. His friends thought he was crazy focusing on his weight gain, saying, "You're just lucky to be alive." He knew that was true, but he couldn't help worrying and obsessing about how he looked. Fortunately, his counselor was aware of the potential side effects associated with Protease Inhibitors and she was able to empathize with his feelings and concerns. It is essential for mental-health professionals to be knowledgeable about the multifaceted psychosocial effects associated with living with HIV.

Living With HIV

Helping clients manage HIV illness may require drastic changes in lifestyle, such as reducing stress; getting enough rest; avoiding drugs like nicotine, alcohol, and recreational drugs; getting regular exercise; eating right; and reducing risk of exposure to diseases.

When working with gay couples, it is important to explore the implicit and explicit contracts regarding monogamy. For an in-depth discussion of the issues related to counseling couples, please review Chapter 5. Mutual monogamy is very safe and requires trust and open communication. If either partner is having unprotected sex outside the relationship and not telling his partner, he could expose his partner to STDs or HIV. Some couples negotiate open relationships, giving permission for either partner to have outside sex as long as it's safe. Since not any type of sex is really safe, this is still a potentially risky situation. Serodiscordant couples, where one is HIV-negative and the other is HIV-positive, must make decisions about their sexual activity. Some practice strict safer sex; others choose not to use any protection. Some HIV-positive men may choose to have unprotected sex with their partners or other men who are also HIV-positive. This is still risky behavior as they may be putting themselves at risk for other STDs such as hepatitis, herpes, or gonorrhea, as well as different strains of the HIV virus.

Therefore, continued condom use is still the safest option in both monogamous and nonmonogamous relationships.

Prevention in the New Millennium

Health educators have historically warned people to avoid being exposed to body fluids, that is, blood, semen, and vaginal fluids. As noted earlier in this chapter, both men and women have been warned to use condoms or other latex barriers if they plan to have vaginal or anal sex, oral–genital contact, or oral sex. Health educators have consistently urged people to use condoms during oral sex even though acknowledging that the risk of infection via oral sex is significantly lower. The potential risk of HIV infection via oral sex remains a controversial topic. HIV is found in saliva; however, studies have failed to prove that unprotected oral sex is a highly risky behavior (DeVincenzi, 1994; Ostrow et al., 1995). Occasionally, however, a case will surface that appears to indicate that HIV infection occurred during oral sex. Recently, a prominent leader in the gay community stated publicly that he is HIV-positive as a result of engaging exclusively in oral sex. Be aware that mental-health practitioners may be asked to clarify what constitutes safer sex, which behaviors are safe and which aren't, and, in particular, whether oral sex is safe sex. Counselors are encouraged to remind clients that the only safe sex is no sex, and encourage clients to practice safer sex.

The following recommendations may be useful for both the clinician and the client (Shalit, 1998).

- Avoid unprotected oral sex if you have any kind of mouth sores, recent dental work, or gum disease.
- Avoid ejaculation during oral sex.
- Use a condom during oral sex, although this is fairly unappealing to most men and women.

Lapses in Safer-Sex Practices

Unfortunately, after 20 years of living under the shadow of HIV, many gay and bisexual men are tired and angry—angry that they've lost so many loved ones, frustrated with a disease that seems to have taken over their sex lives, and sick of dealing with safer-sex practices. Risking HIV infection and other STDs, some men are making decisions to bareback. Reasons cited for barebacking include continued discomfort or difficulty using a condom, internalized homoprejudice, use of drugs or alcohol-impaired judgment, fatalistic thinking such as "I'm gay; I'll be exposed some day," and a sense of complacency that comes from living for over 20 years with an epidemic (Kalichman et al., 1997).

Along with validating clients' feelings of frustration and anger, counselors can play a vital role in helping them negotiate potential lapses. Role-play exercises are particularly useful. Therapists are encouraged to teach clients how to anticipate and handle temptations to lapse into unsafe sex practices, dispel myths about potential risks, and encourage clients to maintain consistent healthy behavior (Kelly et al., 1991).

Counseling Issues Related to HIV

- Be willing to ask about sexual behavior practices and avoid making assumptions based on sexual identity.
- When clients engage in risky behavior, avoid judgment. Encourage clients to get tested for the HIV antibodies.
- Be aware of gay- and lesbian-friendly testing sites. Be able to explain the test to the client, and be familiar with the test procedures. Be prepared to supplement pre- and posttest counseling.
- Explore issues related to disclosure of HIV status. Encourage clients to commit to safer sex both inside and outside the relationship. If the client is HIV-positive, encourage open and honest discussion with potential sexual partners, allowing partners to make informed choices about level of risk.
- The issue of "duty to warn" may be raised if a client continues to engage in risky behavior with unsuspecting or uninformed sexual partners. Seek legal and therapeutic consultation. This issue has not been clearly addressed by the courts, and breaching confidentiality may severely harm the therapeutic relationship. Attempt to use the counseling relationship to change the behavior.

SUBSTANCE ABUSE

Gays and lesbians have long been thought to have alarmingly high rates of alcoholism and other substance abuse problems. In a recent review of the available literature, Bux (1996) cited numerous methodological flaws and limitations in these findings. For example, most studies used small convenient samples that were largely composed of bar patrons.

In fact, the research indicated that gay men are not at any greater risk for drinking heavily or developing a drinking problem than heterosexual men. However, lesbians do appear to drink more heavily than their heterosexual counterparts. Nonetheless, some gays and lesbians have drinking problems. Factors that may contribute to this phenomenon include the effects of internalized and externalized homoprejudice, the tendency to rely on bars for social support, and the absence of events such as having children that help the individual to mature and moderate drinking habits.

Counselors need to be aware of the numerous problems associated with heavy drinking and drug abuse. For example, impairment can lead to unsafe sexual practices and the likelihood of exposure to HIV and other STDs. As mentioned in the case at the beginning of this chapter, recreational drugs such as ecstasy and "Special K" are commonly used at clubs and circuit parties. Ecstasy and "crystal meth" are methamphetamines that cause euphoria, stimulation, and increased sexual energy that may last up to 15 hours. "Special K," or ketamine, is actually an anesthetic that produces hallucinations and dissociation. Taken in large doses, these drugs can be extremely disruptive to one's life, or even lethal. Some clients will become addicted to these or other drugs and develop medical, interpersonal, and emotional problems. When seeking treatment for your clients, find a facility that is supportive and gay- and lesbian-friendly. In addition, be aware that Alcoholics Anonymous (AA) and Narcotics Anonymous (NA) have meetings that are designed specifically to meet the needs of gays and lesbian in recovery.

LIVING HEALTHY

One final note on the connection between mental health and physical health: According to a national survey of lesbians (Bradford, Ryan, & Rothblum, 1994) participants' degree of outness was directly related to health and well-being. In other words, the more out the individual was in her life, the less fear and stress she experienced and the more she enjoyed a greater sense of well-being. Recognizing that it is a luxury to be out to everyone all the time, it is important to note that such behavior would reap both psychological and physical benefits. This is also true for gay men. Specifically, those men who accept their sexual orientation and are out to others experience fewer illnesses and infections (Cole et al., 1996). Clearly, counselors can help clients negotiate the coming out process, deciding to whom and when to come out, and help the client develop a positive self-identity and come out one step at a time.

Tips for Practitioners

Monitor Effects of the Historical Distrust of the Medical Community
Be aware of and sensitive to your client's fear and distrust of the traditional medical community. Maintain a list of competent gay- and lesbian-friendly physicians. In addition, be aware of alternative treatment doctors and therapies. The GLMA has a website with abundant research and information about gay and lesbian health issues. Included in the site is a link to a provider referral list.

Address the Effects of Internalized and External Homoprejudice   Be aware of the link between the effects of oppression and poor health. Encourage clients to come out and live out as they are able; greater visibility has been linked to better health.

Encourage a Healthy Lifestyle   Teach clients the benefits of a healthy lifestyle. Encourage clients to maintain good nutrition, exercise regularly, rest, and decrease use of alcohol and other drugs. In addition, encourage clients to avoid tobacco, manage stress, and receive regular medical treatment. Encourage clients to find meaning in their lives through spirituality, intimate relationships, work, and community endeavors.

Be Aware of Safer-Sex Guidelines   Be prepared to educate your clients, being sensitive to cultural differences. Understand and be able to educate your clients about HIV and other STDs. The Centers for Disease Control (CDC) have a website featuring the latest information on HIV/AIDS and STDs.

Serve as a Role Model   Perform self-examinations of your breasts or testes, schedule regular checkups, and find a doctor that you can trust.

Encourage Your Clients to Have Medical and Legal Powers of Attorney
Encourage clients to designate a partner or other loved one to serve as acting medical or legal power of attorney, if the need should arise. You and your client can easily access these forms at the LLDEF website.

BIBLIOGRAPHY

American Medical Association Council on Scientific Affairs. (1996). Health care needs of gay men and lesbians in the United States. *Journal of the American Medical Association, 275,* 1354–1359.

Bradford, J., Ryan, C., & Rothblum, E. D. (1994). National lesbian health care survey: Implications for mental health care. *Journal of Consulting and Clinical Psychology, 62,*(2), 228–242.

Bux, D. A. (1996). The epidemiology of problem drinking in gay men and lesbians: A critical review. *Clinical Psychology Review, 16,*(4), 277–298.

Centers for Disease Control and Prevention. (1999). *HIV/AIDS surveillance report, 11,* 1–42. Atlanta, GA: Centers for Disease Control and Prevention.

Cole, S. W., Kemeny, M. E., Taylor, S. E., & Visscher, B. R. (1996). Elevated physical health risk among gay men who conceal their homosexual identity. *Health Psychology, 15,* 243–251.

DeVincenzi, I. (1994). A longitudinal study of human immunodeficiency virus transmission by heterosexual partners. *New England Journal of Medicine, 331,* 341–346.

Einhorn, L. & Polgar, M. (1994). HIV-risk behavior among lesbians and bisexual women. *AIDS Education and Prevention, 6,* 514–523.

Gay and Lesbian Medical Association and Columbia University Joseph L. Mailman School of Public Health. (2000). *Lesbian, gay, bisexual and transgender health: Findings and concerns.* [on-line] Available: http://www.glma.org/policy/whitepaper/hpwp.html.

Kalichman, S. C., Kelly, J. A., Morgan, M., & Rompa, D. (1997). Fatalism, future outlook, current life dissatisfaction, and risk for human immunodeficiency virus (HIV) infection among gay and bisexual men. *Journal of Consulting and Clinical Psychology, 65,* 542–546.

Kauth, M. R., Hartwig, M. J., & Kalichman, S. C. (2000). Health behavior relevant to psychotherapy with lesbian, gay and bisexual clients. In R. M. Perez, K. A. Debord, & K. J. Bieschke (Eds.), *Handbook of Counseling and Therapy with Lesbians, Gays and Bisexuals.* Washington, DC: American Psychological Association.

Kelly, J. A., Kalichman, S. C., Kauth, M. R., Kilgore, H. G., Hood, H. V., Campos, P. E., Rao, S. M., Brasfield, T. L., & St. Lawrence, J. S. (1991). Situational factors associated with AIDS risk behavior lapses and coping strategies used by gay men who successfully avoid lapses. *American Journal of Public Health, 81,* 1335–1338.

Murphy, T. F. (1992). Redirecting sexual orientation: Techniques and justifications. *Journal of Sex Research, 29,* 501–523.

National Cancer Institute. (2000). NCI cancer facts: Lifetime probability of Breast Cancer in American Women. [on-line] Available: rex.nci.nih.gov/Intrfce_GIFS/INFO_PATS_INTR_DOC.html.

Ostrow, D., DiFranceisco, W., Chmeil, J., Wagstaff, D., & Wesch, J. (1995). A case-control study of human immunodeficiency virus type-1 seroconversion and risk-related behaviors in the Chicago MAC/CCS cohort, 1984–1992. *American Journal of Epidemiology, 142,* 1–10.

Rankow, E. J. (1995). Lesbian health issues for the primary care provider. *Journal of Family Practice, 40,* 486–493.

Rila, M. (1996). Bisexual women and the AIDS crisis. In B. A. Firestein (Ed.), *Bisexuality: The psychology and politics of an invisible minority.* Thousand Oaks, CA: Sage.

Schneider, J. S. & Levin, S. (1999). Uneasy partners: The lesbian and gay health care community and the AMA. *Journal of the American Medical Association, 282,*(13), 1287–1288.

Shalit, P. (1998). *Living well: The gay man's essential health guide.* Los Angeles: Alyson Books.

Solarz, A. L. (Ed.). (1999). *Lesbian health: Current assessments and directions for the future.* Washington, DC: National Academy Press.

Stevens, P. E. (1992). Lesbian health care research: A review of the literature from 1970 to 1990. Special issue, Lesbian health: What are the issues? *Health Care for Women International, 13,* 91–120.

White, J. & Levinson, W. (1993). Primary care of lesbian patients. *Journal of General Internal Medicine, 8,* 41–47.

Resources

THE AMERICAN PSYCHOLOGICAL ASSOCIATION

http://www.apa.org/pi/l&bres.html
http://www.apa.org/pi/preface.html
http://www.apa.org/divisions/div44/

THE AMERICAN COUNSELING ASSOCIATION

http://www.aglbic.org/resources/rt07.htm

GAY PARENTING PAGES

http://www.familypride.org
http://www.gaydads.com/
http://ucl.broward.cc.fl.us/pathfinders/lsbgayprt.htm
http://userwww.service.emory.edu/~librpj/gaydads.html
http://home.swbell.net/dennisf/gamma/gamma.htm
http://www.adlbooks.com/parent.html
http://www.milepost1.com/~gaydad/TOC.html
http://www.blendedfamily.com
http://www.lesbian.org/lesbian-moms
http://www.inthefamily.com

ADOPTION

http://news.mpr.org/features/199711/20_smiths_fertility/part6/index.html
http://www.adoptive.com/
http://www.4adoptions.com
http://www.adoptme.com/gay.htm
http://www.adopt.org/datacenter/faces/articles/gay/gay3.html
http://www.growthhouse.org/gayfams.html

LAMBDA LEGAL DEFENSE AND EDUCATION FUND

http://lldef.org/cgi-bin/pages/search

CHILDREN AND PARENTS

http://www.colage.org
http://www.pflag.org

SPIRITUALITY

http://www.spiritgatherings.org/
http://cu-lbgt-www.cornell.edu/issues/spirituality.html

http://world.std.com/~rice/q-light/links.html
http://www.whitecranejournal.com/
http://userwww.sfsu.edu/~rbarzan/welcome.htm/main.htm
http://www.suite101.com/welcome.cfm/gay_lesbian_spirituality
http://www.religioustolerance.org
http://www.truluck.com/
http://www.amazon.com
http://www.godlovesgays.com

BISEXUALITY

http://www.bisexual.org
http://www.biresource.org

TRANSGENDER

http://tgforum.com
http:/www.ifge.org
http://www.tgni.com

COUNSELING LESBIANS

http://www.lesbianation.com
http://www.InfiniteResource.net
http://www.nclrights.org
http://www.goodvibes.com

HEALTH ISSUES

The Mautner Project for Lesbians with Cancer: http://www.mautnerproject.org
The Gay Men's Health Crisis: http://gmhc.org
Substance Abuse and Addiction: http://www.drugs.indiana.edu

WEB PAGES OF GENERAL INTEREST

Gay, Lesbian, Straight Education Network (GLSEN): http://www.glsen.org
Public Education Regarding Sexual Orientation Naturally: http://youth.org/loco/
     PERSONProject/
Safe Schools Coalition of Washington: http://safeschools~wa.org
National School Board Association's Safe Resources: http://nsba.org/na/safesources.htm
National Gay and Lesbian Task Force: http://www.ngltf.org
Recovery from Bible Abuse: http://www.truluck.com
E-directory of LesBiGay Scholars: http://newark.rutgers.edu/-lcrew/lbg.edir.html
Scouting for All: http://www.scoutingforall.org
Youth Resources: http://www.youthresource.com
Queer Resources Directory: http://www.qrd.org
Human Rights Campaign: http://www.hrcusa.org
American Civil Liberties Union (ACLU) Lesbian and Gay Rights Project: http://www.aclu.org
National Youth Advocacy Coalition (NYAC): http://www.nyacyouth.org
Gay and Lesbian Association of Retiring Persons: http://www.gaylesbianretiring.org
Seniors Active in a Gay Environment: http://www.sage.org

Index